# THE BILL OF RIGHTS:
## OUR WRITTEN LEGACY

# THE BILL OF RIGHTS:
# OUR WRITTEN LEGACY

by

**Joseph A. Melusky**
**Saint Francis College**
**Loretto, PA**

**Whitman H. Ridgway**
**University of Maryland**
**College Park, MD**

**KRIEGER PUBLISHING COMPANY**
**MALABAR, FLORIDA**
**1993**

Original Edition 1993

Printed and Published by
**KRIEGER PUBLISHING COMPANY**
**KRIEGER DRIVE**
**MALABAR, FLORIDA 32950**

The Bill of Rights : our written legacy / [compiled] by Joseph A.
  Melusky, Whitman H. Ridgway.
      p.   cm.
  Includes bibliographical references.
  ISBN 0-89464-533-1 (cloth) (acid-free paper)
  ISBN 0-89464-827-6 (paperback)
      1. United States—Constitutional law—Amendments—1st–10th-
  -History. 2. Civil rights—United States—History.   I. Melusky,
  Joseph Anthony.   II. Ridgway, Whitman H., 1941–
KF4749.B52   1992
342.73′085—dc20
[347.30285]                                       91-25558
                                                  CIP

10 9 8 7 6 5 4 3 2

For our families

# CONTENTS

Preface                                                                          xi


CHAPTER 1: INDIVIDUAL LIBERTY IN THE
            CONSTITUTIONAL ERA
  I. Introduction                                                                 1
    1. Leonard Levy, "Paradox Resolved"                                           1
  II. Individual Liberty in the Revolutionary Era                                 5
    2. Virginia Declaration of Rights (1776)                                      5
  III. The Demand for a Bill of Rights                                            7
    3. Thomas Jefferson to James Madison (1787)                                   8
    4. Letters from the Federal Farmer to the Republican
       (1787)                                                                     8
    5. A Friend of Liberty and Union to the Freeman of
       Philadelphia (1788)                                                       11
  IV. The Federalist Defense of a Constitution without a
      Bill of Rights                                                             12
    6. Address to a Meeting of the Citizens of Philadelphia,
       James Wilson (1787)                                                       12
    7. *The Federalist*, Number 84, Alexander Hamilton,
       (1788)                                                                    14
    8. James Madison to Thomas Jefferson (1788)                                  17
    9. Unsigned Comment in Philadelphia Paper (1789)                             18
   10. Unsigned Comment in Philadelphia Paper (1790)                             19
  V. The Passage of the Bill of Rights                                           20
   11. The Conversion of James Madison (1789)                                    20
   12. Madison's Initial Resolution (1789)                                       21
   13. Report by a Pennsylvanian, Tench Coxe (1789)                              23
   14. Twelve-Part Bill of Rights Submitted to States (1789)                     24


CHAPTER 2: THE BILL OF RIGHTS AND THE STATES:
            THE FOURTEENTH AMENDMENT
  I. Due Process and Privileges and Immunities                                   27
   15. *Barron v. Baltimore* (1833)                                              27

16. *Slaughterhouse Cases* (1873) 29
17. *Gitlow v. New York* (1925) 33
18. Justice Black's Dissent in *Adamson v. California* (1947) 37
II. Equal Protection of the Laws 39
19. *Civil Rights Cases* (1873) 39
20. *Plessy v. Ferguson* (1896) 44
21. *Brown v. Board of Education* (1954) 49
22. *Craig v. Boren* (1976) 53
23. *Regents of University of California v. Bakke* (1978) 55
24. *Rostker v. Goldberg* (1981) 64
III. Equal Rights Amendments 67
25. U.S. Equal Rights Amendment: Amendment XXVII
  (Proposed) 67
26. State ERAS 67


CHAPTER 3: CRIMINAL JUSTICE AND THE RIGHTS
     OF THE ACCUSED
I. Excerpts from State Constitutions 69
27. Pennsylvania (1776) 69
28. New York Ratification Convention (1788) 70
II. Unreasonable Searches and Seizures 71
29. *Katz v. United States* (1967) 71
30. *Terry v. Ohio* (1968) 75
31. *Michigan v. Sitz* (1990) 79
III. Self-Incrimination and the Right to Counsel 82
32. *Powell v. Alabama* (1932) 82
33. *Gideon v. Wainwright* (1963) 86
34. *Miranda v. Arizona* (1966) 88
IV. The Exclusionary Rule 92
35. *Mapp v. Ohio* (1961) 92
36. *United States v. Leon* (1984) 96
V. Cruel and Unusual Punishment 100
37. *Gregg v. Georgia* (1976) 100


CHAPTER 4: FREEDOM OF EXPRESSION
I. The Revolutionary Era 109
38. The Right of Assembly and Petition: Excerpts from
  State Constitutions 109

39. Freedom of Speech and the Press: Excerpts from
State Constitutions     110
40. Limits on the Freedom of Speech: Excerpt from a
State Constitution     111
II. Restrictions on Freedom of Speech     111
41. John Stuart Mill *On Liberty* (1859)     111
42. *Schenck v. United States* (1919)     114
43. *Near v. Minnesota* (1931)     116
44. *Dennis v. United States* (1951)     117
45. *New York Times Co. v. United States* (1971)     120
III. Symbolic Speech     125
46. *United States v. O'Brien* (1968)     125
47. *Texas v. Johnson* (1989)     127
IV. Obscenity and Freedom of Expression     132
48. *Roth v. United States* (1957)     132
49. *Miller v. California* (1973)     134
50. *F.C.C. v. Pacifica* (1978)     136

CHAPTER 5: FREEDOM OF RELIGION
I. Religion and the States During the Revolutionary Era     141
51. Establishment of Religion: State Constitutions     142
52. Free Exercise of Religion: State Constitutions     143
53. Virginia's "Act for Establishing Religious Freedom"
(1785)     143
II. Separation of Church and State in the Early National
Period     145
54. President Washington's Thanksgiving Proclamation
(1789)     145
55. President Jefferson to a Committee of the Danbury
Baptist Association (1802)     146
56. President Jefferson to Attorney General Levi Lincoln
(1802)     147
III. Judicial Interpretations of Religious Freedom     147
57. *West Virginia State Board of Education v. Barnette*
(1943)     147
58. *Zorach v. Clausen* (1952)     151
59. *Engel v. Vitale* (1962)     154
60. *Abington School District v. Schempp* (1963)     158
61. *Lemon v. Kurtzman* (1971)     160
62. *Lynch v. Donnelly* (1984)     165

CHAPTER 6: THE RIGHT OF PRIVACY

I. Early Analysis of the Concept 171
   63. Natural Law and the Revolutionary Generation 171
   64. The Supreme Court and Natural Law 173
   65. Justice Brandeis's Dissent in *Olmstead v. United States* (1927) 177
II. Modern Trends 180
   66. Justice Harlan's Dissent in *Poe v. Ullman* (1961) 180
   67. *Griswold v. Connecticut* (1965) 183
   68. *Loving v. Virginia* (1967) 185
   69. *Roe v. Wade* (1973) 186
   70. *Maher v. Roe* (1977) 189
   71. Justice O'Connor's Dissent in *Akron v. Akron Center for Reproductive Health* (1983) 191
   72. *Webster v. Reproductive Health Services* (1989) 194
III. The Expansion of the Right to Privacy 201
   73. *Bowers v. Hardwick* (1986) 201
   74. *Cruzan v. Director, Missouri Department of Health* (1990) 206

APPENDIX A: The Constitution of the United States 211

APPENDIX B: The Bill of Rights: A Very Selective Bibliography 231

APPENDIX C: Readings for Students 239

APPENDIX D: Filmography 243

APPENDIX E: Chronology for the Bill of Rights 249

# PREFACE

Should a written Bill of Rights be attached to the U.S. Constitution? As the powers of the national government were described in writing, should not the rights of individuals also be spelled out? Such questions stimulated much debate over two hundred years ago. Written guarantees promised explicit standards against which governmental actions could be judged and protections for people who offended the prevailing sentiments of their contemporaries. The fact that something was popular would not necessarily mean that it was constitutionally permissible. In light of the persuasiveness of such arguments, the first ten amendments to the Constitution were ratified in 1791.

The 1991 Bicentennial of the ratification of this Bill of Rights inspired various programs aimed at public education. With the support of an Exemplary Award from the National Endowment for the Humanities, the Pennsylvania Humanities Council developed one such program. Based on the success of their previous reading-and-discussion program, "The Constitution: Our Written Legacy," the PHC again recruited political scientists and historians to moderate discussion groups for the general public and in-service courses for teachers in communities throughout Pennsylvania. We prepared an anthology entitled, *To Preserve These Rights: The Bill of Rights, 1791–1991*, for use in these programs. This book is an expanded and modified outgrowth of the PHC anthology, adapted to make it as suitable for the undergraduate classroom as it is for the community discussion group.

This book has several distinctive features. First, it relies almost exclusively on primary source materials. Books written about the Framers and their historical context abound, but books presenting the original thoughts and words of the Federalists and Anti-Federalists, earlier works that influenced them, key documents of their times, and so on are less common. This book's reliance on primary materials will enable readers to draw their own conclusions without being overly dependent upon and influenced by the opinions of secondary commentators.

Second, this book is relatively brief. While subjectivity is undeniable in selecting readings, we tried to include only fundamentally important sources. For example, if a case established a landmark principle or applied such a principle in a novel context, it was a strong candidate for inclusion. If, on the other hand, a case was one of a series of decisions that gradually altered the application of some landmark principle, it was excluded. Some cases falling between these two extremes were discussed in introductory passages preceding other selections. Readings were also edited in the interest of brevity. Only material essential to understanding the main point of a selection was included.

Third, coverage of this book is broad. In addition to cases, we included documents, letters, newspaper articles, state constitutional provisions, and other writings that shed light on the historical, evolving, and contemporary meaning of the Bill of Rights.

Fourth, this book is designed to be accessible to diverse audiences. Selections are heavily edited to make them understandable to a general readership and to students with little or no experience in the subject area. Most selections are short and brief introductory passages provide background information and context. This "user friendly" collection should be suitable for various courses. Depending on instructor objectives, student level, time constraints, and the like, it would be fairly easy to adapt this book by using only certain sections or, conversely, by supplementing it with outside readings such as this book's companion anthology, *The Constitution: Our Written Legacy*.

Fifth, this book combines thematic and chronological organization. Six major topics are covered and selections are arranged chronologically within each topic area. Five appendixes follow the main text. We hope that our arrangement of the materials proves convenient and that instructors will use the book in ways that suit their own needs.

The Bill of Rights continues to generate debate and controversy. Does the First Amendment permit a protestor to burn an American flag? Does a right of privacy exist and, if so, does it extend to a woman's decision to obtain an abortion? Does it extend to a right to die? What about the rights of persons accused of crimes? The Framers wrote down some general principles, but they left the precise meaning of their words to future generations. Courts interpret and reinterpret these provisions, but the provisions are sufficiently ambiguous that different judges can interpret them differently. This flexibility both enables the Bill of Rights to remain viable and ensures that it will remain subject to disagreement and discussion. It is the aim of this book to assist readers as they evaluate opposing arguments and act as informed participants in such discussions.

We extend our thanks to the Pennsylvania Humanities Council staff, principally, Dr. Craig Eisendrath, Executive Director; Dr. Joseph J. Kelly, Associate Director; Christie Balka, Executive Program Officer; and Alice E. Ginsberg and Nancy Alexander Ellis, Program Officers. Special thanks to Dr. Kelly for his assistance in obtaining permissions, Ms. Ginsberg for her substantial editorial and administrative contributions, Darlene King of the University of Maryland—College Park for typing portions of an early draft, and Pam Sherry of Saint Francis College for her typing of the final version of this manuscript. Needless to say, the responsibility for any errors of fact or judgment is ours.

Joseph A. Melusky
Whitman H. Ridgway

# CHAPTER 1:

# INDIVIDUAL LIBERTY IN
# THE CONSTITUTIONAL ERA

## I. INTRODUCTION

*The Founders were divided as to the need for a national Bill of Rights. Some argued that it was unnecessary and that the enemies of the proposed Constitution were using the demand for a Bill of Rights as a pretext to undermine the ratification process. Others believed that this same Constitution endangered liberties guaranteed by the state constitutions, so that there was an immediate need for some sort of protection. As you read the material in this chapter, consider the meaning of James Madison's observation: "But whatever might have been the opinions entertained in forming the Constitution, it was the duty of all to support it in its true meaning, as understood by the nation at the time of its ratification."*

## 1. Leonard W. Levy, "Paradox Resolved"

*Democrats believe in self-government and majority rule but there are also limits on the power of popular majorities. The Bill of Rights reflects the belief that the rights of individuals and minorities deserve constitutional protection. In this selection, Levy describes James Madison's treatment of this paradox.*

\* \* \* \* \* \* \* \* \* \* \* \* \* \* \* \* \* \* \* \* \* \* \* \* \* \* \* \* \* \* \*

Why do we have the Bill of Rights? The answer presents a paradox in American constitutional theory. We are a self-governing people who believe in the democratic principle that the majority should rule; at the same time we understand that we must limit the power of the majority, keeping it bitted and bridled by constitutional restraints.

Thus, we believe in self-government by majority rule and also in limits on majority rule. This paradox is resolved when we realize that the purpose both of self-government and of limitations is the same: to ensure our freedom.

We have a bill of rights because we know that man is free if the state is not. The state, even the democratic state, cannot be trusted. A bill of rights is a bill of restraint upon the state.

The purpose of a bill of rights is to remove certain rights from political controversy, and place them as fundamental legal principles.

One's rights to life, liberty or property, to freedom of speech and press, to freedom of worship and assembly, to the equal protection of the laws, do not or should not depend upon the outcome of any elections. By giving them and other rights—the great ideals of liberty, equality and fairness—constitutional status, we declare them to be rights that government cannot impair or deny, and we entrust a special body of defenders, the courts, to protect them.

Through the system, we protect ourselves, too, against the assault of opportunism, the expediencies of the moment and the erosion of small encroachments; we protect ourselves against both the excesses of government and of those among us who are intolerant of differences of race, religions or opinion.

The importance of the Bill of Rights for the maintenance of the civil liberties of all of us as individuals and as members of minority groups— (we are all members of some minority)— seems apparent.

More significant, and not so readily apparent, is the importance of civil liberties to our society as a whole, as part of our machinery of self-government.

Democracy as a form of government cannot work without protecting the personal dignity of individuals; it cannot work without also promoting a dangerous degree of freedom of expression even for the thoughts we hate.

Of all our rights, the one that is, perhaps, essential to all the rest, and to the very idea of self-government or majority rule, is intellectual freedom, guaranteed in the Constitution as freedom of speech, press, assembly and religion.

Essential as intellectual freedom is to individuals and minorities, it is even more essential to the majority. The welfare of the nation, depends, after all, upon the wisdom of our decisions as a people.

Any restraint upon the access of the whole people to the information that may be a factor in its decisions is a restraint upon democracy itself—a restraint upon the rule of the majority, because the will of the majority cannot be really known if any opinion is denied expression.

Given the opportunity to hear other opinions on public issues, a different majority might be constituted among the people, or the same majority might modify or change its public policy by legislation.

Moreover, majority rule in a democracy means not just that a majority decides the course of national action, but that the political minority, those who lose, retain the chance of becoming majority. Democracy works successfully and peaceably because a minority view can become a majority view.

Minorities accept the decisions of a majority when the chance to argue back and convert the majority is present. A society that closes the avenues of opinion and action from minorities, by limiting freedom of expression, forecloses the reality of democratic majority rule, and makes inevitable the use of force and violence by the minority that has been suppressed.

More than a century ago, John Stuart Mill declared: "A state which dwarfs its men, in order that they may be more docile instruments in its hands, will find that with small men, no great thing can really be accomplished." The Bill of Rights exists to prevent us from dwarfing ourselves.

James Madison, who understood that, rose in the first Congress on June 8, 1789, to make a speech recommending that the new Constitution be amended to protect "the great rights of mankind." Madison's purpose was to correct what he, almost alone, conceived as a dangerous political situation.

With the government created by the new Constitution less than a year old, four disaffected states, including Virginia and New York, had called for a second constitutional convention. Its purpose, Madison feared, would be to "mutilate the system," especially by reducing the federal government's power to tax.

The opposition party had earlier exploited the absence of a Bill of Rights in the Constitution. Madison believed that most people who had opposed ratification of the Constitution really would favor it if there were a bill of rights to bridle the new government.

His strategy was to win these people over by persuading the first Congress to adopt protections of civil liberties. That would alleviate the public's anxieties, provide popularity and stability for the government and isolate those anti-federalists whose foremost objective, Madison thought, was "subverting the fabric . . . if not the Union itself."

The anti-federalists had previously used the bill of rights issue as a smokescreen for objections to the Constitution that had less popular appeal. They realized that adoption of a bill of rights would sink the movement for a second convention and make unlikely additional constitutional amendments that would cripple the substantive powers of the federal government. Hence, they sought to scuttle Madison's proposals in Congress.

They began by stalling. Later, they proposed amendments increasing state powers, and finally, they deprecated the importance of the very protections of individual liberty they had once demanded as guarantees from tyranny.

In his memorable speech of June 8, Madison introduced amendments taken mainly from state constitutions and proposals made by state ratifying conventions. All power, he argued, is subject to abuse. To guard against this abuse, the Constitution should secure "the great rights of mankind."

Madison acknowledged that the government had only limited powers, but he noted that the government was authorized to pass all laws "necessary and proper" to carry its powers into operation. Unless prohibited, the government might abuse its discretion.

In Britain, bills of rights had erected barriers only against the powers of the crown, leaving the powers of Parliament "altogether indefinite," Madison said. Above all, the British constitution left unguarded the "choicest" rights of the press and of conscience.

His great objective, Madison declared, was to limit the powers of government, thus preventing legislative as well as executive abuse of power, and above all preventing abuses by "the body of the people, operating by the majority against the minority."

In debate, Madison responded to arguments that a bill of rights was unnecessary because the state governments constitutionally protected freedom. He responded that some states had no bill of rights, that others had "very defective ones," and that the states posed a greater danger to liberty than the new national government.

To address that danger, he proposed an amendment: "No state shall violate the equal rights of conscience or the freedom of the press, or the trial by jury in criminal cases." This, Madison declared, was "the most valuable amendment in the whole list."

To the contention that the protection of specific rights would jeopardize those not protected, Madison replied that the danger could be avoided by adopting the proposal that became the Ninth Amendment. It declared that the enumeration of some rights does not deny the existence of others.

If his amendments were incorporated into the Constitution, Madison concluded, "independent tribunals of justice will consider themselves ... the guardians of those rights, they will be an impenetrable bulwark against every assumption of power in the legislature or executive; they will be naturally led to resist every encroachment upon rights expressly stipulated for in the constitution. ... "

Madison's speech stirred no immediate support in the House. Many federalists thought the House had more important tasks, like the passage of tonnage duties and a judiciary bill, and for six weeks the House ignored him in favor of other business. But Madison would not be put off. He pleaded; he was insistent, compelling and unyielding. Finally, he was triumphant. By the end of the summer Congress proposed to the states the amendments that became the Bill of Rights, limiting the national government only. Madison's accomplishment in the face of congressional opposition and apathy entitles him to be remembered as "father of the Bill of Rights" even more than as "father of the Constitution."

*Source: Leonard W. Levy, "Paradox Resolved," The Philadelphia Inquirer, May 12, 1987.*

## II. INDIVIDUAL LIBERTY IN THE REVOLUTIONARY ERA

*The Revolution forced almost all the states to reformulate their social compact and to define individual liberty in constitutional conventions. Eleven of the thirteen former colonies rewrote their constitutions during this period; six included a specific Declaration or Bill of Rights (seven if New Hampshire's 1784 constitution is counted), while four others protected some individual liberties in the constitution itself. An important example of this process was the Virginia Declaration of Rights (1776), written by George Mason (1725–1792):*

\* \* \* \* \* \* \* \* \* \* \* \* \* \* \* \* \* \* \* \* \* \* \* \* \* \* \* \* \* \*

### 2. Virginia Declaration of Rights (12 June 1776)

A Declaration of Rights made by the Representatives of the good people of Virginia, assembled in full and free Convention; which rights do pertain to them and their posterity, as the basis and foundation of Government.

1. That all men are by nature equally free and independent, and have certain inherent rights, of which, when they enter into a state of society, they cannot, by any compact, deprive or divest their posterity; namely, the enjoyment of life and liberty, with the means of acquiring and possessing property, and pursuing and obtaining happiness and safety.

2. That all power is vested in, and consequently derived from, the People; that magistrates are their trustees and servants, and at all times amenable to them.

3. That Government is, or ought to be, instituted for the common benefit, protection, and security of the people, nation, or community;—of all the various modes and forms of Government that is best which is capable of producing the greatest degree of happiness and safety, and is most ef-

fectually secured against the danger of mal-administration;—and that, whenever any Government shall be found inadequate or contrary to these purposes, a majority of the community hath an indubitable, unalienable, and indefeasible right, to reform, alter, or abolish it, in such manner as shall be judged most conducive to the public weal.

4. That no man, or set of men, are entitled to exclusive or separate emoluments and privileges from the community, but in consideration of public services; which, not being descendible, neither ought the offices of Magistrate, Legislator, or Judge to be hereditary.

5. That the Legislative and Executive powers of the State should be separate and distinct from the Judicative; and, that the members of the two first may be restrained from oppression, by feeling and participating the burdens of the people, they should, at fixed periods, be reduced to a private station, return into that body from which they were originally taken, and the vacancies be supplied by frequent, certain, and regular elections, in which all, or any part of the former members, to be again eligible, or ineligible, as the law shall direct.

6. That elections of members to serve as Representatives of the people, in Assembly, ought to be free; and that all men, having sufficient evidence of permanent common interest with, and attachment to, the community, have the right of suffrage, and cannot be taxed or deprived of their property for public uses without their own consent or that of their Representative so elected, nor bound by any law to which they have not, in like manner, assented, for the public good.

7. That all power of suspending laws, or the execution of laws, by any authority, without consent of the Representatives of the people, is injurious to their rights, and ought not to be exercised.

8. That in all capital or criminal prosecutions a man hath a right to demand the cause and nature of his accusation, to be confronted with the accusers and witnesses, to call for evidence in his favor, and to a speedy trial by an impartial jury of his vicinage, without whose unanimous consent he cannot be found guilty, nor can he be compelled to give evidence against himself; that no man be deprived of his liberty except by the law of the land, or the judgment of his peers.

9. That excessive bail ought not to be required, nor excessive fines imposed, nor cruel and unusual punishment inflicted.

10. That general warrants, whereby any officer or messenger may be commanded to search suspected places without evidence of a fact committed, or to seize any person or persons not named, or whose offense is not particularly described and supported by evidence, are grievous and oppressive, and ought not to be granted.

11. That in controversies respecting property, and in suits between man and man, the ancient trial by Jury is preferable to any other, and ought to be held sacred.

12. That the freedom of the Press is one of the greatest bulwarks of liberty, and can never be restrained but by despotic Governments.

13. That a well-regulated Militia, composed of the body of the people, trained to arms, is the proper, natural, and safe defence of a free State; that Standing Armies, in time of peace, should be avoided as dangerous to liberty; and that, in all cases, the military should be under strict subordination to, and governed by, the civil power.

14. That the people have a right to uniform Governments, and, therefore, that no Government separate from, or independent of, the Government of Virginia, ought to be erected or established within the limits thereof.

15. That no free Government, or the blessing of liberty, can be preserved to any people but by a firm adherence to justice, moderation, temperance, frugality, and virtue, and by frequent recurrence to fundamental principles.

16. That Religion, or the duty which we owe to our Creator, and the manner of discharging it, can be directed only by reason and conviction, not by force or violence; and, therefore, all men are equally entitled to the free exercise of religion, according to the dictates of conscience; and that it is the mutual duty of all to practice Christian forbearance, love, and charity, towards each other.

*Source: Robert A. Rutland, ed.* The Papers of George Mason. *3 vols. (Chapel Hill, N. C.: University of North Carolina Press, 1970), I: 287–89.*

## III. THE DEMAND FOR A BILL OF RIGHTS

*A major Anti-Federalist objection to the proposed Constitution was stated by George Mason, a Virginia delegate to the Philadelphia Convention who refused to sign the document: "There is no Declaration of Rights, and the laws of the general government being paramount to the laws and constitution of the several States, the Declaration of Rights in the separate States are no security." Anti-Federalists were particularly concerned with the implications of the Supremacy Clause in Article VI and the indefinite meaning of the "necessary and proper" clause of Article I Section 8. The following readings represent opinion on the necessity of a federal Bill of Rights.*

### 3. Thomas Jefferson to James Madison (20 December 1787)

*Thomas Jefferson (1743–1826) was serving as a diplomat in Paris during the debate over the Constitution. Recognizing need for a stronger national government, he nonetheless shared some of the Anti-Federalist concerns about individual liberty under the new system, and believed that a Bill of Rights was absolutely necessary.*

\* \* \* \* \* \* \* \* \* \* \* \* \* \* \* \* \* \* \* \* \* \* \* \* \* \* \* \* \* \* \*

. . . . I will now add what I do not like. First the omission of a bill of rights providing clearly and without the aid of sophisms for freedom of religion, freedom of the press, protection against standing armies, restriction against monopolies, the eternal and unremitting force of the habeas corpus laws, and trials by jury in all matters of fact triable by the laws of the land and not by the law of Nations. To say, as Mr. Wilson does that a bill of rights was not necessary because all is reserved in the case of the general government which is not given, while in the particular ones all is given which is not reserved might do for the Audience to whom it was addressed, but is surely gratis dictum, opposed by strong inferences from the body of the instrument, as well as from the omission of the clause of our present confederation which had declared that in express terms. It was a hard conclusion to say because there has been no uniformity among the states as to the cases triable by jury, because some have been so incautious as to abandon this mode of trial, therefore the more prudent states shall be reduced to the same level of calamity. It would have been much more just and wise to have concluded the other way that as most of the states had judiciously preserved this palladium, those who had wandered should be brought back to it, and to have established general right instead of general wrong. Let me add that a bill of rights is what the people are entitled to against every government on earth, general or particular, and what no just government should refuse or rest on inference.

*Source: Julian P. Boyd, et al., ed.* The Papers of Thomas Jefferson, *22 vols. to date (Princeton, N.J.: Princeton University Press, 1950–), XII: 440.*

### 4. Letters from the Federal Farmer to the Republican, No. IV (12 October 1787)

*The Federal Farmer is acknowledged as being one of the most insightful Anti-Federalist writers. Once thought to be written by Richard Henry Lee of Virginia, modern scholars are less certain of the author's identity. The following section explains why the Constitution would endanger individual liberties, currently protected by state constitutions, and why a federal Bill of Rights was required.*

\* \* \* \* \* \* \* \* \* \* \* \* \* \* \* \* \* \* \* \* \* \* \* \* \* \* \* \*

... 4th. There are certain rights which we have always held sacred in the United States, and recognized in all our constitutions, and which, by the adoption of the new constitution in its present form, will be left unsecured. By article 6, the proposed constitution, and the laws of the United States ... and all treaties made ... shall be the supreme law of the land; and the judges in every state shall be bound thereby; any thing in the constitution or laws of any state to the contrary notwithstanding.

It is to be observed that when the people shall adopt the proposed constitution it will be their last and supreme act; it will be adopted not by the people of New-Hampshire, Massachusetts, etc. but by the people of the United States; and whenever this constitution, or any part of it, shall be incompatible with the ancient customs, rights, the laws or the constitutions heretofore established in the United States, it will entirely abolish them and do them away: And not only this, but the laws of the United States which shall be made in pursuance of the federal constitution will be also supreme laws, and wherever they shall be incompatible with those customs, rights, laws or constitutions heretofore established, they will also entirely abolish them and do them away. ...

It is said, that when the people make a constitution, and delegate powers that all powers not delegated by them to those who govern is reserved in the people; and that the people, in the present case, have reserved in themselves, and in their state governments, every right and power not expressly given by the federal constitution to those who shall administer the national government. It is said on the other hand, that the people, when they make a constitution, yield all power not expressly reserved to themselves. The truth is, in either case, it is mere matter of opinion and men usually take either side of the argument, as will best answer their purposes:

But the general presumption being, that men who govern, will, in doubtful cases, construe laws and constitutions most favorably for increasing their own powers; all wise and prudent people, in forming constitutions, have drawn the line, and carefully described the powers parted with and the powers reserved. By the state constitutions, certain rights have been reserved in the people; or rather, they have been recognized and established in such a manner, that state legislatures are bound to respect them, and to make no laws infringing upon them. The state legislatures are obliged to take notice of the bills of rights of their respective states.

The bills of rights, and the state constitutions, are fundamental compacts only between those who govern, and the people of the same state.

In the year 1788, the people of the United States make a federal constitution, which is a fundamental compact between them and their federal rulers; these rulers, in the nature of things, cannot be bound to take notice of any other compact. It would be absurd for them, in making laws, to look over thirteen, fifteen, or twenty state constitutions, to see what rights are established as fundamental, and must not be infringed upon in making laws in the society.... In fact, the 9th and 10th Sections in Art. I in the proposed constitution, are no more nor less, than a partial bill of rights; they establish certain principles as part of the compact upon which the federal legislators and officers can never infringe. It is here wisely stipulated, that the federal legislature shall never pass a bill of attainder, or *ex post facto* law; that no tax shall be laid on articles exported, etc. The establishing of one right implies the necessity of establishing another and similar one.

On the whole, the position appears to me to be undeniable, that this bill of rights ought to be carried farther, and some other principles established, as a part of this fundamental compact between the people of the United States and their federal rulers.

It is true, we are not disposed to differ much, at present, about religion; but when we are making a constitution, it is to be hoped, for ages and millions yet unborn, why not establish the free exercise of religion, as a part of the national compact. There are other essential rights, which we have justly understood to be the rights of freemen; as freedom from hasty and unreasonable search warrants, warrants not founded on oath, and not issued with due caution, for searching and seizing men's papers, property, and persons. The trials by jury in civil causes, it is said, varies so much in the several states, that no words could be found for the uniform establishment of it. If so, the federal legislation will not be able to establish it by any general laws ... When I speak of the jury trial of the vicinage, or the trial of the fact in the neighborhood,—I do not lay so much stress upon the circumstance of our being tried by our neighbors ... but the trial of facts in the neighborhood is of great importance in other respects. Nothing can be more essential than the cross examining witnesses, and generally before the triers of the facts in question. The common people can establish facts with much more ease with oral than written evidence; when trials of facts are removed to a distance from the homes of the parties and witnesses, oral evidence becomes intolerably expensive, and the parties must depend on written evidence, which to the common people is expensive and almost useless. ...

The trial by jury in the judicial department, and the collection of the people by their representatives in the legislature, are those fortunate inventions which have procured for them, in this country, their true proportion of influence, and the wisest and most fit means of protecting themselves in the community. Their situation, as jurors and representatives, enables them to acquire information and knowledge in the affairs and government of the society; and to come forward, in turn, as the centennials and guardians of each other. . . .

I confess I do not see in what cases the congress can, with any pretence of right, make a law to suppress the freedom of the press; though I am not clear, that congress is restrained from laying any duties whatever on printing, and from laying duties particularly heavy on certain pieces printed, and perhaps congress may require large bonds for the payment of these duties. . . .

It is not my object to enumerate rights of inconsiderable importance; but there are others, no doubt, which ought to be established as a fundamental part of the national system. . . .

*Source: Herbert J. Storing, ed.* The Complete Anti-Federalist, *7 vols. (Chicago and London: The University of Chicago Press, 1981), II. 246–51.*

## 5. A Friend of Liberty and Union to the Freeman of Philadelphia (November 1788)

*The following represents one of many unsigned pieces which appeared in the popular press during the debate over the Constitution. By this time the Constitution had been ratified, but Anti-Federalists still hoped for election to the first federal Congress when the new government would be organized.*

\* \* \* \* \* \* \* \* \* \* \* \* \* \* \* \* \* \* \* \* \* \* \* \* \* \* \* \*

Another defect in the federal constitution is equally alarming. No security is provided for the rights of individuals: no bill of rights is framed, nor is any privilege of freemen secured from the invasion of the governors. Trust me, my fellow citizens! we shall not be more powerful or respected abroad, for being liable to oppression at home; but on the contrary, the freest states have been the most powerful. Yet with us no barriers will remain against slavery, under the new continental government, if it be not amended: the State governments, by the express terms of the constitution, can afford no protection to their citizens, and not even a single right is defined or stipulated, which the subject may appeal to against the will and pleasure of the moment.

*Source: Philadelphia* Freeman's Journal, *12 November 1788.*

## IV. THE FEDERALIST DEFENSE OF THE CONSTITUTION WITHOUT A BILL OF RIGHTS

*Most Federalists saw no need for a federal Bill of Rights. Politically, they believed that the Anti-Federalists were using the issue to frighten the people so as to defeat the ratification of the Constitution. If the Anti-Federalists could prevent nine states from ratifying it, or secure enough public support to call a Second Convention, the Constitution would be lost. Many Federalists believed that the new government only possessed those powers enumerated in the Constitution, and since nothing was said in it about restricting freedom of the press or trial by jury, the concern for such traditional liberties was much ado about nothing. Some ridiculed the idea of drafting one bill of rights from the conflicting proposals made during the ratification controversy. In the words of one newspaper comment: "So many absurdities and contradictions have been pointed out in the supposed amendments, that if they should be brought forward on the floor of Congress, it will not be necessary to oppose them. They will immediately, like Swifts' books, give battle to each other, and soon destroy themselves." Others, however, recognized a legitimate public concern, and recommended that the Constitution might be amended according to Article V once the new government was in place.*

### 6. Address to a Meeting of the Citizens of Philadelphia (6 October 1787)

*James Wilson (1742–1798)—a Philadelphia lawyer, signer of the Declaration of Independence, delegate to the Philadelphia Convention, and future member of the Supreme Court—was a firm advocate of a stronger national government. This early defense of the Constitution argued that a Bill of Rights is unnecessary because the federal Constitution gives only enumerated powers to the new government. This became a standard Federalist answer to a demand for a bill of rights. Thomas Jefferson in his letter cited above found this argument unconvincing.*

\* \* \* \* \* \* \* \* \* \* \* \* \* \* \* \* \* \* \* \* \* \* \* \* \* \* \* \* \* \*

... It will be proper ... before I enter into the refutation of the charges that are alleged, to mark the leading discrimination between the state constitutions, and the constitution of the United States. When the people established the powers of legislation under their separate governments, they invested their representatives with every right and authority which they did not in explicit terms reserve: and therefore upon every question, respecting the jurisdiction of the house of assembly, if the frame of government is silent, the jurisdiction is efficient and complete. But in delegating federal powers, another criterion was necessarily introduced: and the congressional authority is to be collected, not from tacit implication, but from the positive grant, expressed in the instrument of union. Hence, it is evident, that in the former case, everything which is not reserved, is given: but in the latter, the reverse of the proposition prevails, and every thing which is not given, is reserved. This distinction being recognized, will furnish an answer to those who think the omission of a bill of rights, a defect in the proposed constitution: for it would have been superfluous and absurd, to have stipulated with a federal body of our own creation, that we should enjoy those privileges, of which we are not divested either by the intention or the act that has brought that body into existence. For instance, the liberty of the press, which has been a copious subject of declamation and opposition: what control can proceed from the federal government, to shackle or destroy that sacred palladium of national freedom? ... In truth, then, the proposed system possess no influence whatever upon the press; and it would have been merely nugatory to have introduced a formal declaration upon the subject; nay, that very declaration might have been construed to imply that some degree of power was given, since we undertook to define its extent.

Another objection that has been fabricated against the new constitution, is expressed in this disingenuous form—"the trial by jury is abolished in civil cases" ... The cases open to a jury, differed in the different states; it was therefore impracticable, on that ground, to have made a general rule ... How, then, was the line of discrimination to be drawn? The convention found the task too difficult for them: and they left the business as it stands—in the fullest confidence, that no danger could possibly ensue, since the proceedings of the supreme court are to be regulated by the congress, which is a faithful representation of the people: and the oppression of government is effectually barred, by declaring that in all criminal cases, the trial by jury shall be preserved. ...

After all, my fellow-citizens, it is neither extraordinary nor unexpected, that the constitution offered to your consideration, should meet with opposition. It is the nature of man to pursue his own interest, in preference to the public good; and I do not mean to make any personal reflection, when I add, that it is the interest of a very numerous, powerful, and respectable body, to counteract and destroy the excellent work produced by the late convention. ... If there are errors, it should be remembered, that the seeds of reformation are sown in the work itself, and the concurrence of two thirds of the congress may at any time introduce alterations and amendments. Regarding it, then, in every point of view, with a candid and disinterested mind, I am bold to assert, that it is the BEST FORM OF GOVERNMENT WHICH HAS EVER BEEN OFFERED TO THE WORLD.

*Source: Paul L. Ford, ed.* Pamphlets on the Constitution of the United States *(Brooklyn, New York: n.p., 1888), pp. 155–61.*

## 7. *The Federalist,* No. 84

*In* The Federalist, *Number 78, Alexander Hamilton predicted that the judiciary would be the "least dangerous" branch of the national government. He noted that it would possess neither "the sword or the purse." He believed that it would have "neither force nor will, but merely judgment." In a system governed by a "limited constitution" that restrains the authority of the elected legislature, however, the judiciary's role is very important. Hamilton observed that courts "are to be considered as the bulwarks of a limited constitution against legislative encroachments." In this light, he rejected the notion that federal judges should be popularly elected and that they should serve limited terms. Instead, he maintained that they should be appointed and enjoy permanent tenure. Although Hamilton was a vocal opponent to a national bill of rights, his views reflected a recognition that there are legitimate limits on the majority's right to rule in a constitutional system and his dependence on the courts to enforce those limits.*

*In* The Federalist, *Number 84, Hamilton responded more directly to those who advocated a written national bill of rights. He disagreed, contending that the Constitution already provided adequate protection for civil rights and liberties. Additionally, he suggested that such a bill of rights might even prove dangerous.*

\* \* \* \* \* \* \* \* \* \* \* \* \* \* \* \* \* \* \* \* \* \* \* \* \* \* \* \* \* \* \*

The most considerable of the remaining objections is, that the plan of the convention contains no bill of rights. Among other answers given to this, it has been upon different occasions remarked that the constitutions of several of the States are in a similar predicament. I add that New York is of the number. And yet opposers of the new system . . . are among the most intemperate partisans of a bill of rights. To justify their zeal in this matter they allege two things: one is that, though the constitution of New York has no bill of rights prefixed to it, yet it contains in the body of it, various provisions in favor of particular privileges and rights which, in substance, amount to the same thing; the other is that the Constitution adopts, in their full extent, the common and statute law of Great Britain, by which many other rights, not expressed in it are equally secured.

To the first I answer that the Constitution offered by the convention contains, as well as the constitution of this State, a number of such provisions.

Independent of those which relate to the structure of the government, we find the following: Article I, section 3, clause 7. "Judgment in cases of impeachment shall not extend further than to removal from office, and disqualification to hold and enjoy any office of honor, trust, or profit under the United States; but the party convicted shall, nevertheless, be liable and subject to indictment, trial, judgment, and punishment, according to law." Section 9 of the same article clause 2. "The privilege of the writ of *habeas corpus* shall not be suspended, unless when in cases of rebellion or invasion the public safety may require it." Clause 3. "No bill of attainder or *ex post facto* law shall be passed." Clause 7. "No title of nobility shall be granted by the United States; and no person holding any office of profit or trust under them, shall, without the consent of the Congress, accept of any present, emolument, office, or title of any kind whatever, from any king, prince, or foreign states." Article III, section 2, clause 3. "The trial of all crimes, except in cases of impeachment, shall be by jury; and such trial shall be held in the State where the said crimes shall have been committed; but when not committed within any State, the trial shall be at such place or places as the Congress may by law have directed." Section 3 of the same article. "Treason against the United States shall consist only in levying war against them, or in adhering to their enemies, giving them aid and comfort. No person shall be convicted of treason, unless on the testimony of two witnesses to the same overt act, or on confession in open court." And clause 3 of the same section. "The Congress shall have power to declare the punishment of treason; but no attainder of treason shall work corruption of blood, or forfeiture, except during the life of the person attained."

It may well be a question, whether these are not, upon the whole, of equal importance with any which are to be found in the constitution of this State. The establishment of the writ of *habeas corpus*, the prohibition of *ex post facto* laws, and of TITLES OF NOBILITY, *to which we have corresponding provisions in our Constitution*, are perhaps greater securities to liberty and republicanism than any it contains. The creation of crimes after the commission of the fact, or, in other words, the subjecting of men to punishment for things which, when they were done, were breaches of no law and the practice of arbitrary imprisonments have been, in all ages, the favorite and most formidable instruments of tyranny. . . .

It has been several times truly remarked, that bills of rights are . . . reservations of rights not surrendered to the prince. Such was MAGNA CHARTA. . . . Here, in strictness, the people surrender nothing; and as they retain everything they have no need of particular reservations. "WE THE PEOPLE of the United States, to secure the blessings of liberty to ourselves and our posterity do *ordain and establish* this Constitution for the United States of America." Here is a better recognition of popular rights than volumes of those aphorisms which make the principal figure in several of our State bills of rights and which would sound much better in a treatise of ethics than in a constitution of government.

But a minute detail of particular rights is certainly far less applicable to a Constitution like that under consideration, which is merely intended to regulate the general political interests of the nation, than to a Constitution which has the regulation of every species of personal and private concerns. If, therefore, the loud clamors against the plan of the convention, on this score, are well founded, no epithets of reprobation will be too strong for the constitution of this State. But the truth is that both of them contain all which, in relation to their objects, is reasonably to be desired.

I go further and affirm that bills of rights . . . are not only unnecessary in the proposed Constitution, but would even be dangerous. They would contain various exceptions to powers which are not granted; and on this very account, would afford a colorable pretext to claim more than were granted. For why declare that things shall not be done which there is no power to do? Why, for instance, should it be said that the liberty of the press shall not be restrained, when no power is given by which restrictions may be imposed? I will not contend that such a provision would confer a regulating power; but it is evident that it would furnish, to men disposed to usurp, a plausible pretense for claiming that power. They might urge with a semblance of reason that the Constitution ought not to be charged with the absurdity of providing against the abuse of an authority which was not given, and that the provision against restraining the liberty of the press afforded a clear implication that a power to prescribe proper regulations concerning it was intended to be vested in the national government. This may serve as a specimen of the numerous handles which would be given to the doctrine of constructive powers, by the indulgence of an injudicious zeal for bills of rights. . . .

There remains but one other view of this matter to conclude the point. The truth is . . . that the Constitution is itself . . . A BILL OF RIGHTS. . . . Is it one object of a bill of rights to declare and specify the political privileges of the citizens in the structure and administration of the government? This is done in the most ample and precise manner in the plan of the convention; comprehending various precautions for the public security, which are not to be found in any of the State constitutions. Is another object of a bill of rights to define certain immunities and modes of proceeding, which are relative to personal and private concerns? This we have seen has also been attended to in a variety of cases in the same plan. Adverting therefore to the substantial meaning of a bill of rights, it is absurd to allege that it is not to be found in the work of the convention. It may be said that it does not go far enough though it will not be easy to make this appear; but it can with no propriety be contended that there is no such thing. It certainly must be immaterial what mode is observed as to the order of declaring the rights of the citizens if they are to be found in any part of the instrument which establishes the government. And hence it must be apparent that much of what has been said on this subject rests merely on verbal and nominal distinctions, entirely foreign to the substance of the thing. . . .

Source: *Clinton Rossiter, ed.,* The Federalist Papers *(New York: New American Library, 1961), pp. 510–20.*

## 8. James Madison to Thomas Jefferson (17 October 1788)

*James Madison (1751–1836), recognized as the father of the Constitution and one of its most articulate defenders in the ensuing ratification debate, shared James Wilson's belief that a Bill of Rights was superfluous. He opposed the last minute move by George Mason and Elbridge Gerry to consider a Bill of Rights in the Philadelphia Convention, and the later effort by Richard Henry Lee to attach a Bill of Rights when the Constitution was being considered by Congress prior to sending it to the states for ratification. His position is best stated in his reply to Thomas Jefferson's letter, cited above:*

\* \* \* \* \* \* \* \* \* \* \* \* \* \* \* \* \* \* \* \* \* \* \* \* \* \* \* \* \* \* \*

. . . My own opinion has always been in favor of a bill of rights; provided it be so framed as not to imply powers not meant to be included in the enumeration. At the same time I have never thought the omission as a material defect, nor been anxious to supply it even by **subsequent** amendment, for any other reason than that it is anxiously desired by others. I have favored it because I supposed it might be of use, and if properly executed could not be of disservice. I have not viewed it in an important light 1. because I conceive that in a certain degree, though not in the extent argued by Mr. Wilson, the rights in question are reserved by the manner in which the federal powers are granted. 2. because there is great reason to fear that a positive declaration of some of the most essential rights could not be obtained in the requisite latitude. I am sure that the rights of Conscience in particular, if submitted to public definition would be narrowed much more than they are ever to be by an assumed power. One of the objections in New England was that the Constitution by prohibiting religious tests opened a door for Jews Turks & infidels. 3. because the limited powers of the federal Government and the jealousy of the subordinate Governments, afford a security which has not existed in the case of the State Governments, and exists in no other. 4. because experience proves the inefficacy of a bill of rights on those occasions when its controul is most needed. Repeated violations of these parchment barriers have been committed by overbearing majorities in every State. In Virginia I have seen the bill of rights violated in every instance where it has been opposed to a popular current. . . . Wherever the real power in a Government lies, there is danger of oppression. In our Governments the real power lies in the majority of the Community, and the invasion of private rights is chiefly to be apprehended, not from acts of Government contrary to the sense of its constituents, but from acts in which the Government is the mere instrument of the major number of the constituents. This is a truth of great importance, but not yet sufficiently attended to. . . . Wherever there is an interest and power to do wrong, wrong will generally be done, and not less readily by a powerful and interested party than by a powerful and interested prince. . . . What use then it may be asked can a bill of rights serve in popular Governments? I answer the two following which though less essential than in other Governments, sufficiently recommend the precaution. 1. The political truths declared in that solemn manner acquire by degrees the character of fundamental maxims of free Government, and as they become incorporated with the national sentiment, counteract the impulses of interest and passion. 2. Altho' it be generally true as above stated that the danger of oppression lies in the interested majorities of the people rather than in usurped acts of the Government, yet there may be occasions on which the evil may spring from the latter sources; and on such, a bill of rights will be a good ground for an appeal to the sense of the community. . . . It is a melancholy reflection that liberty should be equally exposed to danger whether the Government have too much or too little power, and that the line which divides these extremes should be so inaccurately defined by experience.

*Source: Robert A. Rutland, et al., ed.* The Papers of James Madison, *17 vols. to date (Chicago and Charlottesville: The University of Chicago and the University of Virginia Presses, 1956) XI: 297–99*

## 9. Unsigned Comment in Philadelphia Paper (1789)

*The following was an unsigned comment in a Philadelphia paper. The author does not share our contemporary veneration for the Bill of*

*Rights; rather he dismissed the very idea as a popular folly. If parchment barriers are inadequate to protect individual liberty, how can it be protected? Are the rights of the minority also secure?*

\* \* \* \* \* \* \* \* \* \* \* \* \* \* \* \* \* \* \* \* \* \* \* \* \* \* \* \* \* \*

Every age and nation in the world has been marked by some peculiar follies, which have disgraced human understanding. The worship of the ox, the crocodile, and the cat in ancient times, and the belief in astrology and witchcraft by more modern nations, did not prostrate human understanding more than the numerous absurdities, which have been published by some of the states, under the ideas of **amendments** of the new constitution. The liberties of a country depend only upon **two** articles in any government, viz.—upon **equal** representation chosen by the people, and upon checks. These are the two pillars of a free and durable constitution. Every thing else is mere form and ornament, calculated only to please vulgar and weak minds. Where there is a defect in representation, history proves that the most splendid and extensive declaration of rights has not been able to restrain rulers, and where representation has existed, no declaration of rights has been found necessary. Checks are equally necessary to secure liberty; for men possessing supreme power without a check, are apt to be intoxicated, and in a little while exhibit all the phenomena of a balloon.

*Source:* Philadelphia Federal Gazette, *25 February 1789.*

## 10. Unsigned Comment in Philadelphia Paper (1790)

*Another unsigned article in the same paper argued that there is no place for a Bill of Rights in a democratic government. He asserted that the people need a bill of rights in a monarchy but not in a democracy. As "One of the People" observed: "A bill of rights has been demanded in England, because in that country the kings confer liberty on the people."*

\* \* \* \* \* \* \* \* \* \* \* \* \* \* \* \* \* \* \* \* \* \* \* \* \* \* \* \* \* \*

A bill of rights for freemen appears to be a contradiction in terms. From whom are they received? From themselves? Do freemen relinquish those rights that are not specified in a bill? To whom do they relinquish them? To themselves, or their rulers? Who are their rulers but the creatures of their own forming? If freemen retain no rights but those specified in a bill, they divest themselves of THOUSANDS, where they retain ONE. What avails a bill of rights to those who violate the laws? and in a free country, every right of human nature, which are as numerous as sands upon the sea shore, belong to the quiet peaceable citizen.

Bills of rights owe their origin to circumstances no ways honorary to the national independence, and dignity of human nature. Success on the part of the barons, in their war with King John extorted that boasted instrument called the bill of rights. But it may be enquired, whether the powers NOT SURRENDERED by the king, were not supposed to be vested in him. In that case, what was granted, must be viewed in that light of a concession on his part. Its being extorted or voluntary, makes no difference in the degrading idea that connects itself with the transaction.

*Source:* Philadelphia Federal Gazette, *5 January 1790*

## V. THE PASSAGE OF THE BILL OF RIGHTS

*The adoption of a Bill of Rights by the first federal Congress was not a foregone conclusion. Many Federalists argued that there were far more important and less controversial questions which had to be settled first. Some even felt that the system ought to be tried before changing it. James Madison, however, believed that the public expected the first Congress to adopt a Bill of Rights. Working from the amendments proposed by seven ratifying conventions, Madison proposed a set of amendments in June 1789. The matter was sent to a committee which reported a nineteen part bill at the end of July. The House of Representatives finally agreed to a seventeen part measure which was sent to the Senate at the end of August. The Senate returned its version in mid-September and the final draft of twelve amendments was sent to the states on 28 September 1789. The Bill of Rights was ratified in 1791.*

### 11. The Conversion of James Madison

*One of the most remarkable effects of the debate over the Constitution was the conversion of James Madison from opposing a bill of rights to becoming one of its warmest advocates. While it is evident from his private correspondence cited above that he was reconsidering his position on the question, he did not publicly declare his support for one until January 1789 when he wrote a local Baptist minister during his campaign for Congress:*

\* \* \* \* \* \* \* \* \* \* \* \* \* \* \* \* \* \* \* \* \* \* \* \* \* \* \* \* \*

I freely own that I have never seen in the Constitution as it now stands those serious dangers which have alarmed many respectable Citizens. Accordingly whilst it remained unratified, and it was necessary to unite the

States in some one plan, I opposed all previous alterations as calculated to throw the States in to dangerous contentions, and to furnish the secret enemies of the Union with an opportunity of promoting its dissolution. Circumstances are now changed: The Constitution is established on the ratification of eleven States and a very great majority of the people of America; and amendments, if pursued with a proper moderation and in a proper mode, will be not only safe, but may serve the double purpose of satisfying the minds of well meaning opponents, and of providing additional guards in favor of liberty. Under this change of circumstances, it is my sincere opinion that the Constitution ought to be revised, and that the first Congress meeting under it, ought to prepare and recommend to the States for ratification, the most satisfactory provisions for all essential rights, particularly the rights of Conscience in the fullest latitude, the freedom of the press, trials by jury, security against general warrants &c. I think it will be proper also to provide expressly in the Constitution, for the periodical increase of the number of Representatives until the amount shall be entirely satisfactory. . . .

I have intimated that the amendments ought to be proposed by the first Congress. I prefer this mode to that of a General Convention, 1st. because it is the most expeditious mode. A convention must be delayed, until 2/3 of the State Legislatures have applied for one; and afterwards the amendments must be submitted to the States; whereas if the business be undertaken by Congress the amendments may be prepared and submitted in March next. 2ndly, because it is the most certain mode. There are not a few States who will absolutely reject the proposal of a Convention, and yet not to be adverse to amendments in the other mode. Lastly, it is the safest mode. The Congress, who will be appointed to execute as well as to amend the Government, will probably be careful not to destroy or endanger it. A convention, on the other hand, meeting in the present ferment of parties, and containing perhaps insidious characters from different parts of America, would at least spread a general alarm, and be but too likely to turn everything into confusion and uncertainty. It is to be observed however that the question concerning a General Convention, will not belong to the federal Legislature. If 2/3 of the States apply for one, Congress can not refuse to call it; if not, the other mode of amendments must be pursued. . . .

*Source: Rutland,* The Papers of James Madison, *XI: 404–5*

## 12. Madison's Initial Resolution (1789)

*The following are selections from the Madison's initial Resolution calling for a Bill of Rights (8 June 1789). He proposed making corrections into the body of the Constitution itself. The ensuing debate showed a remarkable veneration for the product of the Philadelphia Convention and a consensus that amendments should be added to it. As Congressman Jackson observed: "The Constitution of the Union has been ratified and established by the people; let their act remain inviolable; if any thing we can do has a tendency to improve it, let it be done, but without mutilating and defacing the original." Madison's Fifth Proposal was remarkable in that it restricted state action and anticipated the Fourteenth Amendment. This idea was included in the House Bill but deleted by the Senate. The Eighth Proposal reflected a minimal response to the Anti-Federalist demand to restrict the authority of the national government and to reassert the power of the states.*

\* \* \* \* \* \* \* \* \* \* \* \* \* \* \* \* \* \* \* \* \* \* \* \* \* \* \* \*

Excerpts from Madison's Resolution of 8 June 1789:

**Fourthly.** That in article 1st, section 9, between clauses 3 and 4, be inserted these clauses, to wit: The civil rights of none shall be abridged on account of religious belief or worship, nor shall any national religion be established, nor shall the full and equal rights of conscience be in any manner, or on any pretext infringed. . . . [followed by the enumeration of other individual rights later included in the Bill of Rights].

The exceptions here or elsewhere in the constitution, made in favor of particular rights, shall not be construed as to diminish the just importance of other rights retained by the people; or as to enlarge the powers delegated by the constitution; but either as actual limitations of such powers, or as inserted merely for greater caution. **Fifthly.** That in article 1st, section 10, between clauses 1 and 2, be inserted this clause, to wit:

No state shall violate the equal rights of conscience, or the freedom of the press, or the trial by jury in criminal cases.

**Eighthly.** That immediately after article 6th, be inserted, as article 7th, the clauses following, to wit:

The powers delegated by this constitution, and appropriated to the departments to which they are respectively distributed: so that the legislative department shall never exercise the powers vested in the executive or judicial; nor the executive exercise the powers vested in the legislative or judicial; nor the judicial exercise the powers vested in the legislative or executive departments.

The powers not delegated by this constitution, nor prohibited by it to the states, are reserved to the states respectively.

*Source: Helen E. Veit, Kenneth R. Bowling, and Charlene B. Bickford, ed. Creating The Bill of Rights, (Baltimore & London, The Johns Hopkins University Press, 1991), pp. 11–14.*

## 13. Report by a Pennsylvanian (1789)

*There was remarkably little contemporary comment on the various proposals for a Bill of Rights. The major Anti-Federalist presses reported each version as it was presented in Congress, but Anti-Federalists complained that the Federalist press was ignoring the question. The following edited report by Tench Coxe (1755–1824), writing as A PENNSYLVAN-IAN, concerned Madison's initial proposal in June.*

* * * * * * * * * * * * * * * * * * * * * * * * * * * * *

The manifestation of good faith, which this motion carries, is a matter of no dishonorable reflection on the friends of the new Constitution, and the ingeniousness and moderation discovered by the gentlemen of the house, who have desired amendments, excites feelings of the most comfortable nature. The people must rejoice to find, that their rulers, of however diversified opinions, are equally anxious for their country's happiness. . . .

The [Fourth] article establishes religious liberty, and all those political rights, which by various tricks of state have been wounded through its means, on the firmest grounds. The tender, the almost sacred rights of conscience, says this inestimable article, shall by no means, on no account be abridged or interfered with. No self-righteous or powerful church shall set up its impious domination over all the rest. Every pious man may pay to the divine author of his existence the tribute of thanksgiving and adoration, in the manner of his forefathers.

The following paragraph declares the freedom of the press to be a main bulwark of liberty, and reasoning unanswerably from its usefulness and indispensable necessity, declares that it shall be inviolable.

As civil rulers, not having their duty to the people duly before them, may attempt to tyrannize, and as the military forces which must be occasionally raised to defend our country, might pervert their power to the injury of their fellow-citizens, the people are confirmed by the next article in their right to keep and bear their private arms. . . .

It has been argued by many against a bill of rights, that the omission of some in making the detail would one day draw into question those that should not be particularized. It is therefore provided, that no inference of that kind shall be made, so as to diminish, much less to alienate an ancient tho' unnoticed right, nor shall either of the branches of the Federal Government argue from such an omission any increase or extension of their powers.

The fifth proposition is an admirable thought. The Congress of the United States not only declare that liberty of conscience—the freedom of the press—and trial by jury are due from them to the people of this

Union, but deeming them as precious as the republican form of government, they declare, that no State under pretense of a separate jurisdiction, shall violate either of them. How insurmountable are the obstructions to the progress of tyranny, which this inestimable proposition will create? . . .

The wisdom of every free country has adopted that rule of civil policy, which separates the legislative, executive, and judicial powers, and renders them as far as possible, independent of each other. The eighth proposition therefore, wisely declares that to be the intention of the American people, in constructing their frame of general government; and upon all future questions regarding this point, the article proposed, will dictate such mode of proceedings, as shall most perfectly conform with the explained spirit of the original constitution.

To render more distinct and indelible the line which is drawn between the powers of the several States, and those of the general government, it is proposed by Congress to declare, that the States respectively, retain all such powers as are not delegated to Congress, or the exercise of which is not prohibited by the federal constitution. This must remove all apprehensions that the government of the States will be absorbed by that of the Union.

Whatever may be the fate of some of these propositions, either in Congress, or in the State Legislatures, every ingenious citizen of America will admit, that they manifest an attentive regard to the convenience, and a virtuous solicitude for the safety and happiness of the people, while they leave unimpaired those wholesome and necessary powers which the freemen of the United States have wisely granted to their national government.

*Source:* Philadelphia Federal Gazette, *18, 30 June 1789.*

## 14. Twelve-Part Bill of Rights Submitted to States (1789)

*The following twelve-part Bill of Rights was submitted to the states for ratification on September 28, 1789. Nine states ratified within a year and Virginia satisfied the three-fourths requirement of Article V in 1791. The first two proposed amendments were not ratified; the last ten were renumbered. Three of the original thirteen states—Massachusetts, Connecticut, and Georgia—did not ratify the Bill of Rights until the sesquicentennial celebration in 1939. In 1992 Article the Second was ratified after a passage of more than two hundred years to become the 27th Amendment. The fact that it was ratified after such a lapse of time surprised some Constitutional experts, but the effort of Congress to raise its salary in 1989 and the House banking scandals of 1992 created a popular sentiment to hold Congress accountable that was impossible to resist. The Archivist of the United States certified Michigan's ratification as satisfying Article V and Congress quickly added its endorsement.*

\* \* \* \* \* \* \* \* \* \* \* \* \* \* \* \* \* \* \* \* \* \* \* \* \* \* \* \* \* \* \*

Article the First [not ratified]: After the first enumeration required by the first Article of the Constitution, there shall be one Representative for every thirty thousand, until the number shall amount to one hundred, after which, the proportion shall be so regulated by Congress, that there shall be not less than one hundred Representatives, not less than one Representative for every forty thousand persons, until the number of Representatives shall amount to two hundred, after which the proportion shall be so regulated by Congress, that there shall not be less than two hundred Representatives, not more than one Representative for every fifty thousand persons.

Article the Second [not ratified]: No law, varying the compensation for the services of the Senators and Representatives, shall take effect, until an election of Representatives shall have intervened.

Article the Third [Amendment I]: Congress shall make no law respecting an establishment of religion, or prohibiting the free exercise thereof; or abridging the freedom of speech, or of the press, or the right of the people peaceably to assemble, and to petition the Government for a redress of grievances.

Article the Fourth [Amendment II]: A well regulated militia, being necessary to the security of a free State, the right of the people to keep and bear arms, shall not be infringed.

Article the Fifth [Amendment III]: No Soldier shall, in time of peace be quartered in any House, without the consent of the owner, nor in time of war, but in a manner to be prescribed by law.

Article the Sixth [Amendment IV]: The right of the people to be secure in their persons, houses, papers, and effects, against unreasonable searches and seizures, shall not be violated, and no warrants shall issue, but upon probable cause, supported by oath or affirmation, and particularly describing the place to be searched, and the persons or things to be seized.

Article the Seventh [Amendment V]: No person shall be held to answer for a capital, or otherwise infamous crime, unless on a presentment or indictment of a Grand Jury, except in cases arising in the land or naval forces, or in the militia, when in actual service in time of war or public danger; nor shall any person be subject for the same offence to be twice put in jeopardy of life or limb; nor shall be compelled in any criminal case to be witness against himself, nor deprived of life, liberty, or property, without due process of law; nor shall private property be taken for public use, without just compensation.

Article the Eighth [Amendment VI]: In all criminal prosecutions, the accused shall enjoy the right to a speedy and public trial, by an impartial jury of the State and district wherein the crime shall have been committed; which district shall have been previously ascertained by law, and to be informed of the nature and cause of the accusation; to be confronted with the witnesses against him; to have compulsory process for obtaining witnesses in his favor, and to have the assistance of counsel for his defense.

Article the Ninth [Amendment VII]: In suits at common law, where the value in controversy shall exceed twenty dollars, the right or trial by jury shall be preserved, and no fact tried by a jury, shall be otherwise re-examined in any Court of the United States, than according to the rules of the common law.

Article the Tenth [Amendment VIII]: Excessive bail shall not be required, nor excessive fines imposed, nor cruel and unusual punishments inflicted.

Article the Eleventh [Amendment IX]: The enumeration in the Constitution, of certain rights, shall not be construed to deny or disparage others retained by the people.

Article the Twelfth [Amendment X]: The powers not delegated to the United States by the Constitution, nor prohibited by it to the States, are reserved to the States respectively, or to the people.

*Source: Veit, Bowling, and Bickford, ed. Creating the Bill of Rights, 3–4.*

# CHAPTER 2:

# THE BILL OF RIGHTS
# AND THE STATES––
# THE FOURTEENTH AMENDMENT

## I. DUE PROCESS AND PRIVILEGES AND IMMUNITIES

### 15. *Barron v. Baltimore*
### 7 Peters 243; 8 L.Ed. 672 (1833)

*The First Amendment says that Congress shall make no law abridging freedom of religion, speech, press, or assembly. Likewise, additional portions of the Bill of Rights make no explicit reference to state and local governments. Did the Bill of Rights limit the national government alone?*

*While paving its streets, the City of Baltimore diverted some streams from their natural courses. As a result, deposits of sand and gravel built up near Barron's Wharf rendering the water shallow and the wharf useless. Barron sued on the Fifth Amendment ground that he had been deprived of his property for public use without just compensation. In this, his last constitutional decision, Chief Justice Marshall agreed that Barron had been denied effective use of his property without just compensation. But he held that the Fifth Amendment only affords this protection against the national government.*

*Barron has not been overruled. Today, however, the Fourteenth Amendment would protect citizens against similar injuries suffered at the hands of the state and local governments.*

\* \* \* \* \* \* \* \* \* \* \* \* \* \* \* \* \* \* \* \* \* \* \* \* \* \* \* \*

Mr. Chief Justice **Marshall** delivered the opinion of the Court:

The plaintiff in error contends that it comes within the clause in the fifth amendment . . . which inhibits the taking of private property for public use without just compensation. He insists that this amendment, being in favor of the liberty of the citizen, ought to be so construed as to restrain the legislative power of a State, as well as that of the United States. If this proposition be untrue, the court can take no jurisdiction of the cause.

The question thus presented is, we think, of great importance, but not of much difficulty.

The Constitution was ordained and established by the people of the United States for themselves, for their own government, and not for the government of the individual States. Each State established a constitution for itself, and in that constitution provided such limitations and restrictions on the powers of its particular government as its judgment dictated. The people of the United States framed such a government for the United States as they supposed best adapted to their situation, and best calculated to promote their interests. The powers they conferred on this government were to be exercised by itself; and the limitations on power, if expressed in general terms, are naturally, and, we think, necessarily applicable to the government created by the instrument. They are limitations of power granted in the instrument itself; not of distinct governments, framed by different persons and for different purposes.

If these propositions be correct, the fifth amendment must be understood as restraining the power of the general government, not as applicable to the States. In their several constitutions they have imposed such restrictions on their respective governments as their own wisdom suggested; such as they deemed most proper for themselves. It is a subject on which they judge exclusively, and with which others interfere no farther than they are supposed to have a common interest.

. . . Had the framers of these amendments intended them to be limitations on the powers of the State governments they would have imitated the framers of the original Constitution, and have expressed that intention. Had Congress engaged in the extraordinary occupation of improving the constitutions of the several States by affording the people additional protection from the exercise of power by their own governments in matters which concerned themselves alone, they would have declared their purpose in plain and intelligible language.

But it is universally understood, it is part of the history of the day, that the great revolution which established the Constitution of the United States was not effected without immense opposition. Serious fears were extensively entertained that those powers which the patriot statesmen who then watched over the interests of our country, deemed essential to the union, and to the attainment of those invaluable objects for which union was sought, might be exercised in a manner dangerous to liberty. In almost every convention by which the Constitution was adopted, amendments to guard against the abuse of power were recommended. These amendments demanded security against the apprehended encroachments of the general government—not against those of the local government.

In compliance with a sentiment thus generally expressed, to quiet fears thus extensively entertained, amendments were proposed by the required majority in Congress, and adopted by the States. These amendments contain no expression indicating an intention to apply them to the State governments. This court cannot so apply them.

We are of the opinion that the provision in the fifth amendment to the Constitution, declaring that private property shall not be taken for public use without just compensation, is intended solely as a limitation on the exercise of power by the government of the United States, and is not applicable to the legislation of the States. We are therefore of the opinion that there is no repugnancy between the several acts of the General Assembly of Maryland . . . and the Constitution of the United States. . . .

### 16. *The Slaughterhouse Cases*
### 16 Wallace 36; 21 L.Ed. 394 (1873)

*Until the ratification of the Fourteenth Amendment, only state constitutions and state laws protected basic liberties against encroachment by state and local governments. In 1868, however, additional limitations were placed upon state power. The Fourteenth Amendment prohibits states from denying persons "the privileges and immunities of citizens of the United States" or depriving them of "life, liberty, or property without due process of law." Some of the Amendment's authors hoped that it would protect at the state and local level the kinds of rights and liberties found in the Bill of Rights. Over the years this hope has been at least partially fulfilled as courts have used the Fourteenth Amendment to, in effect, "nationalize" portions of the Bill of Rights.*

*In* Chicago, Burlington and Quincy Railroad Co. v. Chicago *(166 U.S. 226, 1897), the unanimous Supreme Court held that states must supply just compensation to owners when private property is taken for a public purpose. Here for the first time the Court used the due process clause of the Fourteenth Amendment to apply a right found in the Bill of Rights— the Fifth Amendment's just compensation provision in this case—to restrict state action.*

*In* Twining v. New Jersey *(211 U.S. 78, 1908), the Court rejected a claim that the self-incrimination provision of the Fifth Amendment applies against states through the Fourteenth Amendment. However, the Court indicated that some rights similar to those in the Bill of Rights were among the liberties protected by the Fourteenth Amendment: "It is possible that some of the personal rights safeguarded by the first eight*

*Amendments against national action may also be safeguarded against state action, because a denial of them would be a denial of due process of law." Controversy over whether or not a particular right is of such a nature so as to be "included in the conception of due process" has been frequent and intense.*

*A series of subsequent decisions effectively nationalized the First Amendment. In* Gitlow v. New York *(268 U.S. 652, 1925), the Court upheld Mr. Gitlow's conviction for advocating the violent overthrow of the government, but it declared that freedom of speech and the press are among the fundamental liberties protected by the due process clause. In* Stromberg v. California *(283 U.S. 358, 1931), the Court ruled that the Fourteenth Amendment protects freedom of speech and in* Near v. Minnesota *(283 U.S. 687, 1931), it held that freedom of the press is likewise protected against state actions.* DeJonge v. Oregon *(299 U.S. 253, 1937) nationalized the right of assembly and petition,* Cantwell v. Connecticut *(310 U.S. 296, 1940) nationalized the free exercise of religion, and* Everson v. Board of Education of Ewing Township, N.J. *(330 U.S. 1, 1947) nationalized the prohibition against establishment of religion.* Hamilton v. Board of Regents *(293 U.S. 245, 1934) also protected freedom of religion via the Fourteenth Amendment.*

*Some of the rights of the accused have also been protected under the Fourteenth Amendment. For example, in* Moore v. Dempsey *(261 U.S. 86, 1923), the Court observed that due process entitles state criminal defendants to fair trials. In* Powell v. Alabama *(287 U.S. 45, 1932) the right to counsel in capital cases was applied at the state level and in* Brown v. Mississippi *(297 U.S. 278, 1936) a state criminal defendant was protected against coerced confessions. In these cases the Court ruled that the defendants had been denied their due process rights because they had been treated unfairly. The Court did not unequivocally establish that these rights would apply in all state cases exactly as they apply in federal cases. But the line of precedents continued to build and more and more criminal rights were nationalized through the Fourteenth Amendment. See, for example,* Wolf v. Colorado *(338 U.S. 25, 1949) and* Mapp v. Ohio *(367 U.S. 643, 1961) regarding unreasonable searches and seizures and the exclusionary rule;* Robinson v. California *(370 U.S. 660, 1962) concerning cruel and unusual punishment;* Gideon v. Wainwright *(372 U.S. 335, 1963) with respect to the right to counsel in all criminal cases;* Malloy v. Hogan *(378 U.S. 1, 1964) regarding protection against compulsory self-incrimination;* Pointer v. Texas *(380 U.S. 400, 1965) concerning the right to confront hostile witnesses;* Klopfer v. North Carolina *(386 U.S. 213, 1967) with respect to the right to a speedy trial;* Washington v. Texas *(388 U.S. 14, 1967) regarding the right to subpoena favorable witnesses;* Duncan v. Louisiana *(391 U.S. 145, 1968) concerning the right to a jury trial; and* Benton v. Maryland *(395 U.S. 784, 1969) with respect to the protection against double jeopardy.*

*Not all of the rights in the Bill of Rights have been made applicable to the states. For example, the right to grand jury indictment has not been absorbed into the Fourteenth Amendment. But most of the rights contained in the Bill of Rights do now bind the states as well as the national government. In this sense, the Fourteenth Amendment might be regarded almost as a second bill of rights for the states.*

*Shortly after the Fourteenth Amendment went into effect, the privileges and immunities clause appeared to offer promise as a significant mechanism for protecting individual rights against state abridgment. It prohibits states from enacting laws that restrict the privileges and immunities of United States citizenship. What did these "privileges and immunities" entail? Did they include all or parts of the Bill of Rights? In the* Slaughterhouse Cases, *the Court answered that they did not.*

*The Louisiana legislature passed a law in 1869 that provided that all livestock slaughtering in New Orleans would be done by a single corporation. Other butchers objected that this monopoly grant deprived them of the privilege of engaging in the business of their choice. Writing for a five-to-four majority, Justice Miller concluded that United States citizenship conferred no such right on individuals to be enforced against states by way of the Fourteenth Amendment.*

\* \* \* \* \* \* \* \* \* \* \* \* \* \* \* \* \* \* \* \* \* \* \* \* \* \* \*

Mr. Justice **Miller** delivered the opinion of the Court:

... The 1st section of the 14th article, to which our attention is ... invited, opens with a definition of citizenship—not only citizenship of the United States, but citizenship of the states.

... "All persons born or naturalized in the United States and subject to the jurisdiction thereof are citizens of the United States and of the state wherein they reside."

... It declares that persons may be citizens of the United States without regard to their citizenship of a particular state, and it overturns the Dred Scott decision by making all persons born within the United States and subject to its jurisdiction citizens of the United States. That its main purpose was to establish the citizenship of the negro can admit of no doubt. ... [T]he distinction between citizenship of the United States and citizenship of a state is clearly recognized and established. Not only may a man be a citizen of the United States without being a citizen of a state, but an important element is necessary to convert the former into the latter.

He must reside within the state to make him a citizen of it, but it is only necessary that he should be born or naturalized in the United States to be a citizen of the Union.

It is quite clear, then, that there is a citizenship of the United States and a citizenship of a state, which are distinct from each other and which depend upon different characteristics or circumstances in the individual.

We think this distinction and its explicit recognition in this Amendment of great weight in this argument, because the next paragraph of this same section, which is the one mainly relied on by the plaintiffs, ... speaks only of privileges and immunities of citizens of the United States, and does not speak of those of citizens of the several states. The arguments, however, in favor of the plaintiffs, rests wholly on the assumption that the citizenship is the same and the privileges and immunities guaranteed by the clause are the same.

The language is: "No state shall make or enforce any law which shall abridge the privileges or immunities of citizens of the United States." It is a little remarkable, if this clause was intended as a protection to the citizen of a state against the legislative power of his own state, that the words "citizen of the state" should be left out when it is so carefully used, and used in contradistinction to "citizens of the United States" in the very sentence which precedes it. It is too clear for argument that the change in phraseology was adopted understandingly and with a purpose.

Of the privileges and immunities of the citizens of the United States, and of the privileges and immunities of the citizen of the state, and what they respectively are, we will presently consider; but we wish to state here that it is only the former which are placed by this clause under the protection of the Federal Constitution, and that the latter, whatever they may be, are not intended to have any additional protection by this paragraph of the Amendment.

... The First and the leading case on the subject is that of *Corfield v. Coryell,* decided by Mr. Justice Washington in the circuit court for the district of Pennsylvania in 1823.

"The inquiry," he says, "is, what are the privileges and immunities of citizens of the several states? We feel no hesitation in confining these expressions to those privileges and immunities which are fundamental; which belong of right to the citizens of all free governments, and which have at all times been enjoyed by citizens of the several states which compose this Union.... "They may all, ... be comprehended under the following general heads: protection by the government, with the right to acquire and possess property of every kind, and to pursue and obtain happiness and safety, subject, nevertheless, to such restraints as the government may prescribe for the general good of the whole."

... They are, in the language of Judge Washington, those rights which are fundamental. Throughout his opinion, they are spoken of as rights belonging to the individual as a citizen of a state. . . . And they have always been held to be the class of rights which the state governments were created to establish and secure. . . .

. . . [The] sole purpose [of the privileges and immunities clause] was to declare to the several states, that whatever those rights, as you grant or establish them to your own citizens, or as you limit or qualify, or impose restrictions on their exercise, the same, neither more nor less, shall be the measure of the rights of citizens of other states within your jurisdiction.

. . . Was it the purpose of the 14th Amendment, by the simple declaration that no state should make or enforce any law which shall abridge the privileges and immunities of citizens of the United States, to transfer the security and protection of all . . . civil rights . . . from the states to the Federal government?

. . . We are convinced that no such results were intended by the Congress which proposed these amendments, nor by the legislatures of the states, which ratified them. . . .

Mr. Justice **Field**, with whom Mr. Chief Justice **Chase**, Mr. Justice **Swayne**, and Mr. Justice **Bradley** concurred, dissented:

The Amendment does not attempt to confer any new privileges or immunities upon citizens or to enumerate or define those already existing. It assumes that there are such privileges and immunities which belong of right to citizens as such, and ordains that they shall not be abridged by state legislation. If this inhibition has no reference to privileges and immunities of this character, but only refers, as held by the majority of the court in their opinion, to such privileges and immunities as were before its adoption specially designated in the Constitution or necessarily implied as belonging to citizens of the United States, it was a vain and idle enactment, which accomplished nothing, and most unnecessarily excited Congress and the people on its passage. With privileges and immunities thus designated no state could ever have interfered by its laws, and no new constitutional provision was required to inhibit such interference. The supremacy of the Constitution and the laws of the United States always controlled any state legislation of that character. But if the Amendment refers to the natural and inalienable rights which belong to all citizens, the inhibition has a profound significance and consequence. . . .

## 17. *Gitlow v. New York*
### 268 U.S. 652; 45 S.Ct. 625; 69 L.Ed. 1138 (1925)

*This case stands as an early example of how the Fourteenth Amendment's due process clause was used to nationalize portions of the Bill of Rights. A New York State Criminal Anarchy Statute prohibited advocating the violent overthrow of organized government. Benjamin Gitlow was convicted in New York for distributing a document that argued along these lines. Justice Sanford, writing for a seven-to-two majority, held that freedom of speech and the press are protected by the Fourteenth Amendment. Contending that such rights are not absolute and that states can punish those who abuse these freedoms, however, the Court upheld Gitlow's conviction.*

\* \* \* \* \* \* \* \* \* \* \* \* \* \* \* \* \* \* \* \* \* \* \* \* \* \*

Mr. Justice **Sanford** delivered the opinion of the Court:

Benjamin Gitlow was indicted in the supreme court of New York, with three others, for the statutory crime of criminal anarchy. . . .

The contention here is that the statute, by its terms and as applied in this case, is repugnant to the due process clause of the 14th Amendment. Its material provisions are:

"& 160. Criminal anarchy defined. -Criminal anarchy is the doctrine that organized government should be overthrown by force or violence, or by assassination of the executive head or of any of the executive officials of government, or by any unlawful means. The advocacy of such doctrine either by word of mouth or writing is a felony.

. . . The indictment was in two counts. The first charged that the defendants had advocated, advised, and taught the duty, necessity, and propriety of overthrowing and overturning organized government by force, violence, and unlawful means, by certain writings therein set forth, entitled: "The Left Wing Manifesto"; the second, that he had printed, published, and knowingly circulated and distributed a certain paper called "The Revolutionary Age," containing the writings set forth in the first count, advocating, advising, and teaching the doctrine that organized government should be overthrown by force, violence, and unlawful means.

. . . There was no evidence of any effect resulting from the publication and circulation of the Manifesto.

. . . The sole contention here is, essentially, that, as there was no evidence of any concrete result flowing from the publication of the Manifesto, or of circumstances showing the likelihood of such result, the statute as construed and applied by the trial court penalizes the mere utterance, as such, of "doctrine" having no quality of incitement, without regard either to the circumstance of its utterance or to the likelihood of unlawful consequences; and that, as the exercise of the right of free expression with relation to government is only punishable "in circumstances involving likelihood of substantive evil," the statute contravenes the due process clause of the Fourteenth Amendment. The argument in support of this contention rests primarily upon the following proposition; 1st, that the "liberty" protected by the 14th Amendment includes the liberty of speech and of the press; and 2nd, that while liberty of expression "is not absolute," it may be restrained "only in circumstances where its exercise bears a causal relation with some substantive evil, consummated, attempted, or likely"; and as the statute "takes no account of circumstances," it unduly restrains this liberty, and is therefore unconstitutional.

The precise question presented . . . then, is whether the statute, as construed and applied in this case by the state courts, deprived the defendant of his liberty of expression, in violation of the due process clause of the 14th Amendment.

The statute does not penalize the utterance or publication of abstract "doctrine" or academic discussion having no quality of incitement to any concrete action. . . . What it prohibits is language advocating, advising, or teaching the overthrow of organized government by unlawful means. These words imply urging to action. . . .

. . . The Manifesto, plainly, is neither the statement of abstract doctrine nor, as suggested by counsel, mere prediction that industrial disturbances and revolutionary mass strikes will result spontaneously in an inevitable process of evolution in the economic system. It advocates and urges in fervent language mass action which shall progressively foment industrial disturbances, and, through political mass strikes and revolutionary mass action, overthrow and destroy organized parliamentary government. . . .

For present purposes we may and do assume that freedom of speech and of the press—which are protected by the 1st Amendment from abridgment by Congress—are among the fundamental personal rights and "liberties" protected by the due process clause of the 14th Amendment from impairment by the states. . . .

It is a fundamental principle long established, that freedom of speech and of the press which is secured by the Constitution does not confer an absolute right to speak or publish, without responsibility, whatever one may choose. . . .

That a state, in the exercise of its police power, may punish those who abuse this freedom by utterances inimical to the public welfare, tending to corrupt public morals, incite to crime, or disturb the public peace, is not open to question. . . .

. . . [A] state may punish utterances endangering the foundations of organized government and threatening its overthrow by unlawful means. . . .

By enacting the present statute the state has determined, through its legislative body, that utterances advocating the overthrow of organized government by force, violence, and unlawful means, are so inimical to the general welfare, and involve such danger of substantive evil, that they may be penalized in the exercise of its police power. That determination must be given great weight. . . . .That utterances inciting to the overthrow of organized government by unlawfull means present a sufficient danger of substantive evil to bring their punishment within the range of legislative discretion is clear. . . . The state cannot reasonably be required to measure the danger from every such utterance in the nice balance of a jeweler's scale. A single revolutionary spark may kindle a fire that, smoldering for a time, may burst into a sweeping and destructive conflagration. It cannot be said that the state is acting arbitrarily or unreasonably when, in the exercise of its judgment as to the measures necessary to protect the public peace and safety, it seeks to extinguish the spark without waiting until it has enkindled the flame or blazed into the conflagration. It cannot reasonably be required to defer the adoption of measures for its own peace and safety until the revolutionary utterances lead to actual disturbances of the public peace or imminent and immediate danger of its own destruction; but it may, in the exercise of its judgment, suppress the threatened danger in its incipiency. . . .

We cannot hold that the present statute is an arbitrary or unreasonable exercise of the police power of the state, unwarrantably infringing the freedom of speech or press; and we must and do sustain its constitutionality. . . .

Mr. Justice **Holmes** dissented:

Mr. Justice Brandeis and I are of the opinion that this judgment should be reversed. The general principle of free speech, its seems to me, must be taken to be included in the 14th Amendment, in view of the scope that has been given to the word "liberty" as there used. . . . If I am right, then I think that the criterion sanctioned by the full court in *Schenck v. United States,* applies: "The question in every case is whether the words used are used in such circumstances and are of such a nature as to create a clear and present danger that they will bring about the substantive evils that [the state] has a right to prevent." . . . [I]t is manifest that there was no present danger of an attempt to overthrow the government by force on the part of the admittedly small minority who shared the defendant's views. . . . [W]hatever may be thought of the redundant discourse before us, it had no chance of starting a present conflagration. . . .

If the publication of this document had been laid as an attempt to induce an uprising against government at once, and not at some indefinite time in the future, it would have presented a different question. The object would have been one with which the law might deal, subject to the doubt whether there was any danger that the publication could produce any result; or, in other words, whether it was not futile and too remote from possible consequences. But the indictment alleges the publication and nothing more.

### 18. Justice Black's Dissent in *Adamson v. California* 332 U.S. 46; 67 S.Ct. 1672; 91 L.Ed. 1903 (1947)

*In* Palko v. Connecticut *(302 U.S. 319, 1937), the Court ruled that while the Fifth Amendment prohibits double jeopardy at the national level, the Fourteenth Amendment does not apply the same restriction against the states. Writing for an eight-to-one majority, Justice Cardozo summarized previous rulings on the applicability of the Bill of Rights to the states and tried to explain the principles on which such decisions rest. The Fourteenth Amendment, he claimed, nationalizes only those provisions that are "of the very essence of a scheme of ordered liberty." These are rights "so rooted in the traditions and conscience of our people as to be ranked as fundamental." He concluded that Palko had not suffered a "hardship so acute and shocking that our polity will not endure it."*

*Recall that the protection against double jeopardy was seen as fundamentally important by a later court in* Benton v. Maryland *(1969). This development underscores the subjectivity associated with attempts to distinguish rights that are sufficiently important to be absorbed into the Fourteenth Amendment from those that are not.*

*In this case, Adamson claimed that the state of California deprived him of his Fifth Amendment protection against compulsory self-incrimination. By a five-to-four vote, the Supreme Court decided that he had not suffered an unendurable hardship. Justice Black's dissent, however, is especially noteworthy. He considered the Cardozan approach to be too subjective. As with natural law philosophy, the problem is to show that "fundamental principles" actually rest on objective standards and not just on the personal preferences of individual judges. He cited history to support his claim that the authors of the Fourteenth Amendment wanted it to apply all of the Bill of Rights to the states (see, for example, Congressman John Bingham of Ohio and Senator Jacob Howard of Michigan). Black's "total incorporation" would nationalize the entire Bill of Rights and would apply these guarantees to the states exactly as they were applied at the national level. But while Black's position promises more objectivity, it also poses problems. For example, Black's view of the Seventh Amendment would require states to provide jury trials in civil cases involving paltry sums of money.*

*Black's position won four votes. It has never commanded majority support. Most of his ends, however, have been achieved in reality. Without adopting the philosophy of total incorporation, the Court has applied most of the guarantees of the Bill of Rights to the states. A case in point is the Court's decision to overturn* Adamson *in* Malloy v. Hogan *(1964).*

\* \* \* \* \* \* \* \* \* \* \* \* \* \* \* \* \* \* \* \* \* \* \* \* \* \* \* \* \* \* \*

Mr. Justice **Black** dissenting:

This decision reasserts a constitutional theory spelled out in *Twining v. New Jersey* . . . that this Court is endowed by the Constitution with boundless power under "natural law" periodically to expand and contract constitutional standards to conform the Court's conception of what at a particular time constitutes "civilized decency" and "fundamental liberty and justice." Invoking this *Twining* rule, the Court concludes that although comment upon testimony in a federal court would violate the Fifth Amendment, identical comment in a state court does not violate today's fashion in civilized decency and fundamentals and is therefore not prohibited by the Federal Constitution as amended.

. . . I would not reaffirm the *Twining* decision. I think that decision and the "natural law" theory of the Constitution upon which it relies degrade the constitutional safeguards of the Bill of Rights and simultaneously appropriate for this Court a broad power which we are not authorized by the Constitution to exercise. . . .

My study of the history events that culminated in the Fourteenth Amendment, and the expressions of those who sponsored and favored, as well as those who opposed its submission and passage, persuades me that one of the chief objects that the provisions of the Amendment . . . were intended to accomplish was to make the Bill of Rights applicable to the states. With full knowledge of the import of the *Barron* decision, the framers and backers of the Fourteenth Amendment proclaimed its purpose to be to overturn the constitutional rule that case had announced.

. . . In my judgment . . . history conclusively demonstrates that the language of the first section of the Fourteenth Amendment . . . was thought by those responsible for its submission, sufficiently explicit to guarantee that thereafter no state could deprive its citizens of the privileges and protections of the Bill of Rights. . . . [T]he "natural law" formula which the Court uses to reach its conclusion in this case should be abandoned as an incongruous excrescence on our Constitution. I believe that formula to be itself a violation of our Constitution, in that it subtly conveys to courts, at the expense of legislatures, ultimate power over public policies in fields where no specific provision of the Constitution limits legislative power. . . .

. . . In my judgment the people of no nation can lose their liberty so long as a Bill of Rights like ours survives and its basic purposes are conscientiously interpreted, enforced and respected so as to afford continuous protection against old, as well as new, devices and practices which might thwart those purposes. I fear to see the consequences of the Court's practice of substituting its own concepts of decency and fundamental justice for the language of the Bill of Rights as its point of departure in interpreting and enforcing that Bill of Rights. If the choice must be between the selective process of the *Palko* decision applying some of the Bill of Rights to the States, or the *Twining* rule applying none of them, I would choose the *Palko* selective process. But rather than accept either of these choices, I would follow what I believe was the original purpose of the Fourteenth Amendment—to extend to all the people of the nation the complete protection of the Bill of Rights. To hold that this Court can determine what, if any, provisions of the Bill of Rights will be enforced, and if so to what degree, is to frustrate the great design of a written Constitution.

Conceding the possibility that this Court is now wise enough to improve on the Bill of Rights by substituting natural law concepts for the Bill of Rights, I think the possibility is entirely too speculative to agree to take that course. I would therefore hold in this case that the full protection of the Fifth Amendment's proscription against compelled testimony must be afforded by California. This I would do because of reliance upon the original purpose of the Fourteenth Amendment. . . .

To pass upon the constitutionality of statutes by looking to particular standards enumerated in the Bill of Rights and other parts of the Constitution is one thing; to invalidate statutes because of application of "natural law" deemed to be above and undefined by the Constitution is another. In the one instance, courts proceeding within clearly marked constitutional boundaries seek to execute policies written into the Constitution; in the other they roam at will in the limitless area of their own beliefs as to reasonableness and actually select policies, a responsibility which the Constitution entrusts to the legislative representatives of the people.

## II. EQUAL PROTECTION OF THE LAWS

### 19. *The Civil Rights Cases*
### 109 U.S. 3; 3 S.Ct. 18; 27 L.Ed. 835 (1883)

*The equal protection clause of the Fourteenth Amendment does not bear the same kind of direct relationship to the Bill of Rights that the due process clause does, but it is an important weapon in the battle*

*against racial and other forms of discrimination. In light of the fact that
the Bill of Rights is an expression of fundamentally important rights and
in view of the fact that discriminatory treatment is widely regarded as
fundamentally unfair, it is sensible to extend this present examination
of the Fourteenth Amendment to the equal protection area before proceeding to other topics.*

*The Thirteenth, Fourteenth, and Fifteenth Amendments were enacted
to protect the rights of freed slaves. In the closing days of the Reconstruction, however, many in Congress thought that specific laws were necessary to ensure that the rights of blacks would be respected by—and
protected against—whites who were regaining control of Southern state
governments. One such law was the Civil Rights Act of 1875. The Act
made it both a crime and a civil wrong for any person to deny any
other person "the full and equal enjoyment of any of the accommodations, advantages, facilities and privileges of inns, public conveyances
on land or water, theaters and other places of public amusement" on
racial grounds.*

*The Supreme Court's decision in this case, based on five cases that
were grouped together, seriously undermined the civil rights effort of this
period. The Court found the Act unconstitutional. Justice Bradley, writing for the majority, ruled that the Thirteenth Amendment did not authorize Congress to pass this law because racial discrimination is not the
same as involuntary servitude. Furthermore, he claimed that the Fourteenth Amendment gave Congress the power to prevent discrimination
by states, but it did not authorize Congress to prohibit discrimination by
private parties.*

*As the sole dissenter in this case, Justice Harlan rejected the majority's
view of the Thirteenth Amendment. He argued that the burdens of racial
discrimination "constitute badges of slavery and servitude" and that the
Act was an appropriate measure to protect former slaves against such
racial injuries. Years later, in the case of* Jones v. Alfred H. Mayer, Co.
*(392 U.S. 409, 1968), the Court accepted Harlan's reasoning. In* Jones,
*Justice Stewart, writing for the Court, said that the Thirteenth Amend-
ment permits Congress to prohibit private racial discrimination because
the Amendment was intended to remove badges of slavery from this
Nation. In Stewart's words,*

*... Congress has the power under the Thirteenth Amendment ration-
ally to determine what are the badges and the incidents of slavery
and the authority to translate that determination into effective legislation.... [W]hen racial discrimination herds men into ghettos and
makes their ability to buy property turn on the color of their skin,*

*then it too is a relic of slavery.... The Thirteenth Amendment includes the right to buy whatever a white man can, the right to live wherever a white man can live....*

\* \* \* \* \* \* \* \* \* \* \* \* \* \* \* \* \* \* \* \* \* \* \* \* \* \* \* \*

Mr. Justice **Bradley** delivered the opinion of the Court:

... [T]he primary and important question in all the cases is the constitutionality of law....

The essence of the law is, not to declare boldly that all persons shall be entitled to the full and equal enjoyment of the accommodation, advantages, facilities, and privileges of inns, public conveyances, and theaters; but that such enjoyment shall not be subject to any conditions applicable only to citizens of a particular race or color....

Has Congress constitutional power to make such a law? Of course, no one will contend that the power to pass it was contained in the Constitution before the adoption of the last three amendments. The power is sought, first, in the Fourteenth Amendment, and the views and arguments of distinguished Senators, advanced whilst the law was under consideration, claiming authority to pass it by virtue of that amendment, are the principal arguments adduced in favor of the power....

The first section of the Fourteenth Amendment..., after declaring who shall be citizens of the United States, and of the several States, is prohibitory in its character, and prohibitory upon the States. It declares that:

No State shall make or enforce any law which shall abridge the privileges or immunities of citizens of the United States; nor shall any State deprive any person of life, liberty, or property without due process of law; nor deny to any person within its jurisdiction the equal protection of the laws.

It is State action of a particular character that is prohibited. Individual invasion of individual rights is not the subject matter of the amendment. It has a deeper and broader scope. It nullifies and makes void all State legislation, and State action of every kind, which impairs the privileges and immunities of citizens of the United States, or which injures them in life, liberty or property without due process of law, or which denies to any of them the equal protection of the laws. It not only does this, but, in order that the national will, thus declared, may not be a mere *brutum fulmen*, the last section of the amendment invests Congress with power to enforce it by appropriate legislation. To enforce what? To enforce the prohibition. To adopt appropriate legislation for correcting the effects of such prohibited State laws and State acts, and thus to render them effectually null, void, and innocuous. This is the legislative power conferred upon Congress, and this is the whole of it. . . . Positive rights and privileges are undoubtedly secured by the Fourteenth Amendment; but they are secured by way of prohibition against State laws and State proceedings affecting those rights and privileges, and by power given to Congress to legislate for the purpose of carrying such prohibition into effect. . . .

[U]ntil some State law has been passed, or some State action through its officers or agents has been taken, adverse to the rights of citizens sought to be protected by the Fourteenth Amendment, no legislation of the United States under said amendment, nor any proceedings under such legislation, can be called into activity; for the prohibitions of the amendment are against State laws and acts done under State authority. . . . In fine, the legislation which Congress is authorized to adopt in this behalf is not general legislation upon the rights of the citizen, but corrective legislation, that is, such as may be necessary and proper for counteracting such laws as the States may adopt or enforce, and which, by the amendment, they are prohibited from making or enforcing, or such acts and proceedings as the States may commit or take, and which, by the amendment, they are prohibited from committing or taking. . . . It is sufficient for us to examine whether the law in question is of that character.

An inspection of the law shows that it makes no reference whatever to any supposed or apprehended violation of the Fourteenth Amendment on the part of the States. It is not predicated on any such view. It proceeds *ex directo* to declare that certain acts committed by individuals shall be deemed offenses, and shall be prosecuted and punished by proceedings in the courts of the United States. It does not profess to be corrective of any constitutional wrong committed by the States. . . . In other words, it steps into the domain of local jurisprudence, and lays down rules for the conduct of individuals in society towards each other, and imposes sanctions for the enforcement of those rules, without referring in any manner to any supposed action of the State or its authorities.

If this legislation is appropriate for enforcing the prohibitions of the amendment, it is difficult to see where it is to stop. . . . The truth is, that the implication of a power to legislate in this manner is based upon the assumption that if the States are forbidden to legislate or act in a particular way on a particular subject, and power is conferred upon Congress to enforce the prohibition, this gives Congress power to legislate generally upon that subject, and not merely power to provide modes of redress against such State legislation or action. The assumption is certainly unsound. It is repugnant to the Tenth Amendment of the Constitution. . . .

In this connection it is proper to state that civil rights, such as are guaranteed by the Constitution against State aggression, cannot be impaired by the wrongful acts of individuals, unsupported by State authority in the shape of laws, customs, or judicial or executive proceedings. The wrongful act of an individual, unsupported by any such authority, is simply a private wrong, or a crime of that individual.... An individual cannot deprive a man of his right to vote...; he may, by force or fraud, interfere with the enjoyment of the right in a particular case...; but unless protected in these wrongful acts by some shield of State law or State authority, he cannot destroy or injure the right; he will only render himself amenable to satisfaction or punishment; and amenable therefore to the laws of the State where the wrongful acts are committed. Hence, in all those cases where the Constitution seeks to protect the rights of the citizen against discriminative and unjust laws of the State by prohibiting such laws, it is not individual offenses, but abrogation and denial of rights, which it denounces, and for which it clothes the Congress with power to provide a remedy....

We have discussed the question presented by the law on the assumption that a right to enjoy equal accommodation and privileges in all inns, public conveyances, and places of public amusement, is one of the essential rights of the citizen which no State can abridge or interfere with. Whether it is such a right, or not, is a different question which ... it is not necessary to examine....

But the power of Congress to adopt direct and primary, as distinguished from corrective legislation, on the subject in hand, is sought, in the second place, from the Thirteenth Amendment....

This amendment, as well as the Fourteenth, is undoubtedly self-executing without any ancillary legislation, so far as its terms are applicable to any existing state of circumstances. By its own unaided force and effect it abolished slavery, and established universal freedom....

The only question under the present head, therefore, is whether the refusal to any person of the accommodations of an inn, or a public conveyance, or a place of public amusement, by an individual, and without any sanction or support from any State law or regulation, does inflict upon such persons any manner of servitude, or form of slavery, as those terms are understood in this country?...

It would be running the slavery argument into the ground to make it apply to every act of discrimination which a person may see fit to make as to the guests he will entertain, or as to the people he will take into his coach or cab or car, or admit to his concert or theater, or deal with in other matters of intercourse or business.

... We are of opinion, that no countenance of authority for the passage of the law in question can be found in either the Thirteenth or Fourteenth

Amendment of the Constitution; and no other ground of authority for its passage being suggested, it must necessarily be declared void, at least so far as its operation in the several States is concerned....

Mr. Justice **Harlan**, dissenting:

The opinion in these cases proceeds, it seems to me, upon grounds entirely too narrow and artificial....

The Thirteenth Amendment, it is conceded, did something more than to prohibit slavery as an *institution,* resting upon distinctions of race, and upheld by positive law.... Was it the purpose of the nation simply to destroy the institution, and then remit the race, theretofore held in bondage, to the several States for such protection, in their civil rights, ... as those States, in their discretion, might choose to provide? Were the States against whose protest the institution was destroyed, to be left free, so far as national interference was concerned, to make or allow discriminations against that race, as such, in the enjoyment of those fundamental rights which by universal concession, inhere in a state of freedom? ...

That there are burdens and disabilities which constitute badges of slavery and servitude, and that the power to enforce by appropriate legislation the Thirteenth Amendment may be exerted by legislation of a direct and primary character, for the eradication, not simply of the institution, but of its badges and incidents, are propositions which ought to be deemed indisputable.... I hold that since slavery [was] the moving or principal cause of the adoption of the amendment, and since that institution rested wholly upon the inferiority, as a race, of those held in bondage, their freedom necessarily involved immunity from, and protection against, all discrimination against them, because of their race, in respect of such civil rights as belong to freemen of other races. Congress, therefore, under its express power to enforce that amendment, by appropriate legislation, may enact laws to protect that people against the deprivation, because of their race, of any civil rights granted to other freemen in the same State....

### 20. *Plessy v. Ferguson*
### 163 U.S. 537; 16 S.Ct. 1138; 41 L.Ed. 256 (1896)

*After the Reconstruction, some Southern states adopted laws that established and enforced a system of racial segregation. Separate schools, parks, bus and train accommodations, and the like were required by law for blacks and whites. Following the Supreme Court's decision in the 1883* Civil Rights Cases, *no party could raise a constitutional claim when discrimination was practiced by private parties. If the racial discrimination was required by law, however, state action was present and some believed that disadvantaged blacks could bring Fourteenth Amendment based challenges.*

*In 1890, the Louisiana legislature passed a law requiring "that all railway companies carrying passengers in their coaches in this state shall provide equal but separate accommodations for the white and colored races. . . . " Plessy was seven-eighths Caucasian and one-eighth Negroid. He refused to vacate a seat in the white compartment of a railway car and was convicted for violating the law.*

*Justice Henry Brown, writing for a seven-to-one majority, held that the law violated neither the Thirteenth nor Fourteenth Amendments. In the process, the Court endorsed the principle of "separate but equal" facilities for different races. Justice Harlan once again authored a dissenting opinion. In it, he anticipated the eventual reversal of this decision in* Brown v. Board of Education of Topeka *(1954).*

\* \* \* \* \* \* \* \* \* \* \* \* \* \* \* \* \* \* \* \* \* \* \* \* \* \* \* \* \* \*

Mr. Justice **Brown** delivered the opinion of the Court:

. . . This case turns upon the constitutionality of an act of the general assembly of the state of Louisiana, passed in 1890, providing for separate railway carriages for the white and colored races. . . .

The constitutionality of this act is attacked upon the ground that it conflicts both with the 13th Amendment of the Constitution, abolishing slavery, and the 14th Amendment, which prohibits certain restrictive legislation on the part of the states.

1. That it does not conflict with the 13th Amendment, which abolished slavery and involuntary servitude, except as a punishment for crime, is too clear for argument. . . .

A statute which implies merely a legal distinction between the white and colored races—a distinction which is founded in the color of the two races, and which must always exist so long as white men are distinguished from the other race by color—has no tendency to destroy the legal equality of the two races, or re-establish a state of involuntary servitude. Indeed, we do not understand that the 13th Amendment is strenuously relied upon by the plaintiff in error in this connection. . . .

The object of the amendment was undoubtedly to enforce the absolute equality of the two races before the law, but in the nature of things it could not have been intended to abolish distinctions based upon color, or to enforce social, as distinguished from political, equality, or a commingling of the two races upon terms unsatisfactory to either. Laws permitting, and even requiring their separation in places where they are liable to be brought into contact do not necessarily imply the inferiority of either race to the other, and have been generally, if not universally, recognized as within the competency of the state legislatures in the exercise of their police power. The most common instance of this is connected with the establishment of separate schools for white and colored children, which have been held to be a valid exercise of the legislative power even by courts of states where the political rights of the colored race have been longest and most earnestly enforced. . . .

It is claimed by the plaintiff in error that, in any mixed community, the reputation of belonging to the dominant race, in this instance the white race is *property*, in the same sense that a right of action, or of inheritance, is property. Conceding this to be so, for the purposes of this case, we are unable to see how this statute deprives him of, or in any way affects his right to, such property. If he be a white man and assigned to a colored coach, he may have his action for damages against the company for being deprived of his so-called property. Upon the other hand, if he be a colored man and be so assigned, he has been deprived of no property, since he is not lawfully entitled to the reputation of being a white man. . . . .

So far, then, as a conflict with the 14th Amendment is concerned, the case reduces itself to the question whether the statute of Louisiana is a reasonable regulation, and with respect to this there must necessarily be a large discretion on the part of the legislature. In determining the question of reasonableness it is at liberty to act with reference to the established usages, customs, and traditions of the people, and with a view to the promotion of their comfort, and the preservation of the public peace and good order. Gauged by this standard, we cannot say that a law which authorizes or even requires the separation of the two races in public conveyances is unreasonable or more obnoxious to the 14th Amendment than the acts of Congress requiring separate schools for colored children in the District of Columbia, the constitutionality of which does not seem to have been questioned, or the corresponding acts of state legislatures.

We consider the underlying fallacy of the plaintiffs argument to consist in the assumption that the enforced separation of the two races stamps the colored race with a badge of inferiority. If this be so, it is not by reason of anything found in the act, but solely because the colored race chooses to put that construction upon it. The argument necessarily assumes that if, as has been more than once the case, and is not unlikely to be so again, the colored race should become the dominant power in the state legislature, and should enact a law in precisely similar terms, it would thereby relegate the white race to an inferior position. We imagine that the white race, at least, would not acquiesce in this assumption. The argument also assumes that social prejudice may be overcome by legislation, and that equal rights cannot be secured to the Negro except by an enforced commingling of the two races. We cannot accept this proposition. If the two races are to meet on terms of social equality, it must be the result of natural affinities, a mutual appreciation of each other's merits and a voluntary consent of individuals. . . . Legislation is powerless to eradicate racial instincts or to abolish distinctions based upon physical differences, and the attempt to do so can only result in accentuating the difficulties of the present situation. If the civil and political right of both races be equal, one cannot be inferior . . . to the other civilly or politically. If one race be inferior to the other socially, the Constitution of the United States cannot put them upon the same plane.

Mr. Justice **Harlan**, dissenting:

. . . In respect of civil rights, common to all citizens, the Constitution . . . does not, I think, permit any public authority to know the race of those entitled to be protected in the enjoyment of such rights. Every true man has pride of race, and under appropriate circumstances, when the rights of others, his equals before the law, are not to be affected, it is his privilege to express such pride and to take such action based upon it as to him seems proper. But I deny that any legislative body or judicial tribunal may have regard to the race of citizens when the civil rights of those citizens are involved. Indeed such legislation as that here in question is inconsistent, not only with that equality of rights which pertains to citizenship, national and state, but with their personal liberty enjoyed by every one within the United States. . . .

In my opinion, the judgment this day rendered will, in time, prove to be quite as pernicious as the decision made by this tribunal in the *Dred Scott* Case. It was adjudged in that case that the descendants of Africans who were imported into this country and sold as slaves were not included nor intended to be included under the word "citizens" in the Constitution, and could not claim any of the rights and privileges which that instrument provided for and secured to citizens of the United States; that at the time of the adoption of the Constitution they were "considered as a subordinate and inferior class of beings, who had been subjugated by the dominant race, and, whether emancipated or not, yet remained subject to their authority, and had no rights or privileges but such as those who held the power and the government might choose to grant them." The recent amendments of the Constitution, it was supposed, had eradicated these principles from our institutions. But it seems that we have yet, in some of the states, a dominant race, a superior class of citizens, which assumes to regulate the enjoyment of civil rights, common to all citizens, upon the basis of race. The present decision, it may well be apprehended, will not only stimulate aggressions, more or less brutal and irritating, upon the admitted rights of colored citizens, but will encourage the belief that it is possible, by means of state enactments, to defeat the beneficent purposes which the people of the United States had in view when they adopted the recent amendments of the Constitution, by one of which the blacks of this country were made citizens of the United States and of the states in which they respectively reside and whose privileges and immunities, as citizens, the states are forbidden to abridge. Sixty millions of whites are in no danger from the presence here of eight millions of blacks. The destinies of the two races in this country are indissolubly linked together, and the interests of both require that the common government of all shall not permit the seeds of race hate to be planted under the sanction of law. What can more certainly arouse race hate, what more certainly create and perpetuate a feeling of distrust between these races, than state enactments which in fact proceed on the ground that colored citizens are so inferior and degraded that they cannot be allowed to sit in public coaches occupied by white citizens? That, as all will admit, is the real meaning of such legislation as was enacted in Louisiana. . . .

If evils will result from the commingling of the two races upon public highways established for the benefit of all, they will be infinitely less than those that will surely come from state legislation regulating the enjoyment of civil rights upon the basis of race. We boast of the freedom enjoyed by our people above all other peoples. But it is difficult to reconcile that boast with a state of the law which, practically, puts the brand of servitude and degradation upon a large class of our fellow citizens, our equals before the law. The thin disguise of "equal" accommodations for passengers in railroad coaches will not mislead anyone, or atone for the wrong this day done. . . .

I am of opinion that the statute of Louisiana is inconsistent with the personal liberty of citizens, white and black, in that state, and hostile to both the spirit and letter of the Constitution of the United States. If laws of like character should be enacted in the several states of the Union, the effect would be in the highest degree mischievous. Slavery as an institution tolerated by law would, it is true, have disappeared from our country, but there would remain a power in the states, by sinister legislation, to interfere with the full enjoyment of the blessings of freedom; to regulate civil rights, common to all citizens, upon the basis of race; and to place in a condition of legal inferiority a large body of American citizens, now constituting a part of the political community, called the people of the United States, for whom and by whom, through representatives, our government is administered. Such a system is inconsistent with the guarantee given by the Constitution to each state of a republican form of government, and may be stricken down by Congressional action, or by the courts in the discharge of their solemn duty to maintain the supreme law of the land, anything in the Constitution or laws of any state to the contrary notwithstanding.

For the reasons stated, I am constrained to withhold my assent from the opinion and judgment of the majority.

### 21. *Brown v. Board of Education of Topeka*
### 347 U.S. 483; 74 S.Ct. 686; 98 L.Ed. 873 (1954)

*In* Plessy v. Ferguson *(1896), the Supreme Court held that state laws requiring "separate but equal" facilities for blacks and whites did not violate the equal protection clause of the Fourteenth Amendment. In fact, separate facilities provided for blacks were often substandard. Considerable attention was directed towards racially-segregated schools.*

*In* Sweatt v. Painter *(339 U.S. 629, 1950), the Court dealt with the case of a black student who was denied admission to the University of Texas Law School on racial grounds. Instead, he was directed to a separate law school for blacks in Texas. The Court concluded that the black law school was, in fact, not equal to the white law school with respect to library holdings, curriculum, faculty, and alumni attainments. As a result, the Court ordered that the black student be admitted into the University of Texas Law School. The Court did not abandon the separate-but-equal principle in the case; instead, it found that the facilities in question were* not *equal. In* Brown v. Board, *however, the Court did squarely overturn the* Plessy *doctrine.*

*A series of cases from several states challenged the constitutionality of racially-segregated public schools. The Topeka, Kansas case was taken as the nominal leading case, but all of them were determined by a single decision. Writing for the unanimous Court, Chief Justice Warren did not scrutinize the facilities to evaluate their relative quality. Rather, he concluded that separate educational facilities are "inherently unequal." Subsequently, the Court ordered desegregation to proceed with "all deliberate speed."*

*Despite this order, many schools remained racially segregated. In* Swann v. Charlotte-Mecklenburg Board of Education *(402 U.S. 1, 1971), the Court confronted a school system in which two-thirds of the district's black students attended schools that were more than 99% black. The school district and the local district court failed to agree on a desegregation plan. The district court eventually ordered the school district to implement a massive bussing program to effect desegregation. The unanimous Supreme Court upheld the district court's order and supported the use of bussing to combat racial segregation. In such cases, the burden would be placed on school authorities to show that their racial composition is not the result of discriminatory actions.*

*In 1991 (*Board of Education of Oklahoma City Public Schools v. Dowell, *112 L.Ed. 2d 715), the Supreme Court supported a school district's attempt to end a court-ordered desegration plan that had been imposed back in 1972. The Supreme Court held that a district court's finding that the school district was no longer operating in a discriminatory fashion and that the purposes of previous desegration litigation had been accomplished was sufficient to justify the discontinuation of the previously ordered desegration plan.*

\* \* \* \* \* \* \* \* \* \* \* \* \* \* \* \* \* \* \* \* \* \* \* \* \* \* \* \*

Mr. Chief Justice **Warren** delivered the opinion of the Court:

These cases come to us from the states of Kansas, South Carolina, Virginia and Delaware. They are premised on different facts and different local conditions, but a common legal question justifies their consideration together in this consolidated opinion.

In each of the cases, minors of the Negro race through their legal representatives, seek the aid of the courts in obtaining admission to the public schools of their community on a nonsegregated basis. In each instance, they have been denied admission to schools attended by white children under laws requiring or permitting segregation according to race. This segregation was alleged to deprive the plaintiffs of the equal protection of the laws under the Fourteenth Amendment. . . .

The plaintiffs contend that segregated public schools are not "equal" and cannot be made "equal," and that hence they are deprived of equal protection of the laws. . . .

. . . The doctrine of "separate but equal" did not make its appearance in this Court until 1896 in . . . *Plessy v. Ferguson,* . . . involving not education but transportation. American courts have since labored with the doctrine for over half a century. . . .

In the instant cases, that question is directly presented. Here, unlike *Sweatt v. Painter,* there are findings below that the Negro and white schools involved have been equalized, or are being equalized, with respect to buildings, curricula, qualifications and salaries of teachers, and other "tangible" factors. Our decision, therefore, cannot turn on merely a comparison of these tangible factors in the Negro and white schools involved in each of the cases. We must look instead to the effect of segregation itself on public education.

In approaching this problem, we cannot turn the clock back to 1868 when the Amendment was adopted, or even to 1896 when *Plessy v. Ferguson* was written. We must consider public education in the light of its full development and its present place in American life throughout the Nation. Only in this way can it be determined if segregation in public schools deprive these plaintiffs of the equal protection of the laws.

Today, education is perhaps the most important function of the state and local governments. Compulsory school-attendance laws and the great expenditures for education both demonstrate our recognition of the importance of education to our democratic society. It is required in the performance of our most basic public responsibilities, even service in the armed forces. It is the very foundation of good citizenship. Today it is a principal instrument in awakening the child to cultural values, in preparing him for later professional training, and in helping him to adjust normally to his environment. In these days, it is doubtful any child may reasonably be expected to succeed in life if he is denied the opportunity of an education. Such an opportunity, where the state has undertaken to provide it, is a right which must be made available to all on equal terms.

We come then to the question presented: Does segregation of children in public schools solely on the basis of race, even though the physical facilities and other "tangible" factors may be equal, deprive the children of the minority group of equal educational opportunities? We believe that it does.

. . . To separate them from others of similar age and qualifications solely because of their race generates a feeling of inferiority as to their status in the community that may effect their hearts and minds in a way unlikely ever to be undone. The effect of this separation on their educational opportunities was well stated by a finding in the Kansas case by a court which nevertheless felt compelled to rule against the Negro plaintiffs: "Segregation of white and colored children in public schools has a detrimental effect upon the colored children. The impact is greater when it has the sanction of the law; for the policy of separating the races is usually interpreted as denoting the inferiority of the Negro group. A sense of inferiority affects the motivation of a child to learn. Segregation with the sanction of law, therefore, has a tendency to retard the educational and mental development of Negro children and to deprive them of some of the benefits they would receive in a racially integrated school system."

Whatever may have been the extent of psychological knowledge at the time of *Plessy v. Ferguson,* this finding is amply supported by modern authority. Any language in *Plessy v. Ferguson* contrary to this finding is rejected.

We conclude that in the field of public education the doctrine of "separate but equal" has no place. Separate educational facilities are inherently unequal. Therefore, we hold that the plaintiffs and others similarly situated for whom the actions have been brought are, by reason of the segregation complained of, deprived of the equal protection of the laws guaranteed by the Fourteenth Amendment. This disposition makes unnecessary any discussion whether such segregation also violates the Due Process Clause of the Fourteenth Amendment.

Because these are class actions, because of the wide applicability of this decision, and because of the great variety of local conditions, the formulation of decrees in these cases presents problems of considerable complexity. On reargument, the consideration of appropriate relief was necessarily subordinated to the primary questions—the constitutionality of segregation in public education. We have now announced that such segregation is a denial of the equal protection of the laws. In order that we may have the full assistance of the parties in formulating decrees, the cases will be restored to the docket, and the parties are requested to present further argument on Questions 4 and 5 previously propounded by the Court for the reargument this Term. The Attorney General of the United States is again invited to participate. The Attorneys General of the states requiring or permitting segregation in public education will also be permitted to appear as *amici curiae* [friends of the Court who give advice on matters pending before it] upon request to do so by September 15, 1954, and submission of briefs by October 1, 1954. *Brown v. Board of Education* (Second Case; 1955).

These cases were decided on May 17, 1954. The opinions of that date, declaring the fundamental principle that racial discrimination in public education is unconstitutional, are incorporated herein by reference. All provisions of federal, state, or local law requiring or permitting such discrimination must yield to this principle. There remains for consideration the manner in which relief is to be accorded. . . .

Full implementation of these constitutional principles may require solution of varied local school problems. School authorities have the primary responsibility for elucidating, assessing, and solving these problems; courts will have to consider whether the action of school authorities constitutes good faith implementation of the governing constitutional principles. Because of their proximity to local condition and the possible need for further hearings, the courts which originally heard these cases can best perform this judicial appraisal. Accordingly, we believe it appropriate to remand the cases to those courts.

In fashioning and effectuating the decrees, the courts will be guided by equitable principles. Traditionally, equity has been characterized by a practical flexibility in shaping its remedies and by a facility for adjusting and reconciling public and private needs. These cases call for the exercise of these traditional attributes of equity power. At stake is the personal interest of the plaintiffs in admission to public schools as soon as practicable on a nondiscriminatory basis. To effectuate this interest may call for elimination of a variety of obstacles in making the transition to school systems operated in accordance with the constitutional principles set forth in our May 17, 1954, decision. Courts of equity may properly take into account the public interest in the elimination of such obstacles in a systematic and effective manner. But it should go without saying that the vitality of these constitutional principles cannot be allowed to yield simply because of disagreement with them.

While giving weight to these public and private considerations, the courts will require that the defendants make a prompt and reasonable start toward full compliance with our May 17, 1954 ruling. Once such a start has been made, the courts may find that additional time is necessary to carry out the ruling in an effective manner. The burden rests upon the defendants to establish that such time is necessary in the public interest and is consistent with good faith compliance at the earliest practicable date. . . .

The . . . cases are remanded to the district courts to take such proceedings and enter such orders and decrees consistent with this opinion as are necessary and proper to admit to public schools on a racially nondiscriminatory basis with all deliberate speed the parties to these cases. . . .

## 22. *Craig v. Boren*
### 429 U.S. 190; 97 S.Ct. 451; 50 L.Ed. 2d 397 (1976)

*The Fourteenth Amendment says that no State shall deny persons "the equal protection of the laws." But virtually any law treats certain persons differently. We deny young children the right to drive, vote, and so on. Such "discriminatory" treatment is readily justifiable. But the same could not be said if these rights were denied to blacks or females. The Court has fashioned some standards to employ as it attempts to distinguish permissible legislative classifications from impermissible ones in light of the Equal Protection Clause.*

*For years, the Court deferred to the judgments of legislators about what kinds of economic and social classifications were needed. The Court invalidated laws for compromising equal protection guarantees only if the laws bore no "rational connection" to even some hypothetically "legitimate governmental purpose." The challenging party carried the burden of providing that the law was unreasonable. Most laws could easily survive this minimal judicial scrutiny.*

*During the 1960s, however, the Warren Court used the Equal Protec-*

*tion Clause to protect "fundamental interests" and "suspect classes." If a law affected a suspect class of persons or hampered the exercise of some fundamentally important right, the Court would subject it to "strict scrutiny." To survive, such laws would have to be drawn narrowly (i.e., they had to be "minimally burdensome") and they had to be "necessary" to "compelling governmental interests." Few laws could survive this strict scrutiny.*

*This "two-tier" approach has not been abandoned, but a "newer" approach to equal protection questions has been emerging when a law affects "questionable"--but not suspect—classes or "important"—but not fundamental interests. Such laws are subjected to an "intermediate" level of scrutiny. To survive, such laws must be "substantially related" to "important" governmental interests. The best examples of cases triggering such intermediate review involve sex discrimination.*

*In* Reed v. Reed *(404 U.S. 71, 1972), the Court invalidated an Idaho law that provided that "males must be preferred to females" in determining administrators of estates. The Court found the distinction arbitrary and contrary to the Equal Protection Clause of the Fourteenth Amendment. In* Frontiero v. Richardson *(411 U.S. 671, 1973), the Court ruled that military regulations cannot treat dependents of female members of the armed forces differently than they treat dependents of males. A plurality, though not a majority, wanted to go so far as to regard sex as a suspect classification.*

Craig v. Boren *demonstrates the Court's intermediate scrutiny of a gender-based classification. At issue was an Oklahoma law that prohibited the sale of 3.2 percent beer to males under twenty-one and to females under eighteen years of age. Justice Brennan rejected the State's attempts to justify the distinction by reference to traffic safety and concluded that the law violated the Equal Protection Clause. The case was decided by a vote of seven-to-two. In dissent, Justice Rehnquist emphasized that this law treated males less favorably than females—not the other way around—and that the Court should decide the case by applying the "rational basis" test.*

\* \* \* \* \* \* \* \* \* \* \* \* \* \* \* \* \* \* \* \* \* \* \* \* \* \* \*

Mr. Justice **Brennan** delivered the opinion of the Court:

... To withstand constitutional challenge, previous cases establish that classifications by gender must serve important governmental objectives and must be substantially related to the achievement of those objectives. ...

We accept for purposes of discussion the District Court's identification of the objective underlying [the law] as the enhancement of traffic safety. Clearly, the protection of public health and safety represents an important function of state and local governments. However, appellees' statistics in our view cannot support the conclusion that the gender-based distinction closely serves to achieve that objective and therefore the distinction cannot under *Reed* withstand equal protection challenge.

... [T]he showing offered by the appellees does not satisfy us that sex represents a legitimate, accurate proxy for the regulation of drinking and driving.... [T]he relationship between gender and traffic safety [is] far too tenuous to satisfy *Reed's* requirement that the gender-based difference be substantially related to achievement of the statutory objective....

Mr. Justice **Rehnquist**, dissenting:

... I think the Oklahoma statute challenged here need pass only the "rational basis" equal protection analysis ... and I believe that is constitutional under that analysis.

Subsequent to *Frontiero,* the Court has declined to hold that sex is a suspect class.... However, the Court's application here of an elevated or "intermediate" level of scrutiny, like that invoked in cases dealing with discrimination against females, raises the question of why the statute here should be treated any differently from countless legislative classifications unrelated to sex which have been upheld under a minimum rationality standard....

Most obviously unavailable to support any kind of special scrutiny in this case, is a history or pattern of past discrimination [against males] .... There is no suggestion in the Court's opinion that males in this age group are in any way peculiarly disadvantaged, subject to systematic discriminatory treatment, or otherwise in need of special solicitude from the courts....

The Court's conclusion that a law which treats males less favorably than females "must serve important governmental objectives and must be substantially related to achievement of those objectives" apparently comes out of thin air....

### 23. *Regents of the University of California v. Bakke*
### 438 U.S. 265; 98 S.Ct. 2733; 57 L.Ed. 2d 750 (1978)

*Laws that treat persons differently because of race are generally subjected to strict scrutiny. Hence, most such laws are invalidated. But what about remedial programs? What about laws and voluntary efforts designed to compensate the victims of past racial discrimination for their injuries? Does the Constitution permit such "affirmative action" programs?*

*Opponents of affirmative action say that these programs are a form of reverse discrimination against white persons. They argue that the Constitution requires that society be "color blind" and that such programs violate this principle. Supporters of affirmative action counter that it is not enough to stop discriminating against minorities. Equal opportunity requires that they be compensated for past injustices. For example, suppose that two men—Mr. W and Mr. B—are preparing for a race. Mr. W, a white man, has been training under the guidance of running and nutrition coaches. Mr. B, a black man, has been chained to a tree and fed a steady diet of bread and water. On the day of the race, B's captors release him, apologize, promise never to do it again, and they lead him to the starting line where he takes his place alongside W. Has B been treated fairly? Does he have an equal opportunity to succeed? Supporters of affirmative action programs think that such victims deserve remedial treatment, at least for a time. One of the Supreme Court's most important decisions in this area emerged from Allan Bakke's application to the medical school of the University of California at Davis.*

*The Medical School had two admissions programs for its incoming class of 100 students. The special admissions program set aside 16 seats for minority applicants who did not compete with the 84 other applicants. Bakke, a white male, was rejected despite the fact that he had stronger objective scores (grade point average, MCATs, letters of recommendation, and so on) than minority applicants who were accepted. Bakke contended that this special admissions program violated the California Constitution, Title VI of the Civil Rights Act of 1964 (which prohibits racial discrimination in programs that receive federal funding), and the Equal Protection Clause of the Fourteenth Amendment.*

*Justices Brennan, White, Marshall, and Blackmun found neither constitutional nor Title VI violations and voted to uphold the special admissions program. Justices Stewart, Burger, Rehnquist, and Stevens concluded that the program violated Title VI so they did not address the constitutional questions. Justice Powell's opinion, therefore, proved decisive. He invalidated the Davis program because it operated as a strict racial quota. However, he said that race could be taken into account as one factor when admissions officers screen applicants because racial diversity can enrich an institution. In short, the Court ruled that some special admissions programs might be acceptable but the Davis one was not.*

*In a number of subsequent cases, the Court was supportive of affirmative action programs. (*See, for example, United Steelworkers of America v. Weber, *433 U.S. 193, 1979;* Fullilove v. Klutznick, *448 U.S. 448, 1980;* Sheetmetal Workers Local 28 v. EEOC, *478 U.S. 421, 1986;* United States

v. Paradise, *480 U.S. 149, 1987;* Johnson v. Transportation Agency, Santa Clara County, California, *480 U.S. 616, 1987; and* Metro Broadcasting Corp. v. F.C.C., *111 L.Ed. 2d 445, 1990.) But in other cases, the Court was less supportive. (*See, for example, Memphis Firefighters v. Stotts, *467 U.S. 561, 1984;* Wygant v. Jackson Board of Education, *476 U.S. 267, 1986; and* Richmond v. J. A. Cronson Co., *488 U.S. 469, 1989; and* Wards Cove Packing Co. Inc. et al. v. Atonio. et al., *490 U.S. 642, 1989.) As such, the issue remains unsettled.*

\* \* \* \* \* \* \* \* \* \* \* \* \* \* \* \* \* \* \* \* \* \* \* \* \* \* \* \* \*

Mr. Justice **Powell** stated:

... For the reasons stated in the following opinion, I believe that so much of the judgment of the California court as holds petitioner's special admissions program unlawful and directs that respondent be admitted to the Medical School must be affirmed. For the reasons expressed in a separate opinion, my Brothers The Chief Justice, Mr. Justice Stewart, Mr. Justice Rehnquist, and Mr. Justice Stevens concur in this judgment. I also conclude for the reasons stated in the following opinion that the portion of the court's judgment enjoining petitioner from according any consideration to race in its admissions process must be reversed. For reasons expressed in separate opinions, my Brothers Mr. Justice Brennan, Mr. Justice White, Mr. Justice Marshall, and Mr. Justice Blackmun concur in this judgment.

Because the special admissions program involved a racial classification, the Supreme Court held itself bound to apply strict scrutiny. It then turned to the goals the University presented as justifying the special program. Although the court agreed that the goals of integrating the medical profession and increasing the number of physicians willing to serve members of minority groups were compelling state interests, it concluded that the special admissions program was not the least intrusive means of achieving those goals. Without passing on the state constitutional or the federal statutory grounds cited in the trial court's judgment, the California court held that the Equal Protection Clause required that "no applicant may be rejected because of his race, in favor of another who is less qualified, as measured by standards applied without regard to race"....

### III.

... Petitioner prefers to view ... [the special admissions program] as establishing a "goal" of minority representation in the medical school. Respondent, echoing the courts below, labels it a racial quota. This semantic distinction is beside the point: the special admissions program is undeniably a classification based on race and ethnic background. To the extent that there existed a pool of at least minimally qualified minority applicants to fill the 16 special admissions seats, white applicants could compete only for 84 seats in the entering class, rather than the 100 open to minority applicants. Whether this limitation is described as a quota or a goal, it is a line drawn on the basis of race and ethnic status. . . . Racial and ethnic classifications, however, are subject to stringent examination without regard to these additional characteristics. Racial and ethnic distinctions of any sort are inherently suspect and thus call for the most exacting judicial examination. . . .

Petitioner urges us to adopt for the first time a more restrictive view of the Equal Protection Clause and hold that discrimination against members of the white "majority" cannot be suspect if its purpose can be characterized as "benign." The clock of our liberties, however, cannot be turned back to 1868. . . . It is far too late to argue that the guarantee of equal protection to all persons permits the recognition of special wards entitled to a degree of protection greater than that accorded others. . . .

. . . [T]here are serious problems of justice connected with the idea of preference itself. First, it may not always be clear that a so-called preference is in fact benign. Second, preferential programs may only reinforce common stereotypes holding that certain groups are unable to achieve success without special protection based on a factor having no relationship to individual worth. Third, there is a measure of inequity in forcing innocent persons in respondent's position to bear the burdens of redressing grievances not of their making. Also, the mutability of a constitutional principle, based upon shifting political and social judgments, undermines the chances for consistent application of the Constitution from one generation to the next, a critical feature of its coherent interpretation. . . .

## C.

Petitioner contends that on several occasions this Court has approved preferential classifications without applying the most exacting scrutiny. Most of the cases upon which petitioner relies are drawn from three areas: school desegregation, employment discrimination, and sex discrimination. Each of the cases cited presented a situation materially different from the facts of this case. The school desegregation cases are inapposite. Each involved remedies for clearly determined constitutional violations.

Such preferences also have been upheld where a legislative or administrative body charged with the responsibility made determinations of past discrimination by the industries affected, and fashioned remedies deemed appropriate to rectify the discrimination. But we have never approved preferential classifications in the absence of proven constitutional or statutory violations. . . .

. . . [T]he operation of petitioner's special admissions program is quite different from the remedial measures approved. It prefers the designated minority groups at the expense of other individuals who are totally foreclosed from competition for the 16 special admissions seats in every medical school class. Because of that foreclosure, some individuals are excluded from enjoyment of a state-provided benefit—admission to the medical school—they otherwise would receive. When a classification denies an individual opportunities or benefits enjoyed by others solely because of his race or ethnic background, it must be regarded as suspect.

### IV.

We have held that in "order to justify the use of a suspect classification, a State must show that its purpose or interest is both constitutionally permissible and substantial, and that its use of the classification is 'necessary [to] the accomplishment' of its purpose or the safeguarding of its interest". . . . The special admissions program purports to serve the purposes of: (i) "reducing the historic deficit of traditionally disfavored minorities in medical schools and the medical profession;" (ii) countering the effects of societal discrimination; (iii) increasing the number of physicians who will practice in communities currently underserved; and (iv) obtaining the educational benefits that flow from an ethnically diverse student body. It is necessary to decide which, if any, of these purposes is substantial enough to support the use of a suspect classification.

### A.

If a petitioner's purpose is to assure within its student body some specified percentage of a particular group merely because of its race or ethnic origin, such a preferential purpose must be rejected not as insubstantial but as facially invalid. Preferring members of any one group for no reason other than race or ethnic origin is discrimination for its own sake. This the Constitution forbids. . . .

### B.

The State certainly has a legitimate and substantial interest in ameliorating, or eliminating where feasible, the disabling effects of identified discrimination. . . . We have never approved a classification that aids persons perceived as members of relatively victimized groups at the expense of other innocent individuals in the absence of judicial, legislative, or administrative findings of constitutional or statutory violations. . . . Without such findings of constitutional or statutory violations, it cannot be said that the government has any greater interest in helping one individual than in refraining from harming another. Thus, the government has no compelling justification for inflicting such harm.

Petitioner does not purport to have made, and is in no position to make, such findings. Its broad mission is education, not the formulation of any legislative policy or the adjudication of particular claims of illegality.... Hence, the purpose of helping certain groups whom the faculty of the Davis Medical School perceived as victims of "societal discrimination" does not justify a classification that imposes disadvantages upon persons like respondent, who bear no responsibility for whatever harm the beneficiaries of the special admissions program are thought to have suffered. To hold otherwise would be to convert a remedy heretofore reserved for violations of legal rights into a privilege that all institutions throughout the Nation could grant at their pleasure to whatever groups are perceived as victims of societal discrimination. That is a step we have never approved. ...

## D.

The fourth goal asserted by petitioner is the attainment of a diverse student body. This clearly is a constitutionally permissible goal for an institution of higher education. Academic freedom, though not a specifically enumerated constitutional right, long has been viewed as a special concern of the First Amendment. The freedom of a university to make its own judgments as to education includes the selection of its student body. Thus, in arguing that its universities must be accorded the right to select those students who will contribute the most to the "robust exchange of ideas," petitioner invokes a countervailing constitutional interest, that of the First Amendment. In this light, petitioner must be viewed as seeking to achieve a goal that is of paramount importance in the fulfillment of its mission. It may be argued that there is greater force to these views at the undergraduate level than in a medical school where the training is centered primarily on professional competency. But even at the graduate level, our tradition and experience lend support to the view that the contribution of diversity is substantial.... An otherwise qualified medical student with a particular background—whether it be ethnic, geographic, culturally advantaged or disadvantaged—may bring to a professional school of medicine experiences, outlooks and ideas that enrich the training of its student body and better equip its graduates to render with understanding their vital service to humanity.

Ethnic diversity, however, is only one element in a range of factors a university properly may consider in attaining the goal of a heterogeneous student body.... As the interest of diversity is compelling in the context of a university's admissions program, the question remains whether the program's racial classification is necessary to promote this interest.

### V. A.

It may be assumed that the reservation of a specified number of seats in each class for individuals from the preferred ethnic groups would contribute to the attainment of considerable ethnic diversity in the student body. But petitioner's argument that this is the only effective means of serving the interest of diversity is seriously flawed. In a most fundamental sense the argument misconceives the nature of the state interest that would justify consideration of race or ethnic background. It is not an interest in simple ethnic diversity, in which a specified percentage of the student body is in effect guaranteed to be members of selected ethnic groups, with the remaining percentage an undifferentiated aggregation of students. The diversity that furthers a compelling state interest encompasses a far broader array of qualifications and characteristics of which racial or ethnic origin is but a single though important element. Petitioner's special admissions program focused *solely* on ethnic diversity, would hinder rather than further attainment of genuine diversity. Nor would the state interest in genuine diversity be served by expanding petitioner's two-track system into a multitrack program with a prescribed number of seats set aside for each identifiable category of applicants. Indeed, it is inconceivable that a university would thus pursue the logic of petitioner's two-track program to the illogical end of insulating each category of applicants with certain desired qualifications from competition with all other applicants.

The experience of other university admissions programs, which take race into account in achieving the educational diversity valued by the First Amendment, demonstrates that the assignment of a fixed number of places to a minority group is not a necessary means toward that end. An illuminating example is found in the Harvard College Program:

"In recent years Harvard College has expanded the concept of diversity to include students from disadvantaged economic, racial and ethnic groups. Harvard College now recruits not only Californians or Louisianans but also blacks and Chicanos and other minority students. . . .

In practice, this new definition of diversity has meant that race has been a factor in some admission decisions. When the Committee on Admissions reviews the large middle group of applicants who are 'admissible' and deemed capable of doing good work in their courses, the race of an applicant may tip the balance in his favor just as geographic origin or a life spent on a farm may tip the balance in other candidates' cases. A farm boy from Idaho can bring something to Harvard College that a Bostonian cannot offer. Similarly, a black student can usually bring something that a white person cannot offer.

"In Harvard College admissions the Committee has not set target-quotas for the number of blacks, or of musicians, football players, physicists or Californians to be admitted in a given year. [But in] choosing among thousands of applicants who are not only 'admissible' academically but have other strong qualities, the Committee, with a number of criteria in mind, pays some attention to distribution among many types and categories of students."

In such an admissions program, race or ethnic background may be deemed a "plus" in a particular applicant's file, yet it does not insulate the individual from comparison with all other candidates for the available seats. The file of a particular black applicant may be examined for his potential contribution to diversity without the factor of race being decisive when compared, for example, with that of an applicant identified as an Italian-American if the latter is thought to exhibit qualities more likely to promote beneficial educational pluralism. Such qualities could include exceptional personal talents, unique work or service experience, leadership potential, maturity, demonstrated compassion, a history of overcoming disadvantage, ability to communicate with the poor, or other qualifications deemed important. In short, an admissions program operated in this way is flexible enough to consider all pertinent elements of diversity in light of the particular qualifications of each applicant, and to place them on the same footing for consideration, although not necessarily accounting them the same weight. Indeed, the weight attributed to a particular quality may vary from year to year depending upon the "mix" both of the student body and the applicants for the incoming class.

This kind of program treats each applicant as an individual in the admissions process. The applicant who loses out on the last available seat to another candidate receiving a "plus" on the basis of ethnic background will not have been foreclosed from all consideration for that seat simply because he was not the right color or had the wrong surname. It would mean only that his combined qualifications, which may have included similar nonobjective factors, did not outweigh those of the other applicant. His qualifications would have been weighed fairly and competitively, and he would have no basis to complain of unequal treatment under the 14th Amendment.

It has been suggested that an admissions program which considers race only as one factor is simply a subtle and more sophisticated—but no less effective—means of according racial preference than the Davis program. A facial intent to discriminate, however, is evident in petitioner's preference program and not denied in this case. No such facial infirmity exists in an admissions program where race or ethnic background is simply one element—to be weighed fairly against other elements—in the selection process. And a Court would not assume that a university, professing to employ a facially nondiscriminatory admissions policy, would operate it as a cover for the functional equivalent of a quota system.

### B.

In summary, it is evident that the Davis special admissions program involves the use of an explicit racial classification never before countenanced by this Court. It tells applicants who are not Negro, Asian, or "Chicano" that they are totally excluded from a specific percentage of the seats in an entering class. No matter how strong their qualifications, quantitative and extracurricular, including their own potential for contribution to educational diversity, they are never afforded the chance to compete with applicants from the preferred groups for the special admission seats. At the same time, the preferred applicants have the opportunity to compete for every seat in the class. The fatal flaw in petitioner's preferential program is its disregard of individual rights as guaranteed by the 14th Amendment. . . . Such rights are not absolute. But when a State's distribution of benefits or imposition of burdens hinges on the color of a person's skin or ancestry, that individual is entitled to a demonstration that the challenged classification is necessary to promote a substantial state interest. Petitioner has failed to carry this burden. For this reason, that portion of the California court's judgment holding petitioner's special admissions program invalid under the 14th Amendment must be affirmed.

### C.

In enjoining petitioner from ever considering the race of any applicant, however, the courts below failed to recognize that the State has a substantial interest that legitimately may be served by a properly devised admissions program involving the competitive consideration of race and ethnic origin. For this reason, so much of the California court's judgment as enjoins petitioner from any consideration of the race of any applicant must be reversed.

### VI.

With respect to respondent's entitlement to an injunction directing his admission to the Medical School, petitioner has conceded that it could not carry its burden of proving that, but for the existence of its unlawful special admissions program, respondent still would not have been admitted. Hence, respondent is entitled to the injunction, and that portion of the judgment must be affirmed.

## 24. *Rostker v. Goldberg*
### 453 U.S. 57; 101 S.Ct. 2646; 69 L.Ed. 2d 478 (1981)

*Strict scrutiny almost invariably leads to the invalidation of the challenged law; this is not necessarily the case with intermediate scrutiny. The Court sometimes upholds gender-based classifications that further important governmental interests. In* Rostker, *the Court ruled that preparing for a draft of combat troops is such an interest. At issue was a challenge to the Military Selective Service Act (MSSA) that authorized the president to require draft registration for males but not for females. Writing for a six-to-three majority, Justice Rehnquist rejected arguments that the law violated equal-protection guarantees.*

*The Persian Gulf war (1991) again focused attention on the role of women in combat. Because women are serving in many non-traditional roles in the all-volunteer military, such as pilots or support personnel, they found themselves more directly in harm's way than ever before. Of the 35,000 women who participated in the Gulf war, fifteen were killed, and two were captured. Citing such figures, and the fact that military rules restrict women from combat roles, which also hampers their professional development and advancement, women's advocates demanded in post-war congressional hearings that such restrictions be eliminated. The chiefs of the military services, arguing that front line duty and combat were unsuitable for women, did not want to alter existing policy.*

\* \* \* \* \* \* \* \* \* \* \* \* \* \* \* \* \* \* \* \* \* \* \* \* \* \* \* \* \* \*

Justice **Rehnquist** delivered the opinion of the Court:

The question presented is whether the Military Selective Service Act, ... violates the Fifth Amendment to the United States Constitution in authorizing the President to require the registration of males and not females. ...

This is not, however, merely a case involving the customary deference accorded congressional decisions. The case arises in the context of Congress's authority over national defense and military affairs, and perhaps in no other area has the Court accorded Congress greater deference. ... This Court has consistently recognized Congress's "broad constitutional power" to raise and regulate armies and navies. *Schlesinger v. Ballard,* 419 U.S. 498, 510 (1975). As the Court noted in considering a challenge to the selective service laws, "The constitutional power of Congress to raise and support armies and to make all laws necessary and proper to that end is broad and sweeping." *United States v. O'Brien,* 391 U.S. 367, 377 (1968). ...

Not only is the scope of Congress's constitutional power in this area broad, but the lack of competence on the part of the courts is marked. In *Giligan v. Morgan,* 413 U.S. 1, 10 (1973), the Court noted:

> It is difficult to conceive of an area of governmental activity in which the courts have less competence. The complex, subtle and professional decisions as to the composition, training, equipping, and control of a military force are essentially professional military judgments, subject always to civilian control of the Legislative and Executive branches.

None of this is to say that Congress is free to disregard the Constitution when it acts in the area of military affairs. . . . We of course do not abdicate our ultimate responsibility to decide the constitutional question but simply recognize that the Constitution itself requires such deference to congressional choice. In deciding the question before us we must be particularly careful not to substitute our judgment of what is desirable for that of Congress. . . .

No one could deny that under the test of *Craig v. Boren,* . . . the Government's interest in raising and supporting armies is an "important governmental interest." Congress and its committees carefully considered and debated two alternative means of furthering that interest: the first was to register only males for potential conscription, and the other was to register both sexes. Congress chose the former alternative. When that decision is challenged on equal protection grounds, the question a court must decide is not which alternative it would have chosen, had it been the primary decision maker, but whether that chosen by Congress denies equal protection of the laws.

. . . [T]he decision to exempt women from registration was not the "accidental by-product of a traditional way of thinking about women." . . . The issue was considered at great length and Congress clearly expressed its purpose and intent. . . .

Congress determined that any future draft, which would be facilitated by the registration scheme, would be characterized by a need for combat troops. . . .

Women as a group, however, unlike men as a group, are not eligible for combat. The restrictions on the participation of women in combat in the Navy and Air Force are statutory. . . . The Army and Marine Corps preclude the use of women in combat as a matter of established policy. Congress specifically recognized and endorsed the exclusion of women from combat in exempting women from registration. . . .

The reason women are exempt from registration is not because military needs can be met by drafting men. This is not a case of Congress arbitrarily choosing to burden one of two similarly situated groups, such as would be the case with an all black or all white, or an all Catholic or all Lutheran, or an all Republican or all Democratic registration. Men and women, because of the combat restrictions on women, are simply not similarly situated for purposes of a draft or registration for a draft.

Congress's decision to authorize the registration of only men, therefore, does not violate the Due Process Clause.... The fact that Congress and the Executive have decided that women should not serve in combat fully justifies Congress in not authorizing their registration, since the purpose of registration is to develop a pool of potential combat troops. As was the case in *Schlesinger v. Ballard*... "the gender classification is not invidious, but rather realistically reflects the fact that the sexes are not similarly situated" in this case.... The Constitution requires that Congress treat similarly situated persons similarly, not that it engage in gestures of superficial equality....

...Justice **Marshall** with whom Justice **Brennan** joins, dissenting:

The Court today.... upholds a statute that requires males but not females to register for the draft, and which thereby categorically excludes women from a fundamental civic obligation.... I dissent.

...[Statutes] like the MSSA, which discriminate on the basis of gender, must be examined under the "heightened" scrutiny mandated by *Craig v. Boren*.... Under this test, a gender-based classification cannot withstand constitutional challenge unless the classification is substantially related to the achievement of an important governmental objective....

...[T]he Government must show that registering women would substantially impede its efforts to prepare for a draft. Under our precedents, the Government cannot meet this burden without showing that a gender neutral statute would be a less effective means of attaining this end.... In this case, the Government makes no claim that preparing for a draft of combat troops cannot be accomplished just as effectively by registering both men and women but drafting only men if only men turn out to be needed....

...[T]he majority simply assumes that registration prepares for a draft in which every draftee must be available for assignment to combat. But the majority's draft scenario finds no support in either the testimony before Congress, or more importantly, in the findings of the Senate Report. ...[E]ven the Government represents only that "in the event of mobilization, approximately two-thirds of the demand of the induction system would be for combat skills."...

This review of the findings contained in the Senate Report ... demonstrates that there is no basis for the Court's representation that women are ineligible for all the positions that would need to be filled in the event of a draft.

... Congressional enactments in the area of military affairs must like all other laws, be *judged* by the standards of the Constitution.

... In some 106 instances since this Court was established it has determined that congressional action exceeded the bounds of the Constitution. I believe the same is true of this statute.

## III. EQUAL RIGHTS AMENDMENTS

### 25. U.S. Equal Rights Amendment: Amendment XXVII (Proposed)

*As part of an overall campaign to end discrimination against women, a demand grew to ensure women's equality under the law through an Equal Rights Amendment to the Constitution. After languishing in Congress for 49 years, two-thirds of both houses of Congress approved the Amendment and it was submitted to the states on March 22, 1972. Ratification of constitutional amendments requires the approval of three-fourths of the state legislatures. Thirty-eight states, therefore, were needed to ratify. The first state ratified the Amendment only 32 minutes after it was submitted and a total of thirty states approved it in the first year. But opponents of the Equal Rights Amendment gained momentum and the ratification drive stalled as concerns about the implications of the Amendment mounted. In October 1978, Congress extended the original seven-year deadline for ratifications until June 30, 1982. In spite of the extension, the Amendment fell three votes short of ratification.*

\* \* \* \* \* \* \* \* \* \* \* \* \* \* \* \* \* \* \* \* \* \* \* \* \* \* \* \* \* \* \* \*

### AMENDMENT XXVII (Proposed)

**SECTION 1**: Equality of rights under the law shall not be denied or abridged by the United States or by any State on account of sex.

**SECTION 2**: The Congress shall have the power to enforce, by, appropriate legislation, the provisions of this article.

**SECTION 3**: This amendment shall take effect two years after the date of ratification.

### 26. State Equal Rights Amendments

*It is important to realize that the federal Constitution is not the sole protector of individual liberty in America. Indeed, considering the Supreme Court's apparent shift from favoring individual liberties to supporting governmental authority, some commentators have observed an emergence of a new judicial federalism, where individual liberty is more secure under some state constitutions than under the federal Constitution. A good example of this is the ERA. Although the national ERA amendment was never ratified, at least seventeen states adopted ERA amendments. The following are examples.*

\* \* \* \* \* \* \* \* \* \* \* \* \* \* \* \* \* \* \* \* \* \* \* \* \* \* \* \* \*

*Alaska Constitution, Article 1, Section 3*

No person is to be denied the enjoyment of any civil or political right because of race, color, creed, sex, or national origin.

*Pennsylvania Constitution, Article 1, Section 28*

Equality of rights under the law shall not be denied or abridged in the Commonwealth of Pennsylvania because of the sex of the individual.

# CHAPTER 3:

# CRIMINAL JUSTICE AND
# THE RIGHTS OF THE ACCUSED

## I. EXCERPTS FROM STATE CONSTITUTIONS

*People of today sometimes question why there is so much concern for the rights of the accused. Some believe that the Warren Court coddled criminals and that the Burger and Rehnquist Courts are merely restoring the proper balance between the rights of society and those of the accused. Others feel that the state has too much power and that it is sometimes abused. They argue that the legal system should be scrupulously fair because people accused of a crime are presumed innocent until proven guilty.*

*The Revolutionary generation shared a broader consensus about the importance of upholding the rights of the accused. They had more immediate experience with the abuses of the inquisitorial and royal prerogative systems of justice—which included extracting confessions by torture, permitting anonymous accusations, secret trials, judges who were allied with the prosecution, and not allowing representation by counsel. They identified closely with the efforts of the English people to protect the rights of the individual by delimiting the power of the crown. From the Magna Carta (1215), though the common law, and the adoption of the English Bill of Rights (1689), a body of fundamental rights of Englishmen evolved. Just as these rights limited the power of the crown, the Revolutionary generation sought to define important individual rights as a protection against the newly created state and federal governments.*

\* \* \* \* \* \* \* \* \* \* \* \* \* \* \* \* \* \* \* \* \* \* \* \* \* \* \* \* \* \* \*

## 27. Pennsylvania (1776)

*Excerpts from the Declaration of Rights*

IX. That in all prosecutions for criminal offenses, a man hath a right to be heard by himself and his council, to demand the cause and nature of his accusation, to be confronted with the witnesses, to call for evidence in his favor, and a speedy public trial, by an impartial jury of the country, without the unanimous consent of which jury he cannot be found guilty; nor can he be compelled to give evidence against himself; nor can any man be justly deprived of his liberty except by the laws of the land, or the judgement of his peers.

X. That the people have a right to hold themselves, their houses, papers, and possessions, free from search and seizure, and therefore warrants without oaths or affirmations first made, affording a sufficient foundation for them, and whereby every officer or messenger may be commanded or required to search suspected places, or to seize any person or person, his or their property, not particularly described, are contrary to that right, and ought not to be granted.

XI. That in controversies respecting property, and in suits between man and man, the parties have a right to trial by jury, which ought to be held sacred.

## Excerpts from the Constitution

Section 25. Trials shall be by jury as heretofore: And it is recommended to Legislature of this state, to provide a law against every corruption or partiality in the choice, return, or appointment of juries.

Section 29. Excessive bail shall not be exacted for bailable offenses: And all fines shall be moderate.

*Source: Thorpe.* Federal and State Constitutions. *V: 3083, 3088, 3089.*

## 28. New York Ratification Convention (1788)

*The concern for the rights of the accused was not limited to those states which had adopted Bills of Rights during the Revolutionary era. The following recommendations were representative of a general Anti-Federalist belief that the new federal Constitution required a bill of rights to protect individual liberties. Five states ratified the Constitution with recommendations to protect individual liberty; minorities from two other state conventions also called for similar action. It is remarkable that the New York ratification convention proposed the following as potential amendments to the Constitution when the state itself had not adopted a declaration of rights when it wrote its Constitution in 1777.*

\* \* \* \* \* \* \* \* \* \* \* \* \* \* \* \* \* \* \* \* \* \* \* \* \* \* \* \* \*

That no Person ought to be taken imprisoned, or disseised of his freehold, or exiled or deprived of his Privileges, Franchises, Life, Liberty, or Property, but by the due process of Law.

That no Person ought to be put twice in Jeopardy of Life or Limb for one and the same Offense, nor, unless in case of impeachment, be punished more than once for the same Offense.

That every Person restrained of his Liberty is entitled to an enquiry into the lawfulness of such restraint, and to a removal thereof if unlawful, and that such enquiry and removal ought not to be denied or delayed, except when on account of Public Danger the Congress shall suspend the privilege of the Writ of Habeas Corpus.

That excessive bail ought not to be required; nor excessive Fines imposed; nor Cruel or unusual Punishments inflicted.

That (except in the Government of the Land and Naval Forces, and on the Militia when in actual Service, and in cases of Impeachment) a Presentment or Indictment by a Grand Jury ought to be observed as a necessary preliminary to the trial of all Crimes cognizable by the Judiciary of the United States and such a Trial should be speedy, public, and by an impartial Jury of the County where the Crime was committed; and that no person can be found Guilty without the unanimous consent of such Jury. And that in all Criminal Prosecutions, the Accused ought to be informed of the cause and nature of his Accusation, to be confronted with his accusers and the Witnesses against him, to have the means of producing his Witnesses, and the assistance of Council for his defense, and should not be compelled to give Evidence against himself.

That the trial by Jury in the extent that it obtains by the Common Law of England is one of the greatest securities to the rights of a free People, and ought to remain inviolate.

*Source: The New York Instrument of Ratification. Record Group 11. National Archives.*

## II. UNREASONABLE SEARCHES AND SEIZURES

### 29. *Katz v. United States*
### 389 U.S. 347; 88 S.Ct. 507; 19 L.Ed. 2d 576 (1967)

*The colonists objected to England's use of general warrants and writs of assistance to justify searches of homes for smugglers and others suspected of violating navigation laws. These general warrants and writs authorized anyone—including private parties—to conduct broad searches without time limit. The Fourth Amendment prohibits "unreasonable searches and seizures." Further, warrants must "particularly describ[e] the place to be searched and the persons or things to be seized." Such warrants must also be supported by a showing of "probable cause." This entails a "belief that the law was being violated on the premises to be searched; and . . . the facts . . . are such that a reasonable discreet and prudent man would be led to believe that there was a commission of the offense charged . . . " (Dumbra v. U.S., 268 U.S. 435, at 441, 1925). The Supreme Court has also ruled that warrants must be issued by detached and neutral magistrates, not by police officers or government enforcement agents. (Johnson v. U.S., 333 U.S. 10, 1948).*

*If an individual who owns or occupies the place to be searched voluntarily consents to the search, no warrant is needed. (U.S. v. Matlock, 415 U.S. 164, 1974). Otherwise, the Court has generally held that searches not accompanied by warrants are unreasonable unless they are supported by special exigencies that make the warrantless search necessary. In other words, warrantless searches may be "reasonable" if they are necessitated by exigent circumstances. Examples include searches conducted incident to a lawful arrest, searches of areas in plain view, searches of automobiles, searches associated with hot pursuit, searches involving readily destructible evidence, and stop-and-frisk practices. With the exception of stop-and-frisk "searches"—which will be discussed separately below—such searches are normally accompanied by probable cause; what is lacking is time to obtain a warrant. Here, the warrant requirement is impractical because a suspect might flee or evidence might be destroyed while a law enforcement officer discussed the matter with a magistrate.*

*What about technological advances? Does the Fourth Amendment apply to airplane overflights, infrared telescope, spike mikes, telephone wiretaps, and other forms of electronic surveillance? Courts have found the Amendment's language sufficiently broad to cover a wide array of "unreasonable" activities. This was not always so.*

*In Olmstead v. United States (277 438, 1928), federal prohibition officers had tapped a telephone used by a bootlegger and obtained incriminating evidence against him as a result. The Supreme Court upheld his conviction over Fourth-Amendment objections. The Court found, first, that no physical trespass into his premises took place, therefore, there had been no "search." Second, he intended to project his voice to distant places when he picked up the phone. Third, no tangible evidence was taken, therefore, there had been no "search." In short, the Court found the Fourth Amendment inapplicable.*

*In Silverman v. United States (365 U.S. 505, 1961), things began to change. Police drove a spike mike into a hot-air duct in a building wall so they could eavesdrop on conversations inside the building. The Court found that here, unlike Olmstead, there had been physical trespass or a "search." On this ground, the Court ruled that the evidence was inadmissible.*

*In* Katz v. United States, *FBI agents used an electronic device to obtain evidence that Katz was violating federal communication statutes. Since no physical trespass occurred and since nothing tangible was seized, the FBI did not get a warrant. Writing for a seven-to-one majority, Justice Stewart held that the Fourth Amendment protects the privacy of persons, not just areas, and its reach should not depend on whether or not there had been some physical trespass.* Olmstead *was overruled. It is interesting to note that Justice Black dissented. His literal approach to constitutional interpretation which so often produced "liberal" results here led him to conclude that the express terms of the Fourth Amendment do not cover wiretapping.*

\* \* \* \* \* \* \* \* \* \* \* \* \* \* \* \* \* \* \* \* \* \* \* \* \* \* \* \* \* \*

Mr. Justice **Stewart** delivered the opinion of the Court:

The petitioner was convicted ... under an eight-count indictment charging him with transmitting wagering information by telephone from Los Angeles to Miami and Boston, in violation of a federal statute. At the trial the Government was permitted, over the petitioner's objection, to introduce evidence of the petitioner's end of telephone conversations, overheard by FBI agents who had attached an electronic listening and recording device to the outside of the public telephone booth from which he had placed his calls....

.... [T]he Fourth Amendment protects people, not places. What a person knowingly exposes to the public even in his own home or office, is not a subject of Fourth Amendment protection.... But what he seeks to preserve as private, even in an area accessible to the public, may be constitutionally protected....

The Government stresses the fact that the telephone booth from which the petitioner made his calls was constructed partly of glass, so that he was as visible after he entered it as he would have been if he had remained outside. But what he sought to exclude when be entered the booth was not the intruding eye—it was the uninvited ear.... One who occupies it, shuts the door behind him, and pays the toll that permits him to place a call, is surely entitled to assume that the words he utters into the mouthpiece will not be broadcast to the world....

The Government contends, however, that the activities of its agents in this case should not be tested by Fourth Amendment requirements, for the surveillance technique they employed involved no physical penetration of the telephone booth from which the petitioner placed his calls. It is true that the absence of such penetration was at one time thought to foreclose further Fourth Amendment inquiry, *Olmstead v. United States*

[1928]. . . . But "[t]he premise that property interests control the right of the Government to search and seize has been discredited." *Warden v. Hayden* [1967]. . . . [O]nce it is recognized that the Fourth Amendment protects people—and not simply "areas"—against unreasonable searches and seizures, it becomes clear that the reach of that Amendment cannot turn upon the presence or absence of a physical intrusion into any given enclosure. . . . The Government's activities in electronically listening to and recording the petitioner's words violated the privacy upon which he justifiably relied while using the telephone booth and thus constituted a "search and seizure" within the meaning of the Fourth Amendment. The fact that the electronic device employed to achieve that end did not happen to penetrate the wall of the booth can have no constitutional significance.

The question remaining for decision, then, is whether the search and seizure conducted in this case complied with constitutional standards. . . .

. . . It is apparent that the agents in this case acted with restraint. Yet the inescapable fact is that this restraint was imposed by the agents themselves, not by a judicial officer. They were not required, before commencing the search, to present their estimate of probable cause for detached scrutiny by a neutral magistrate. They were not compelled, during the conduct of the search itself, to observe precise limits established in advance by a specific-court order. Nor were they directed, after the search had been completed, to notify the authorizing magistrate in detail of all that had been seized. In the absence of such safeguards, this Court has never sustained a search upon the sole ground that officers reasonably expected to find evidence of a particular crime and voluntarily confined their activities to the least intrusive means consistent with that end. Searches conducted without warrants have been held unlawful "notwithstanding facts unquestionably showing probable cause." *Agnello v. United States* [1925], for the Constitution requires "that the deliberate impartial judgment of a judicial officer . . . be interposed between the citizen and the police. . . . " *Wong Sun v. United States* [1963] . . . —subject only to a few specifically established and well-delineated exceptions. . . .

The Government . . . argues that surveillance of a telephone booth should be exempted from the usual requirement of advance authorization by a magistrate upon a showing of probable cause. We cannot agree. Omission of such authorization "bypasses the safeguards provided by an objective predetermination of probable cause and substitutes instead the far less reliable procedure of an after-the-event justification for the . . . search too likely to be subtly influenced by the familiar shortcoming of hindsight judgment." . . .

. . . Wherever a man may be, he is entitled to know that he will remain free from unreasonable searches and seizures. The government agents here ignore "the procedure of antecedent justification . . . that is central to the Fourth Amendment, a procedure that we hold to be a constitutional precondition of the kind of electronic surveillance involved in this case. Because the surveillance here failed to meet that condition, and because it led to the petitioner's conviction, the judgment must be reversed.

Mr. Justice **Black**, dissenting:

If I could agree with the Court that eavesdropping carried on by electronic means (equivalent to wiretapping) constitutes a "search" or "seizure," I would be happy to join the Court's opinion. . . .

My basic objection is twofold: (1) I do not believe that the words of the Amendment will bear the meaning given them by today's decision, and (2) I do not believe that it is the proper role of this Court to rewrite the Amendment in order "to bring it into harmony with the times" and thus reach a result that many people believe to be desirable.

### 30. *Terry v. Ohio*
### 392 U.S. 1; 88 S.Ct. 1868, 20 L.Ed, 2d 889 (1968)

*As noted, it is generally held that a neutral magistrate, not a police officer, should decide when a search and seizure is appropriate. Warrantless searches are usually "unreasonable" unless they are justified by exigent circumstances that make it impractical to get a warrant. For example, if a police officer sees a crime committed, he does not need a warrant to make an arrest and to conduct a search incident to the arrest. But what if a police officer has only a strong suspicion—not probable cause—underlying his or her belief that a crime is about to occur? Writing for an eight-to-one Court in* Terry v. Ohio, *Chief Justice Warren said that when an experienced police officer observes unusual conduct that convinces him that a crime is in the offing, he may frisk the suspect by patting down his outer clothing in search of a weapon because the suspect might endanger the officer and/or the public. If incriminating evidence is uncovered, it is admissible in court.*

\* \* \* \* \* \* \* \* \* \* \* \* \* \* \* \* \* \* \* \* \* \* \* \* \* \* \* \* \* \*

Mr. Chief Justice **Warren** delivered the opinion of the Court:

Petitioner Terry was convicted of carrying a concealed weapon . . . Police Detective Martin McFadden . . . testified that while he was patrolling in plain clothes in downtown Cleveland at approximately 2:30 in the afternoon of October 31, 1963, his attention was attracted by two men. Chilton and Terry, standing on the corner of Huron Road, and Euclid Avenue. He had never seen the two men before, and he was unable to say precisely what first drew his eye to them. However, he testified that he had been a policemen for 39 years and a detective for 35 and that he had been assigned to patrol this vicinity of downtown Cleveland for shoplifters and pickpockets for 30 years. He explained that he had developed routine habits of observation over the years and that he would "stand and watch people or walk and watch people at many intervals of the day." He added: "Now, in this case when I looked over they didn't look right to me at the time."

His interest aroused, Officer McFadden took up a post of observation in the entrance to a store 300 to 400 feet away from the two men. "I got more purpose to watch them when I seen their movements," he testified. He saw one of the men leave the other one and walk . . . past some stores. The man paused for a moment and looked in a store window, then walked on a short distance, turned around and walked back toward the corner, pausing once again to look in the same store window. He rejoined his companion at the corner, and the two conferred briefly. Then the second man went through the same series of motions, strolling down Huron Road, looking in the same window, walking on a short distance turning back, peering in the store window again, and returning to confer with the first man at the corner. The two men repeated this ritual alternately between five and six times apiece—in all, roughly a dozen trips. At one point, while the two were standing together on the corner, a third man approached them and engaged them briefly in conversation. This man then left the two others and walked west . . . Chilton and Terry resumed their measured pacing, peering, and conferring. After this had gone on for 10 to 12 minutes, the two men walked off together . . . following the path taken earlier by the third man.

By this time Officer McFadden had become thoroughly suspicious. He testified that after observing their elaborately casual and oft-repeated reconnaissance . . . , He suspected the two men of "casing a job, a stick-up," and that he considered it his duty as a police office to investigate further. He added that he feared "they may have a gun." Thus, Officer McFadden followed Chilton and Terry and saw them stop in front of Zucker's store to talk to the same man who had conferred with them earlier on the street corner. Deciding that the situation was ripe for direct action, Officer McFadden approached the three men, identified himself as a police officer and asked for their names. At this point his knowledge was confined to what he had observed. He was not acquainted with any of the three men by name or by sight, and he had received no information concerning them from any other source. When the men "mumbled something" in response to his inquiries, Officer McFadden grabbed petitioner Terry, spun him around . . . and patted down the outside of his clothing. In the left breast pocket of Terry's overcoat Officer McFadden felt a pistol. He reached inside the overcoat pocket, but was unable to remove the gun. At this point, keeping Terry between himself and the others, the officer ordered all three men to enter Zucker's store. As they went in he removed Terry's overcoat completely, retrieved a .38 caliber revolver from the pocket and ordered all three men to face the wall with their hands raised. Officer McFadden proceeded to pat down the outer clothing of Chilton and the third man, Katz. He discovered another revolver in the outer pocket of Chilton's overcoat, but no weapons were found on Katz. The officer testified that he only patted the men down to see whether they had weapons, and that he did not put his hands beneath the outer garments of either Terry or Chilton until he felt their guns. . . . Officer McFadden seized Chilton's gun, asked the proprietor of the store to call a police wagon, and took all three men to the station, where Chilton and Terry were formally charged with carrying concealed weapons.

. . . It must be recognized that whenever a police officer accosts an individual and restrains his freedom to walk away, he has "seized" that person. And it is nothing less than sheer torture of the English language to suggest that a careful exploration of the outer surfaces of a person's clothing all over his or her body in an attempt to find weapons is not a "search". . . .

We therefore reject the notions that the Fourth Amendment does not come into play at all as a limitation upon police conduct if the officers stop short of something called "technical arrest" or a "full-blown search."

In this case there can be no question, then, that Officer McFadden seized petitioner and subjected him to a "search" when he took hold of him and patted down the outer surfaces of his clothing. We must decide whether at that point it was reasonable for Officer McFadden to have interfered with petitioner's personal security as he did. . . .

If this case involved police conduct subject to the Warrant Clause of the Fourth Amendment, we would have to ascertain whether "probable cause" existed to justify the search and seizure which took place. However, that is not the case. We do not retreat from our holdings that the police must whenever practicable, obtain advance judicial approval of searches and seizures through the warrant procedure . . . But we deal here with an entire rubric of police conduct—necessarily swift action predicated upon the on-the-spot observations of the officer on the beat—which historically has not been, and as a practical matter could not be, subjected to the warrant procedure. Instead, the conduct involved in this case must be tested by the Fourth Amendment's general proscription against unreasonable searches and seizures.

. . . [A] police officer may in appropriate circumstances and in an appropriate manner approach a person for purposes of investigating possibly criminal behavior even though there is no probable cause to make an arrest. It was this legitimate investigative function Officer McFadden was discharged when he decided to approach petitioner and his companions. . . .

. . . It does not follow that because an officer may lawfully arrest a person only when he is apprised of facts sufficient to warrant a belief that the person has committed or is committing a crime, the officer is equally unjustified absent that kind of evidence, in making any intrusions short of an arrest. Moreover, a perfectly reasonable apprehension of danger may arise long before the officer is possessed of adequate information to justify taking a person into custody for the purpose of prosecuting him for a crime. . . .

. . . [T]here must be a narrowly drawn authority to permit a reasonable search for weapons for the protection of the police officer, where he has reason to believe that he is dealing with an armed and dangerous individual, regardless of whether he has probable cause to arrest the individual for a crime. The officer need not be absolutely certain that the individual is armed; the issue is whether a reasonably prudent man in the circumstances would be warranted in the belief that his safety or that of others was in danger . . . And in determining whether the officer acted reasonably in such circumstances, due weight must be given, not to his inchoate and unparticularized suspicion or "hunch," but to the specific reasonable inferences which he is entitled to draw from the facts in light of his experience. . . .

We think on the facts and circumstances Officer McFadden detailed before the trial judge a reasonably prudent man would have been warranted in believing petitioner was armed and thus presented a threat to the officer's safety while he was investigating his suspicious behavior. . . .

. . . Officer McFadden confined his search strictly to what was minimally necessary to learn whether the men were armed and to disarm them once he discovered the weapons. He did not conduct a general exploratory search for whatever evidence of criminal activity he might find.

. . . At the time he seized petitioner and searched him for weapons, Officer McFadden had reasonable grounds to believe that petitioner was armed and dangerous, and it was necessary for the protection of himself and others to take swift measures to discover the true facts and neutralize the threat of harm if it materialized. The policeman carefully restricted his search to what was appropriate to the discovery of the particular items which he sought . . . We merely hold today that where a police officer observes unusual conduct which leads him reasonably to conclude in light of his experience that criminal activity may be afoot and that the persons with whom he is dealing may be armed and presently dangerous; where in the course of investigating this behavior he identities himself as a policeman and makes reasonable inquiries; and where nothing in the initial stages of the encounter serves to dispel his reasonable fear for his own or others' safety, he is entitled for the protection of himself and others in the area to conduct a carefully limited search of the outer clothing of such persons in an attempt to discover weapons which might be used to assault him. Such a search is a reasonable search under the Fourth Amendment, and any weapons seized may properly be introduced in evidence against the person from whom they were taken.

### 31. *Michigan Department of State Police v. Sitz* 496 U.S. 444; 110 S.Ct. 2481; 110 L.Ed.2d 412 (1990)

*Highway sobriety checkpoints represent a classic Fourth Amendment dilemma. The majority opinion, defining the issue as a reaction to a critical national problem, is quick to apply a balancing test where society's interest in controlling drunk driving is balanced against what is seen as a minimal intrusion into the realm of an individual's protected rights. Being stopped at a checkpoint is no more intrusive, for the majority, than having to stop at an immigration road block. The dissent argues that the balancing test is misapplied and that the proper analysis should focus on the police-officers' individualized suspicion. Absent some articulable reason for a stop, the citizen ought to be free from being stopped under the Fourth Amendment.*

\* \* \* \* \* \* \* \* \* \* \* \* \* \* \* \* \* \* \* \* \* \* \* \* \* \* \* \*

Chief Justice **Rehnquist** delivered the opinion of the Court:

This case poses the question whether a State's use of highway sobriety checkpoints violates the Fourth and Fourteenth Amendments to the United States Constitution. We hold that it does not. . . .

Petitioners . . . established a sobriety checkpoint pilot program in early 1986. . . .

Under the guidelines, checkpoints would be set up at selected sites along state roads. All vehicles passing through a checkpoint would be stopped and their drivers briefly examined for signs of intoxication. In cases where a checkpoint officer detected signs of intoxication, the motorist would be directed to a location out of the traffic flow where an officer would check the motorist's driver's license and car registration and, if warranted, conduct further sobriety tests. Should the field tests and the officer's observations suggest that the driver was intoxicated, an arrest would be made. All other drivers would be permitted to resume their journey immediately. . . .

To decide this case the trial court performed a balancing test derived from our opinion in *Brown v. Texas,* 443 U.S. 47 (1979) . . . [T]he test involved "balancing the state's interest in preventing accidents caused by drunk drivers, the effectiveness of sobriety checkpoints in achieving that goal, and the level of intrusion on an individual's privacy caused by the checkpoints." . . .

In this Court respondents seek to defend the judgment in their favor by insisting that the balancing test . . . was not the proper method of analysis. Respondents maintain that the analysis must proceed from a basis of probable cause or reasonable suspicion and rely for support on language from our decision last Term in *Treasury Employees v. Von Raab,* 489 U.S.— (1989). We said in *Von Raab:*

> "Where a Fourth Amendment intrusion serves special governmental needs, beyond the normal need for law enforcement, it is necessary to balance the individual's privacy expectations against the Government's interests to determine whether it is impractical to require a warrant or some level of individualized suspicion in the particular context." . . .

No one can seriously dispute the magnitude of the drunken driving problem or the States' interest in eradicating it. Media reports of alcohol-related death and mutilation on the Nation's roads are legion. The anecdotal is confirmed by the statistical. . . . For decades, this Court has "repeatedly lamented the tragedy." . . .

Conversely, the weight bearing on the other scale—the measure of the intrusion on motorists stopped briefly at sobriety checkpoints—is slight. We reached a similar conclusion as to the intrusion on motorists subjected to a brief stop at a highway checkpoint for detecting illegal aliens. . . . We see virtually no difference between the levels of intrusion on law-abiding motorists from the brief stops necessary to the effectuation of these two types of checkpoints, which to the average motorist would seem identical save for the nature of the questions the checkpoint officers might ask. . . . [T]he "objective" intrusion, measured by the duration of the seizure and the intensity of the investigation, as minimal. . . .

With respect to what it perceived to be the "subjective" intrusion on motorists, however, the Court of Appeals found such intrusion substantial. . . . The court first affirmed the trial court's finding that the guidelines governing checkpoint operation minimize the discretion of the officers on the scene. But the court also agreed with the trial court's conclusion that the checkpoints have the potential to generate fear and surprise in motorists. This was so because the record failed to demonstrate that approaching motorists would be aware of their option to make U-turns or turnoffs to avoid the checkpoints. On that basis, the court deemed the subjective intrusion from the checkpoints unreasonable. . . .

We believe the Michigan courts misread our cases concerning the degree of "subjective intrusion" and the potential for generating fear and surprise. The "fear and surprise" to be considered are not the natural fear of one who has been drinking over the prospect of being stopped at a sobriety checkpoint but, rather, the fear and surprise egendered in law abiding motorists by the nature of the stop. . . .

The Court of Appeals went on to consider as part of the balancing analysis the "effectiveness" of the proposed checkpoint program. Based on extensive testimony in the trial record, the court concluded that the checkpoint program failed the "effectiveness" part of the test, and that this failure materially discounted petitioncr's strong interest in implementing the program. We think the Court of Appeals was wrong on this point as well.

. . . [F]or purposes of Fourth Amendment analysis, the choice among such reasonable alternatives remains with the governmental officials who have a unique understanding of, and a responsibility for, limited public resources, including a finite number of police officers. . . .

In sum, the balance of the State's interest in preventing drunken driving, the extent to which this system can reasonably be said to advance that interest, and the degree of intrusion upon individual motorists who are briefly stopped, weighs in favor of the state program. We therefore hold that it is consistent with the Fourth Amendment. . . .

Justice **Brennan**, with whom Justice **Marshall** joins dissenting:

Today, the court rejects a Fourth Amendment challenge to a sobriety checkpoint policy in which police stop all cars and inspect all drivers for signs of intoxication without *any* individualized suspicion that a specific driver is intoxicated. The Court does so by balancing "the State's interest in preventing drunken driving, the extent to which this system can reasonably be said to advance that interest, and the degree of intrusion upon individual motorists who arc briefly stopped." . . . [T]he Court misapplies that test by undervaluing the nature of the intrusion and exaggerating the law enforcement need to use the roadblocks to prevent drunken driving. . . .

The majority opinion creates the impression that the Court generally engages in a balancing test in order to determine the constitutionality of all seizures, or at least those "dealing with police stops of motorists on public highways." . . . This is not the case. In most cases, the police must possess probable cause for a seizure to be judged reasonable. . . . Only when a seizure is "*substantially* less intrusive," ... than a typical arrest is the general rule replaced by a balancing test. ... But one searches the majority opinion in vain for any acknowledgement that the *reason* for employing the balancing test is that the seizure is minimally intrusive.

Indeed, the opinion reads as if the minimal nature of the seizure *ends* rather than begins the inquiry into reasonableness. ... The Court ignores the fact that in this class of minimally intrusive searches, we have generally required the Government to prove that it had reasonable suspicion for a minimally intrusive seizure to be considered reasonable. ... Some level of individualized suspicion is a core component of the protection the Fourth Amendment provides against arbitrary government action. ... By holding that no level of suspicion is necessary before the police may stop a car for the purpose of preventing drunken driving, the Court potentially subjects the general public to arbitrary or harassing conduct by the police. ...

... Without proof that the police cannot develop individualized suspicion that a person is driving while impaired by alcohol, I believe the constitutional balance must be struck in favor or protecting the public against even the "minimally intrusive" seizures involved in this case.

... In the face of the "momentary evil" of drunken driving, the Court today abdicates its role as the protector of that fundamental right. I respectfully dissent.

## III. SELF-INCRIMINATION AND THE RIGHT TO COUNSEL

### 32. *Powell v. Alabama*
### 287 U.S. 45; 53 S.Ct. 55; 77 L.Ed. 158 (1932)

*The Sixth Amendment provides that "in all criminal prosecutions, the accused shall enjoy the right ... to have the assistance of counsel for his defense." In fact, many criminal defendants went unrepresented by counsel. For years, this right depended on the ability of defendants to pay for their own attorneys.*

*In* Powell v. Alabama, *this federal right was extended to the state level by way of the Fourteenth Amendment's Due Process Clause. Writing for a seven-to-two majority in the famous "Scottsboro Boys" case, Justice Sutherland concluded that the defendants in a state capital case had been unable to receive fair trials without counsel. Note, however, that Sutherland emphasized the illiteracy of the defendants, the atmosphere of public hostility, and other circumstances of the case at hand in an attempt to limit the scope of his decision.*

*The Court in* Johnson v. Zerbst *(1938) subsequently broadened the right to counsel by ruling that all federal defendants—including those in non-capital cases—are entitled to an attorney. And in* Gideon v. Wainwright *(1963), the Court went on to rule all state defendants should be assisted by counsel in cases involving serious charges.*

\* \* \* \* \* \* \* \* \* \* \* \* \* \* \* \* \* \* \* \* \* \* \* \* \* \* \* \* \*

Mr. Justice **Sutherland** delivered the opinion of the Court:

The petitioners, hereinafter referred to as defendants, are negroes charged with the crime of rape, committed upon the persons of two white girls. . . .

There was a severance upon the request of the state, and the defendants were tried in three several groups. . . . Each of the three trials was completed within a single day. Under the Alabama statute the punishment for rape is to be fixed by jury, and in its discretion may be from ten years' imprisonment to death. The juries found defendants guilty and imposed the death penalty upon all . . .

The record shows that on the day when the offense said to have been committed these defendants, together with a number of other negroes, were upon a freight train on its way through Alabama. On the same train were seven white boys and two white girls. A fight took place between the negroes and the white boys, in the course of which the white boys, with the exception of one named Gilley, were thrown off the train. A message was sent ahead, reporting the fight and asking that every negro be gotten off the train. The participants in the fight, and the two girls, were in an open gondola car. The two girls testified that each of them was assaulted by six different negroes in turn, and they identified the seven defendants as having been among the number. . . .

Before the train reached Scottsboro, Alabama, a sheriff's posse seized the defendants and two other negroes. Both girls and the negroes then were taken to Scottsboro, the county seat. Word of their coming and of the alleged assault had preceded them, and they were met at Scottsboro by a large crowed. It does not sufficiently appear that the defendants were seriously threatened with, or that they were actually in danger of, mob violence; but it does appear that the attitude of the community was one of great hostility. The sheriff thought it necessary to call for the militia to assist in safeguarding the prisoners. . . . Soldiers took the defendants to Gadsden for safekeeping, brought them back to Scottsboro for arraignment, returned them to Gadsden for safekeeping while awaiting trial, escorted them to Scottsboro for trial a few days later, and guarded the courthouse and grounds at every stage of the proceedings. It is perfectly apparent that the proceedings from beginning to end, took place in an atmosphere of tense, hostile and excited public sentiment. During the entire time, the defendants were closely confined or were under military guard... [T]he record clearly indicates that most, if not all, of them were youthful and they are constantly referred to as "the boys." They were ignorant and illiterate. All of them were residents of other states where alone members of their families or friends resided.

However guilty defendants, upon due inquiry might prove to have been, they were, until convicted, presumed to be innocent. It was the duty of the court having their cases in charge to see that they were denied no necessary incident of a fair trial.... The sole inquiry which we are permitted to make is whether the federal Constitution was contravened... and as to that, we confine ourselves... to the inquiry whether the defendants were in substance denied the right of counsel, and if so, whether such denial infringes the due process clause of the Fourteenth Amendment.

... [A] defendant should be afforded a fair opportunity to secure counsel of his own choice. Not only was that not done here, but such designation of counsel as was attempted was either so indefinite or so close upon the trial as to amount to denial of effective and substantial aid in that regard....

... [U]ntil the very morning of the trial, no lawyer had been named or definitely designated to represent the defendants. Prior to that time, the trial judge had "appointed all members of the bar" for the limited "purpose of arraigning the defendants."...

... [D]uring perhaps the most critical period of the proceedings against these defendants, that is to say, from the time of their arraignment until the beginning of their trial, when consultation, thorough-going investigation and preparation were vitally important, the defendants did not have the aid of counsel in any real sense....

... The question... is whether the denial of the assistance of counsel contravenes the due process clause of the Fourteenth Amendment to the federal Constitution....

The Sixth Amendment, in terms, provides that in all criminal prosecutions the accused shall enjoy the right "to have the assistance of counsel for his defense."...

... The fact that the right involved is of such a character that is cannot be denied without violating those "fundamental principles of liberty and justice which lie at the base of all our civil and political institutions," (*Hebert v. Louisiana* [1926]), is obviously one of those compelling considerations which must prevail in determining whether it is embraced within the due process clause of the Fourteenth Amendment, although it be specifically dealt with in another part of the federal Constitution . . . " [I]t is possible that some of the personal rights safeguarded by the first eight Amendments against national action may also be safeguarded against state action, because a denial of them would be a denial of due process of law . . . If this is so, it is not because those rights are enumerated in the first eight Amendments, but because they are of such a nature that they are included in the conception of due process of law." . . . [T]he right to the aid of counsel is of this fundamental character.

. . . What . . . does a hearing include? Historically and in practice, in our own country at least, it has always included the right to the aid of counsel when desired and provided by the party asserting the right . . . Even the intelligent and educated layman has small and sometimes no skill in the science of law . . . Left without the aid of counsel he may be put on trial without a proper charge, and convicted upon incompetent evidence, or evidence irrelevant to the issue or otherwise inadmissible. He lacks both the skill and knowledge adequately to prepare his defense, even though he have a perfect one. He requires the guiding hand of counsel at every step in the proceedings against him. Without it, though he be not guilty, he faces the danger of conviction because he does not know how to establish his innocence. If that be true of men of intelligence, how much more true is it of the ignorant and illiterate, or those of feeble intellect. . . .

In the light of the facts outlined in the forepart of this opinion—the ignorance and illiteracy of the defendants, their youth, the circumstances of public hostility, the imprisonment and the close surveillance of the defendants by the military forces, the fact that their friends and families were all in other states and communication with them necessarily difficult, and above all that they stood in deadly peril of their lives—we think the failure of the trial court to give them reasonable time and opportunity to secure counsel was a clear denial of due process.

. . . [U]nder the circumstances just stated, the necessity of counsel was so vital and imperative that the failure of the trial court to make an effective appointment of counsel was likewise a denial of due process within the meaning of the Fourteenth Amendment. Whether this would be so in other criminal prosecutions, or under other circumstances, we need not determine. All that it is necessary now to decide, as we do decide, is that in a capital case, where the defendant is unable to employ counsel, and is incapable adequately of making his own defense because of ignorance, feeblemindedness, illiteracy, or the like, it is the duty of the court whether requested or not, to assign counsel for him as a necessary requisite of due process of law. . . .

## 33. *Gideon v. Wainwright*
### 372 U.S. 335; 83 S.Ct. 792; 9 L.Ed. 2d 799 (1963)

*In the wake of* Powell v. Alabama, *courts sometimes ruled that defendants received fair trials without the assistance of counsel if they were deemed capable of conducting their own defenses. For example, in* Betts v. Brady *(316 U.S. 455, 1942), the Supreme Court underscored the principle that a state need not necessarily appoint counsel for indigent defendants in all criminal cases. In capital cases, however, the Court consistently held that defendants required counsel.*

*Clarence Gideon had been arrested in Florida for breaking and entering. He appeared in court without a lawyer. He was indigent and asked the court to appoint one to assist him. In light of the fact that Florida law provided for the appointment of counsel for indigents in capital cases only, Gideon's request was refused. He was convicted and appealed his case, claiming that his Sixth Amendment right to counsel had been denied.*

*Rejecting the premise of* Betts, *the Supreme Court agreed with Gideon. Writing for the unanimous Court, Justice Black concluded that criminal defendants cannot be assured of receiving fair trials without the aid of counsel. As a result, the right to counsel was applied to both capital and noncapital criminal cases in state courts. Gideon was retried with a lawyer. This time, he was acquitted.*

Gideon *established that the right to counsel applies to state trials. It did not, however, clearly determine at what stage that right attached. In* Hamilton v. Alabama *(368 U.S. 52, 1961), the Court ruled that the accused is entitled to counsel at arraignment. In* Escobedo v. Illinois *(378 U.S. 478, 1964), the Court ruled that the right attaches when a general investigation becomes accusatory and focuses on an individual as a prime suspect. In* White v. Maryland *(373 U.S. 59, 1963), the Court said that it applied to preliminary hearings. The right was applied to a defendant's first appeal in* Douglas v. California *(372 U.S. 535, 1963) and it was applied to a line-up in* United States v. Wade *(388 U.S. 218, 1967)—a federal case—and* Gilbert v. California *(388 U.S. 263, 1967)— a state case. In short, the right to counsel has evolved to apply to the critical stages of the criminal justice process.*

\* \* \* \* \* \* \* \* \* \* \* \* \* \* \* \* \* \* \* \* \* \* \* \* \* \* \* \* \* \* \*

Mr. Justice **Black** delivered the opinion of the Court:

.... Since 1942, when *Betts v. Brady* was decided by a divided by a Court, the problem of a defendant's federal constitutional right to counsel in a state court has been a continuing source of controversy and litigation...

.... [In *Betts*] [t]he Court said: "Asserted denial [of due process] is to be tested by an appraisal of the totality of the facts in a given case ... "

... [T]he Court held that refusal to appoint counsel under the particular facts and circumstances in the *Betts* Case was not so "offensive to the common and fundamental ideas of fairness" as to amount to a denial of due process.... Upon full reconsideration, we conclude that *Betts v. Brady* should be overruled....

We think the Court in *Betts* had ample precedent for acknowledging that those guarantees of the Bill of Rights which are fundamental safeguards of liberty immune from federal abridgment are equally protected against state invasion by the Due Process Clause of the Fourteenth Amendment.... In many cases ... this Court had looked to the fundamental nature of original Bill of Rights guarantees to decide whether the Fourteenth Amendment makes them obligatory on the States. Explicitly recognized to be of this "fundamental nature" and therefore made immune from state invasion by the Fourteenth, or some part of it, are the First Amendment's freedoms of speech, press, religion, assembly, association, and petition for redress of grievances. For the same reason ... the Court has made obligatory on the States the Fifth Amendment's command that private property shall not be taken for public use without just compensation, the Fourth Amendment's prohibition of unreasonable searches and seizures, and the Eighth's ban on cruel and unusual punishment....

We accept *Betts v. Brady's* assumption based as it was on our prior cases, that a provision of the Bill of Rights which is "fundamental and essential to a fair trial" is made obligatory upon the States by the Fourteenth Amendment. We think the Court in *Betts* was wrong, however in concluding that the Sixth Amendment's guarantee of counsel is not one of these fundamental rights....

... Not only these precedents but also reason and reflection require us to recognize that in our adversary system of criminal justice, any person haled into court, who is too poor to hire a lawyer, cannot be assured a fair trial unless counsel is provided for him. This seems to us to be an obvious truth. Governments, both state and federal, quite properly spend vast sums of money to establish machinery to try defendants accused of crime. Lawyers to prosecute are everywhere deemed essential to protect the public's interest in an orderly society. Similarly, there are few defendants charged with crime, few indeed, who fail to hire the best lawyers they can get to prepare and present their defenses. That government hires lawyers to prosecute and defendants who have the money hire lawyers to defend are the strongest indications of the widespread belief that lawyers in criminal courts are necessities, not luxuries. The right of one charged with crime to counsel may not be deemed fundamental and essential for fair trials in some countries, but it is in ours. . . .

## 34. *Miranda v. Arizona*
## 348. U.S. 436, 86 S.Ct. 1602; 16 L.Ed. 2d 694 1966)

*In cases like Gideon v. Wainwright (1963), Malloy v. Hogan (1964), and Escobedo v. Illinois (1964), the Warren Court expanded the right to counsel and the privilege against compulsory self-incrimination. In some ways, the Court moved to merge these two complementary rights. Because it is difficult to prove what actually happens during police interrogations, the presence of counsel is one way to protect against coerced confessions. The Miranda decision required the police to inform the accused that he need not incriminate himself and that he is entitled to legal counsel.*

*Miranda consolidated four related cases that raised questions about the admissibility of confessions. In the lead case, Ernesto Miranda was suspected of kidnapping and rape. He was arrested at his home and taken to a police station for questioning. He was not advised of his right to remain silent nor of his right to counsel. After two hours of questioning, he provided a written confession. He was subsequently convicted. Writing for a five-to-four majority, Chief Justice Warren ruled that the confession was inadmissible and that such defendants should be informed of their rights.*

*Miranda was retried and was again convicted. Following his eventual release, he got into a card game. A fight erupted and Miranda was stabbed to death. On his person were a number of "Miranda Cards." When police arrived on the scene, the arresting officer read one of Miranda's own cards to the suspect arrested for his murder.*

*The Supreme Court has moved to strengthen one's right to an attorney. In Edwards v. Arizona (451 U.S. 477, 1981), the court recognized that if a person accused of a crime requests an attorney the police must end the interrogation until the attorney is present. There was some question whether the authorities could initiate a new interrogation without an attorney being present by just giving the Miranda warning anew. In Minnick v. Mississippi (111 S.Ct. 486, 1990) the Court reinforced this right by holding that once an accused requests an attorney the authorities may not question him without that attorney.*

\* \* \* \* \* \* \* \* \* \* \* \* \* \* \* \* \* \* \* \* \* \* \* \* \* \* \* \* \*

Mr. Chief Justice **Warren** delivered the opinion of the Court:
The cases before us raise questions which go to the roots of our con-

cepts of American criminal jurisprudence: the restraints society must observe consistent with the Federal Constitution in prosecuting individuals for crime. More specifically, we deal with the admissibility of statements obtained from an individual who is subjected to custodial police interrogation and the necessity for procedures which assure that the individual is accorded his privilege under the Fifth Amendment to the Constitution not to be compelled to incriminate himself.

We start here, as we did in *Escobedo,* with the premise that our holding is not as innovation in our jurisprudence, but is an application of principles long recognized and applied in other settings. We have undertaken a thorough re-examination of the *Escobedo* decision and the principles it announced, and we reaffirm it. That case was but an explication of basic rights that are enshrined in our Constitution—that "No person . . . shall be compelled in any criminal case to be a witness against himself," and that "the accused shall . . . have the Assistance of Counsel"—rights which were put in jeopardy in that case through official overbearing. These precious rights were fixed in our Constitution only after centuries of persecution and struggle. . . .

The constitutional issue we decide in each of these cases is the admissibility of statements obtained from a defendant questioned while in custody or otherwise deprived of his freedom of action in any significant way. In each, the defendant was questioned by police officers, detectives, or a prosecuting attorney in a room in which he was cut off from the outside world. In none of these cases was the defendant given a full and effective warning of his rights at the outset of the interrogation process. In all the cases, the questioning elicited [confessions] which were admitted at their trials. They all thus share salient features—incommunicado interrogation of individuals in a police-dominated atmosphere, resulting in self-incriminating statements without full warning of Constitutional rights. . . .

In these cases, we might not find the defendants' statements to have been involuntary in traditional terms. Our concern for adequate safeguards to protect precious Fifth Amendment rights is, or course, not lessened in the slightest. In each of the cases, the defendant was thrust into an unfamiliar atmosphere and run through menacing police interrogation procedures. The potential for compulsion is forcefully apparent, for example, in *Miranda,* where the indigent Mexican defendant was a seriously disturbed individual with pronounced sexual fantasies. . . .

It is obvious that such an interrogation environment is created for no purpose other than no subjugate the individual to the will of his examiner. The atmosphere carries its own badge of intimidation. . . . The current practice of incommunicado interrogating is at odds with one of our Nation's most cherished principles—that the individual may not be compelled to incriminate himself. Unless adequate protective devices are employed to dispel the compulsion inherent in custodial surroundings, no statement obtained from the defendant can truly be the product of his free choice....

Today, then, there can be no doubt that the Fifth Amendment privilege is available outside of criminal court proceedings and serves to protect persons in all settings in which there freedom of action is curtailed in any significant way from being compelled to incriminate themselves. We have concluded that without proper safeguards the process of in-custody interrogation of persons suspected or accused of crime contains inherently compelling pressures which work to undermine the individual's will to resist and to compel him to speak where he would not otherwise do so freely. In order to combat these pressures and to permit a full opportunity to exercise the privilege against self-incrimination, the accused must be adequately and effectively apprised of his rights and the exercise of those rights must be fully honored.

It is impossible for us to foresee the potential alternative for protecting the privilege which might be devised by Congress or the States in the exercise of their creative rule-making capacities. Therefore we cannot say that the Constitution necessarily requires adherence to any particular solution for the inherent compulsions of the interrogation process as it is presently conducted. Our decision in no way creates a constitutional straitjacket which will handicap sound efforts at reform, nor is it intended to have this effect. We encourage Congress and the States to continue their laudable search for increasingly effective ways of protecting the rights of the individual while promoting efficient enforcement of our criminal laws. However, unless we are shown other procedures which are at least as effective in apprising accused persons of their right of silence and in assuring a continuous opportunity to exercise it, the following safeguards must be observed.

At the outset, if a person in custody is to be subjected to interrogation, he must first be informed in clear and unequivocal terms that he has the right to remain silent. For those unaware of the privilege, the warning is needed simply to make them aware of it—the threshold requirement for an intelligent decision as to its exercise. More important, such a warning is an absolute prerequisite incoming the inherent pressures of the interrogation atmosphere. It is not just the subnormal or woefully ignorant who succumb to an interrogator's imprecations, whether implied or expressly stated, that the interrogation will continue until a confession is obtained or that silence in the face of accusation is itself damning and will bode ill when presented to a jury. Further, the warning will show the individual that his interrogators are prepared to recognized his privilege should be choose to exercise it....

.... More important, whatever the background of the person interrogated, a warning at the time of the interrogation is indispensable to overcome its pressures and to insure that the individual knows he is free to exercise the privilege at that point in time.

The warning of the right to remain silent must be accompanied by the explanation that anything said can and will be used against the individual in court. This warning is needed in order to make him aware not only of the privilege, but also of the consequence of forgoing it. It is only through an awareness of these consequences that there can be any assurance of real understanding and intelligent exercise of the privilege. Moreover, this warning may serve to make the individual more acutely ware that he is faced with a phase of the adversary system—that he is not in the presence of persons acting solely in his interest.

The circumstances surrounding in-custody interrogation can operate very quickly to overbear the will of one merely made aware of his privilege by his interrogators. Therefore, the right to have counsel present at the interrogation is indispensable to the protection of the Fifth Amendment privilege under the system we delineate today. Our aim is to assure that the individual's right to choose between silence and speech remains unfettered throughout the interrogation process. A once-stated warning, delivered by those who will conduct the interrogation, cannot itself suffice to that end among those who most require knowledge of their rights. A mere warning given by the interrogators is not alone sufficient to accomplish that end. Prosecutors themselves claim that the admonishment of the right to remain silent without more "will benefit only the recidivist and the professional. . . ."

Accordingly we hold that an individual held for interrogation must be clearly informed that he has the right to consult with a lawyer and to have the lawyer with him during interrogation under the system for protecting the privilege we delineate today. As with the warnings of the right to remain silent and that anything stated can be used in evidence against him, this warning is an absolute prerequisite to interrogation. No amount of circumstantial evidence that the person may have been aware of this right will suffice to stand in its stead. Only through such a warning is there ascertainable assurance that the accused was aware of this right.

If an individual indicates that he wishes the assistance of counsel before any interrogation occurs, the authorities cannot rationally ignore or deny his request on the basis that the individual does not have or cannot afford a retained attorney. The financial ability of the individual has no relationship to the scope of the rights involved here. The privilege against self-incrimination secured by the Constitution applies to all individuals. The need for counsel in order to protect the privilege exists for the indigent as well as the affluent. . . .

In order fully to apprise a person interrogated of the extent of his rights under this system then, it is necessary to warn him not only that he has the right to consult with an attorney, but also that if he is indigent a lawyer will be appointed to represent him. Without this additional warning, the admonition of the right to consult with counsel would often be understood as meaning only that he can consult with a lawyer if he has one or has the funds to obtain one. The warning of a right to counsel would be hollow if not couched in terms that would convey to the indigent—the person most often subjected to interrogation—the knowledge that he too has a right to have counsel present. As with the warnings of the right to remain silent and of the general right to counsel, only by effective and express explanation to the indigent of this right can there be assurance that he was truly in a position to exercise it.

Once warnings have been given, the subsequent procedure is clear. If the individual indicates in any manner, at any time prior to or during questioning, that he wishes to remain silent, the interrogation must cease. . . . If the individual states that he wants an attorney, the interrogations must cease until an attorney is present. At that time, the individual must have an opportunity to confer with the attorney and to have him present during any subsequent questioning. If the individual cannot obtain an attorney and he indicates that he wants one before speaking to the police, they must respect his decision to remain silent. . . . The requirement of warnings and waiver of rights is a fundamental with respect to the Fifth Amendment privilege and not simply a preliminary ritual to existing methods of interrogation. . . .

The principles announced today deal with the protection which must be given to the privilege against self-incrimination when the individual is first subjected to police interrogation while in custody at the station or otherwise deprived of his freedom of action in any significant way. It is this point that our adversary system of criminal proceedings commences, distinguishing itself at the outset from the inquisitorial system recognized in some countries. . . .

## IV. THE EXCLUSIONARY RULE

### 35. *Mapp v. Ohio*
### 367 U.S. 643; 81 S.Ct. 1684; 6 L.Ed. 2d 1981 (1961)

*In* Weeks v. United States *(232 U.S. 383, 1914), the Court developed the exclusionary rule as a means of enforcing the Fourth Amendment. Evidence gathered by federal agents through unreasonable searches and seizures would not be admissible in federal courts. The exclusionary rule has also been used to bar the use of evidence obtained in violation of the Fifth and Sixth Amendments as well. But the rule did not apply to state courts. In* Wolf v. Colorado *(338 U.S. 25, 1949), the Court ruled that unreasonable searches and seizures conducted by state officials violate the Fourteenth Amendment, but a state can still use this evidence in its own courts if permitted by its own laws.*

*The Court extended the exclusionary rule to states in* Mapp v. Ohio. *Cleveland police officers were seeking a suspect who was reportedly hiding in a certain house where they also expected to find gambling materials. They forced their way into the house without a warrant and searched the premises. They found a trunk containing obscene materials. This evidence was used to convict Miss Mapp on obscenity charges in the state courts. Writing for a six-to-three majority, Justice Clark overruled* Wolf *and held that evidence obtained through unreasonable searches and seizures is inadmissible in state, as well as federal, courts.*

*The exclusionary rule has been very controversial. In 1926, Benjamin Cardozo lamented that "[t]he criminal is to go free because the constable has blundered." Justice Clark replied, "The criminal goes free, if he must, but it is the law that sets him free. Nothing can destroy a government more quickly than its failure to observe its own laws, or worse, its disregard of the charter of its own existence." Chief Justice Burger argued that the rule should be abandoned and replaced with a law authorizing individuals to sue law enforcement officials who violate their rights for monetary damages. Defenders of the exclusionary rule say it is the only effective deterrent to police misconduct. Further, the criminal does not necessarily go free when the constable blunders; a conviction can be obtained on other grounds.*

\* \* \* \* \* \* \* \* \* \* \* \* \* \* \* \* \* \* \* \* \* \* \* \* \* \* \* \*

Mr. Justice **Clark** delivered the opinion of the Court:

Appellant stands convicted of knowingly having had in her possession and under her control certain lewd and lascivious books, pictures and photographs in violation of [Ohio law]. . . .

The Supreme Court of Ohio found that her conviction was valid though "based primarily upon the introduction in evidence of lewd and lascivious books and pictures unlawfully seized during an unlawful search of defendant's home. . . ."

On May 23, 1957, three Cleveland police officers arrived at appellant's residence in that city pursuant to information that "a person [was] hiding out in the home, who was wanted for questioning in connection with a recent bombing, and that there was a large amount of policy paraphernalia being hidden in the home.". . . . Upon their arrival at the house, the officers knocked on the door and demanded entrance but appellant, after telephoning her attorney, refused to admit them without a search warrant. They advised their headquarters of the situation and undertook a surveillance of the house.

The officers again sought entrance some three hours later when four or more additional officers arrived on the scene. When Miss Mapp did not come to the door immediately, at least one of the several doors to the house was forcibly opened and the policemen gained admittance. Meanwhile Miss Mapp's attorney arrived, but the officers, having secured their own entry, and continuing in their defiance of the law, would permit him neither to see Miss Mapp nor to enter the house. It appears that Miss Mapp was halfway down the stairs from the upper floor to the front door when the officers, in this highhanded manner, broke into the hall. She demanded to see the search warrant. A paper claimed to be a warrant, was held up by one of the officers. She grabbed the "warrant" and placed it in her bosom. A struggle ensued in which the officers recovered the piece of paper and as a result of which they handcuffed appellant because she had been "belligerent" in resisting their official rescue of the "warrant" from her person. Running roughshod over appellant, a policeman "grabbed" her, "twisted [her] hand," and she "yelled [and] pleaded with him" because "it was hurting." Appellant in handcuffs, was then forcibly taken upstairs to her bedroom where the officers searched a dresser a chest of drawers, a closet and some suitcases. They also looked into a photo album and through personal papers belonging to the appellant. The search spread to the rest of the second floor including . . . the living room, the kitchen and a dinette. The basement of the building and a trunk found therein were also searched. The obscene materials for possession of which she was ultimately convicted were discovered in the course of that widespread search.

At the trial no search warrant was produced by the prosecution, nor was the failure to produce one explained or accounted for. At best, "There is, in the record, considerable doubt as to whether there ever was any warrant for the search of defendant's home." . . .

The State says that even if the search were made without authority, or otherwise unreasonably it is not prevented from using the unconstitutionally seized evidence at trial, citing *Wolf v. Colorado* [1949], in which this Court did indeed hold "that in a prosecution in a State court for a State crime the Fourteenth Amendment does not forbid the admission of evidence obtained by an unreasonable search and seizure." On this appeal . . . it is urged once again that we review that holding. . . .

In 1929, 35 years after *Weeks* was announced, this Court, in *Wolf, v. Colorado,* again for the first time, discussed the effect of the Fourth Amendment upon the States through the operation of the Due Process Clause of the Fourteenth Amendment . . .

Nevertheless, after declaring that the "security of one's privacy against arbitrary intrusion by the police" is "implicit 'in the concept of ordered liberty' and as such enforceable against the States through the Due Process Clause" . . . the Court decided that the *Weeks* exclusionary rule would not then be imposed upon the States as "an essential ingredient of the right." . . .

. . . Today we once again examine *Wolf's* constitutional documentation of the right to privacy free from unreasonable state intrusion . . . We hold that all evidence obtained by searches and seizures in violation of the Constitution is, by that same authority, inadmissible in a state court.

Since the Fourth Amendment's right of privacy has been declared enforceable against the States through the Due Process Clause of the Fourteenth, it is enforceable against them by the same sanction of exclusion as is used against the Federal Government. Were it otherwise, then . . . the assurance against unreasonable federal searches and seizures would be "a form of words," valueless and undeserving of mention in a perpetual charter of inestimable human liberties, so too, without that rule the freedom from state invasions of privacy would be so ephemeral and so neatly severed from its conceptual nexus with the freedom from all brutish means of coercing evidence as not to merit this Court's high regard as a freedom "implicit in the concept of ordered liberty." . . .

Moreover, our holding that the exclusionary rule is an essential part of both the Fourth and Fourteenth Amendment is not only the logical dictate of prior cases, but it also makes very good sense. There is no war between the Constitution and common sense. Presently a federal prosecutor may make no use of evidence illegally seized, but a State's attorney across the street may, although he supposedly is operating under the enforceable prohibitions of the same Amendment. Thus the State, by admitting evidence unlawfully seized, serves to encourage disobedience to the Federal Constitution which it is bound to uphold. . . .

There are those who say, as did Justice (then Judge) Cardozo, that under our constitutional exclusionary doctrine "[t]he criminal is to go free because the constable has blundered." *People v. Defore,* 242 N.Y., at page 21 [1926]. In some cases this will undoubtedly be the result. But, as was said in *Elkins,* "there is another consideration-the imperative of judicial integrity." The criminal goes free, if he must, but it is the law that sets him free. Nothing can destroy a government more quickly than its failure to observe its own laws, or worse, its disregard of the charter of its own existence. . . .

The ignoble shortcut to conviction left open to the State tends to destroy the entire system of constitutional restraints on which the liberties of the people rest. Having once recognized that the right to privacy embodied in the Fourth Amendment is enforceable against the States, and that the right to be secure against rude invasions of privacy by state officers is therefore, constitutional in origin, we can no longer permit that right to remain an empty promise. . . .

## 36. *United States v. Leon*
### 468 U.S. 897, 104 S. Ct. 3405; 82 L.Ed. 2d 677 (1984)

*The exclusionary rule continues to generate controversy. In* United States v. Leon, *the Court created a "defective warrant" exception to the exclusionary rule. Writing for a six-to-three majority, Justice White held that the rule should not bar evidence obtained by police officers who acted in reasonable reliance on a search warrant issued by a neutral magistrate but ultimately found to be unsupported by probable cause. White observed that the rule is designed to deter improper police conduct; it should not be applied to deter objectively reasonable law enforcement activities. Here the police obtained a warrant in "good faith" but the magistrate made an error in issuing it without sufficient cause. "Penalizing the officer for the magistrate's error, rather than his own, cannot logically contribute to the deterrence of Fourth Amendment violations." Justice Brennan, joined by Justice Marshall, argued in dissent that this decision would instruct police officers and magistrates to take less care in preparing warrant's "since their mistakes will from now on have virtually no consequences."*

*The Court also modified the exclusionary rule in additional ways. In* Nix v. Williams *(467 U.S. 431, 1984), an "inevitable discovery" exception was announced. Here the police told counsel that they would drive a suspect to another city and they would not question him along the way. The police started a conversation during the drive and the suspect made incriminating statements and directed them to a body for which they had been searching. His statements were inadmissible because the right to counsel was violated, but evidence as to the body's location was admitted on the ground that the police would have inevitably found it anyway.*

*The Court again modified the exclusionary rule in* Maryland v. Garrison *(480 U.S. 79, 1987). Here police obtained a warrant to search the third floor of a building where they thought only one apartment—belonging to a suspected drug dealer—was located. There were actually two apartments on the third floor. Calling it an honest mistake, they searched both apartments and found incriminating evidence in Mr. Garrison's apartment. The Court admitted the evidence saying that the police conduct was consistent with reasonable efforts to identify the place to be searched. In effect, an "honest mistakes" exception to the exclusionary rule was created.*

\* \* \* \* \* \* \* \* \* \* \* \* \* \* \* \* \* \* \* \* \* \* \* \* \* \* \* \* \* \*

Justice **White** delivered the opinion of the Court:

This case presents the question whether the Fourth Amendment exclusionary rule should be modified so as not to bar the use in the prosecution's case-in-chief of evidence obtained by officers acting in reasonable reliance on a search warrant issued by a detached and neutral magistrate but ultimately found to be unsupported by probable cause....

In August 1981, a confidential informant of unproven reliability informed an officer of the Burbank Police Department that two persons known to him as "Armando" and " Patsy" were selling large quantities of cocaine and methaqualone from their residence...

On the basis of this information, the Burbank police initiated an extensive investigation.....

A facially valid search warrant was issued in September 1981 by a State Superior Court Judge. The ensuing searches produced large quantities of drugs....

We have concluded that, in the Fourth Amendment context, the exclusionary rule can be modified somewhat without jeopardizing its ability to perform its intended functions....

The Fourth Amendment contains no provision expressly precluding the use of evidence obtained in violation of its commands... [T]he exclusionary rule... operates as "a judicially created remedy designed to safeguard Fourth Amendment rights generally through its deterrent effect, rather than a personal constitutional right of the party aggrieved."...

The substantial social costs exacted by the exclusionary rule for the vindication of Fourth Amendment rights have long been a source of concern... An objectionable collateral consequence of this interference with the criminal justice system's truth-finding function is that some guilty defendants may go free or receive reduced sentences as a result of favorable plea bargains. Particularly when law enforcement officers have acted in objective good faith or their transgressions have been minor, the magnitude of the benefit conferred on such guilty defendants offends basic concepts of the criminal justice system.... Indiscriminate application of the exclusionary rule, therefore, may well "generat[e] disrespect for the law and the administration of justice."...

... [T]he balancing approach that has evolved in various contexts—including criminal trials —"forcefully suggest[s] that the exclusionary rule be more generally modified to permit the introduction of evidence obtained in the reasonable good-faith belief that a search or seizure was in accord with the Fourth Amendment." *Illinois v. Gates*, [1983].

If exclusion of evidence obtained pursuant to a subsequently invalidated warrant is to have any deterrent effect... it must alter the behavior of individual law enforcement officers or the policies or their depart-ment . . . We . . . conclude that suppression of evidence obtained pursuant to a warrant should be ordered only on a case-by-case basis and only in those unusual cases in which exclusion will further the purposes of the exclusionary rule.

We have frequently questioned whether the exclusionary rule can have any deterrent effect when the offending officers acted in the objectively reasonable belief that their conduct did not violate the Forth Amend-ment . . . But even assuming that the rule effectively deters some police misconduct and provides incentive for the law enforcement profession as a whole to conduct itself in accord with the Fourth Amendment, it cannot be expected, and should not be applied to deter objectively reasonable law enforcement activity. . . .

This is particularly true, we believe, when an officer acting with objec-tive good faith has obtained a search warrant from a judge or magistrate and acted within its scope. In most such cases, there is no police illegality and thus nothing to deter. It is the magistrate's responsibility to determine whether the officer's allegations establish probable cause and, if so, to issue a warrant comporting in form with the requirements of the Fourth Amendment. In the ordinary case, an officer cannot be expected to ques-tion the magistrate's probable-cause determination or his judgment that the form of the warrant is technically sufficient. . . . Penalizing the officer for the magistrate's error, rather than his own, cannot logically contribute to the deterrence of Fourth Amendment violations.

We conclude that the marginal or nonexistent benefits produced by suppressing evidence obtained in objectively reasonable reliance on a subsequently invalidated search warrant cannot justify the substantial cost of exclusion. . . .

Suppression therefore remains an appropriate remedy if the magistrate or judge in issuing a warrant was misled by information in an affidavit that the affiant knew was false or would have known was false except for his reckless disregard of the truth. . . . [D]epending on the circumstances of the particular case, a warrant may be so facially deficient—i.e., in failing to particularize the place to be searched or the things to be seized—that the executing officers cannot reasonably presume it to be valid. . . .

. . . The good-faith exception for searches conducted pursuant to war-rants is not intended to signal our unwillingness strictly to enforce the requirements of the Fourth Amendment, and we do not believe that it will have this effect. As we have already suggested, the good-faith exception, turning as it does on objective reasonableness, should not be difficult to apply in practice. When officers have acted pursuant to a warrant, the prosecution should ordinarily be able to establish objective good faith without a substantial expenditure of judicial time. . . .

In the absence of an allegation that the magistrate abandoned his detached and neutral role, suppression is appropriate only if the officers were dishonest or reckless in preparing their affidavit or could not have harbored an objectively reasonable belief in the existence of probable cause. . . .

Justice **Brennan**, with whom Justice **Marshall** joins, dissenting:

Ten years ago in *United States v. Calandra,* 414 U.S. 338 (1974), I expressed the fear that the Court's decision "may signal that a majority of my colleagues have positioned themselves to reopen the door [to evidence secured by official lawlessness] still further and abandon altogether the exclusionary rule in search-and-seizure cases." Id., at 365 (dissenting opinion). Since then, in case after case, I have witnessed the Court's gradual but determined strangulation of the rule. It now appears that the Court's victory over the Fourth Amendment is complete. That today decision represents the *piece de resistance* of the Court's past efforts cannot be doubted, for today the Court sanctions the use in the prosection's case-in-chief of illegally obtained evidence against the individual whose rights have been violated—a result that had previously been thought to be foreclosed.

. . . [T]he Amendment, like other provisions of the Bill of Rights, restrains the power of the government as a whole; it does not specify only a particular agency and exempt all others. The judiciary is responsible, no less than the executive, for ensuring that constitutional rights arc respected. . . .

The flaw in the Court's argument however, is that its logic captures only one comparatively minor element of the generally acknowledged deterrent purposes of the exclusionary rule. To be sure, the rule operates to some extent to deter future misconduct by individual officers who have had evidence suppressed in their own cases. But what the Court overlooks is that the deterrence rationale for the rule is not designed to be, nor should it be thought of as a form of "punishment" of individual police officers for their failure to obey the restraints imposed by the Fourth Amendment. . . . Instead, the chief deterrent function of the rule is its tendency to promote institutional compliance with Fourth Amendment requirement on the part of law enforcement agencies generally. . . .

If the overall educational effect of the exclusionary rule is considered, application of the rule to even those situations in which individual police officers have acted on the basis of a reasonable but mistaken belief that their conduct was authorized can still be expected to have a considerable long-term deterrent effect. If evidence is consistently excluded in these circumstances, police departments will surely be prompted to instruct their officers to devote greater care and attention to providing sufficient information to establish probable cause when applying for a warrant, and to review with some attention the form of the warrent that they have been issued, rather then automatically assuming that whatever document the magistrate has signed will necessarily comport with Fourth Amendment requirements.

After today's decision, however, that institutional incentive will be lost. Indeed, the Court's "reasonable mistake" exception to the exclusionary rule will tend to put a premium on police ignorance of the law. Armed with the assurance provided by today's decisions that evidence will always be admissible whenever an officer has "reasonably" relied upon a warrant, police departments will be encouraged to train officers that if a warrant has simply been signed, it is reasonable without more, to rely on it. . . .

. . . A chief consequence of today's decisions will be to convey a clear and unambiguous message to magistrates that their decisions to issue warrants are now insulated from subsequent judicial review. Creation of this new exception for good faith reliance upon a warrant implicitly tells magistrates that they need not take much care in reviewing warrant applications, since their mistakes will from now on have virtually no consequence: If their decision to issue a warrant was correct, the evidence will be admitted; if their decision was incorrect but the police relied in good faith on the warrant, the evidence will also be admitted. Inevitably, the care and attention devoted to such an inconsequential chore will dwindle. . . .

. . . . In the long run, however, we as a society pay a heavy price for such expcdiency, because as Justice Jackson observed, "the rights guaranteed in the Fourth Amendment are not mere second-class rights but belong in the catalog indispensable freedoms." *Brinegar v. United States,* 338 U.S. 160, 180 (1949) (dissenting opinion). Once lost, such rights are difficult to recover. There is hope, however, that in time this or some later Court will restore these precious freedoms to their rightful place as a primary protection for our citizens against overreaching offcialdom.

## V. CRUEL AND UNUSUAL PUNISHMENT

### 37. *Gregg v. Georgia*
### 428 U.S. 153; 96 S.Ct. 2909; 49 L.Ed 2d 859 (1976)

*The question of what is a "cruel and unusual punishment" is not as simple as it might appear. Today, most people would probably agree that burning at the stake, or breaking someone on the wheel, is cruel and unusual. This was not always the case. Most court decisions now are primarily concerned with whether the punishment fits the crime, or whether the punishment was the one intended by the legislature, when determining if a punishment is "cruel and unusual."*

*There was a concerted attack on the death penalty as being a "cruel and punishment" in the 1960s. The Court rendered several decisions focusing on whether juries could fairly decide the death penalty within legislative guidelines, and then in* Furman v. Georgia *(408 U.S. 238, 1972) it seemed to strike down the death penalty itself. Although there was a majority, this decision revealed a badly-divided Court. The majority could not agree on one opinion and presented five separate concurrences. Justice Douglas argued that death penalties were "cruel and unusual" because they were disproportionately levied against the poor and minorities. Justice Brennan concluded: "When examined by the principles applicable under the Cruel and Unusual Punishments Clause, death stands condemned as fatally offensive to human dignity. The punishment of death is therefore 'cruel and unusual,' and the States may no longer inflect it as a punishment for crimes." Justice Marshall, after agreeing that the poor were more likely to end up on death row, argued that "... the death penalty is an excessive and unnecessary punishment that violates the Eighth Amendment." Chief Justice Burger wrote one of the three dissenting opinions. After pointing out that the majority had not really voided capital punishments, rather it had decided "that the present system of discretionary sentencing in capital cases has failed to produce evenhanded justice," the Chief Justice invited state legislatures to reform their sentencing procedures in order to pass constitutional muster.*

*The case which follows challenged Georgia's effort to alter its sentencing procedures in the wake of* Furman. *A new majority upheld the modified procedures and the spirited dissents of Justices Brennan and Marshall reaffirmed their positions in* Furman.

\* \* \* \* \* \* \* \* \* \* \* \* \* \* \* \* \* \* \* \* \* \* \* \* \* \* \* \*

Mr. Justice **Stewart**, Mr. Justice **Powell**, and Mr. Justice **Stevens** announced the judgment of the Court and filed an opinion delivered by Mr. Justice **Stewart**:

The issue in this case is whether the imposition of the sentence of death for the crime of murder under the law of Georgia violates the Eighth and Fourteenth Amendments.

The petitioner, Troy Gregg, was charged with committing armed robbery and murder. In accordance with Georgia procedure in capital cases, the trial was in two stages, a guilt stage and a sentencing stage. The evidence at the guilt trial established that ... the petitioner and a traveling companion . . . while hitchhiking north in Florida were picked up by Fred Simmons and Bob Moore. . . . [T]he four men interrupted their journey for a rest stop along the highway. The next morning the bodies of Simmons and Moore were discovered in a ditch nearby. . . .

. . . [T]he petitioner and Allen, while in Simmons' car, were arrested in Asheville, N. C. In the search incident to the arrest a .25 caliber pistol, later shown to be that used to kill Simmons and Moore, was found in the petitioner's pocket. After receiving the warnings required by *Miranda v. Arizona* (1966), and signing a written waiver of his rights, the petitioner signed a statement in which he admitted shooting, then robbing Simmons and Moore. He justified the slaying on grounds of self-defense. . . .

The trial judge submitted the murder charges to the jury on both felony murder and nonfelony-murder theories. He also instructed on the issue of self-defense but declined to instruct on manslaughter. He submitted the robbery case to the jury on both an armed-robbery theory and on the lesser included offense of robbery by intimidation. The jury found the petitioner guilty of two counts of armed robbery and two counts of murder.

At the penalty stage, which took place before the same jury, neither the prosecutor nor the petitioner's lawyer offered any additional evidence. Both counsel, however, made lengthy arguments dealing generally with the propriety of capital punishment under the circumstances and with the weight of the evidence of guilt. The trial judge instructed the jury that it could recommend either a death sentence or a life prison sentence on each count. The judge further charged the jury that in determining what sentence was appropriate the jury was free to consider the facts and circumstances, if any, presented by the parties in mitigation or aggravation.

Finally, the judge instructed the jury that it "would not be authorized to consider [imposing] the penalty of death" unless it first found beyond a reasonable doubt one of these aggravation circumstances:

"One—That the offense of murder was committed while the offender was engaged in the commission of two other capital felonies, to-wit the armed robbery of [Simmons and Moore].

"Two—That the offender committed the offense of murder for the purpose of receiving money and the automobile described in the indictment.

"Three—The offense of murder was outrageously and wantonly vile, horrible and inhuman, in that they [sic] involved the depravity of [the] mind of the defendant."

Finding the first and second of these circumstances, the jury returned verdicts of death on each count.

The Supreme court of Georgia affirmed the convictions and the imposition of the death sentences for murder. . . . The death sentences imposed for armed robbery, however, were vacated on the grounds that the death penalty had rarely been imposed in Georgia for that offense and that the jury improperly considered the murders as aggravating circumstances for the robberies after having considered the armed robberies as aggravating circumstances for the murders. . . .

### III. . . .

It is clear from the foregoing precedents that the Eighth Amendment has not been regarded as a static concept. As Mr. Chief Justice Warren said, in an off-quoted phrase, "[t]he Amendment must draw its meaning from the evolving standards of decency that mark the progress of a maturing society." *Trop v. Dulles* [1958]. . . . Thus, an assessment of temporary values concerning the infliction of a challenged sanction is relevant to the application of the Eighth Amendment. As we develop below more fully, this assessment does not call for a subjective judgment. It requires, rather, that we look to objective indicia that reflect the public attitude toward a given sanction.

But our cases also make clear that public perceptions of standards of decency with respect to criminal sanctions are not conclusive. A penalty also must accord with "the dignity of man," which is the "basic concept underlying the Eighth Amendment." *Trop v. Dulles*. This means, at least, that the punishment not be "excessive." When a form of punishment in the abstract (in this case, whether capital punishment may ever be imposed as a sanction for murder) rather than in the particular (the propriety of death as a penalty to be applied to a specific defendant for a specific crime) is under consideration, the inquiry into "excessiveness" has two aspects. First, the punishment must not involve the unnecessary and wanton infliction of pain. *Furman v. Georgia* (Burger, C. J. dissenting). . . . Second, the punishment must not be grossly out of proportion to the severity of the crime. *Trop v. Dulles*. . . .

### C.

. . . We now consider specifically whether the sentences of death for the crime of murder is a per se violation of the Eighth and Fourteenth Amendments to the Constitution. We note first that history and precedent strongly support a negative answer to this question.

The imposition of the death penalty for the crime of murder has a long history of acceptance both in the United States and in England. . . .

It is apparent from the text of the Constitution itself that the existence of capital punishment was accepted by the Framers. At the time the Eighth Amendment was ratified, capital punishment was a common sanction in every State. Indeed, the First Congress of the United States enacted legislation providing death as the penalty for specified crimes . . . And the Fourteenth Amendment, adopted over three quarters of the century later, similarly contemplates the existence of the capital sanction in providing that no State shall deprive any person of "life, liberty or property" without due process of law. . . .

Four years ago, the petitioners in *Furman* and its companion cases predicated their argument primarily upon the asserted proposition that standards of decency had evolved to the point where capital punishment no longer could be tolerated. The petitioners in those cases said, in effect, that the evolutionary process had come to an end, and that standards of decency required that the Eighth Amendment be construed finally as prohibiting capital punishment for any crime regardless of its depravity and impact on society. This view was accepted by two Justices. Three other justices were unwilling to go so far, focusing on the procedures by which convicted defendants were selected for the death penalty rather than on the actual punishment inflicted, they jointed in the conclusion that the statutes before the Court were constitutionally invalid.

The petitioners in the capital cases before the Court today renew the "standards of decency" argument, but developments during the four years since *Furman* have undercut substantially the assumptions upon which their argument rested. . . .

The most marked indication of society's endorsement of the death penalty for murder is the legislative response to *Furman*. The legislatures of at least 35 States have enacted new statues that provide for the death penalty for at least some crimes that result in the death of another person. And the Congress of the United States, in 1974, enacted a statute providing the death penalty for aircraft conspiracy that results in death. These recently adopted statutes have attempted to address the concerns expressed by the Court in *Furman* primarily (i) by specifying the factors to be weighed and the procedures to be followed in deciding when to impose a capital sentence, or (ii) by making the death penalty mandatory for specified crimes. . . .

In the only statewide referendum occurring since *Furman* and brought to our attention, the people of California adopted a constitutional amendment that authorized capital punishment, in effect negating a prior ruling by the Supreme Court of California . . . that the death penalty violated the California Constitution. . . .

. . . [T]he Eighth Amendment demands more than that a challenged punishment be acceptable to contemporary society. The Court also must ask whether it comports with the basic concept of human dignity at the core of the Amendment. . . .

In part, capital punishment is an expression of society's moral outrage at particularly offensive conduct. This function may be unappealing to many, but it is essential in an ordered society that asks its citizens to rely on legal processes rather than self-help to vindicate their wrongs. . . .

Statistical attempts to evaluate the worth of the death penalty as a deterrent to crimes by potential offenders have occasioned a great deal of debate. The results simply have been inconclusive. . . .

In sum, we cannot say that the judgment of the Georgia legislature that capital punishment may be necessary in some cases is clearly wrong. . . .

Finally, we must consider whether the punishment of death is disproportionate in relation to the crime for which it is imposed. . . .

We hold that the death penalty is not a form of punishment that my never be imposed, regardless of the circumstances of the offense, regardless of the character of the offender, and regardless of the procedure followed in reaching the decision to impose it.

### IV.

We now consider whether Georgia may impose the death penalty on the petitioner in this case.

### A. . . .

*Furman* mandates that where discretion is afforded a sentencing body on a matter so grave as the determining of whether a human life should be taken or spared, that discretion must be suitably directed and limited so as to minimize the risk of wholly arbitrary and capricious action. . . .

Jury sentencing has been considered desirable in capital cases in order "to maintain a link between contemporary community values and the penal system—a link without which the determination of punishment could hardly reflect 'the evolving standards of decency that mark the progress of a maturing society.' But it creates special problems . . . Those who have studied the question suggest that a bifurcated procedure—one in which the question of sentence is not considered until the determination of guilt has been made—is the best answer." . . .

### B.

We now turn to consideration of the constitutionality of Georgia's capital-sentencing procedures. In the wake of *Furman*, Georgia amended its capital punishment statute, but chose not to narrow the scope of its murder provisions. Thus, now as before *Furman*, in Georgia "[a] person commits murder when he unlawfully and with malice aforethought, either express or implied, causes the death of another human being." All persons convicted of murder "shall be punished by death or by imprisonment for life."

Georgia did act, however, to narrow the class of murderers subject to capital punishment by specifying 10 statutory aggravating circumstances, one of which must be found by the jury to exist beyond a reasonable doubt before a death sentence can ever be imposed. In addition, the jury is authorized to consider any other appropriate aggravating or mitigating circumstances. The jury is not required to find any mitigating circumstances in order to make a recommendation of mercy that is binding on the trial court, but it must find a *statutory* aggravating circumstances before recommending a sentence of death.

These procedures require the jury to consider the circumstances of the crime and the criminal before it recommends sentence ... [T]he jury's attention is directed to the specific circumstances of the crime: Was it committed in the course of another capital felony? Was it committed for money? Was it committed upon a peace officer or judicial officer? Was it committed in a particularly heinous way or in a manner that endangered the lives of many persons? In addition, the jury's attention is focused on the characteristics of the person who committed the crime: Does he have a record of prior convictions for capital offenses? Are there any special facts about this defendant that mitigate against imposing capital punishment (e.g. his youth, the extent of his cooperation with the police, his emotional state at the time of the crime)....

### 3.

Finally, the Georgia statute has an additional provision designed to assure that the death penalty will not be imposed on a capriciously selected group of convicted defendants. The new sentencing procedures require that the state supreme court review every death sentence....

It is apparent that the Supreme Court of Georgia has taken its review responsibilities seriously.... Although armed robbery is a capital offense under Georgia law, the Georgia court concluded that the death sentences imposed in this case for that crime were "unusual in that they are rarely imposed for [armed robbery]. Thus, under the test provided by statutes ... they must be considered to be excessive or disproportionate to the penalties imposed in similar cases. The Court therefore vacated Gregg's death sentences for armed robbery and has followed a similar course in every other armed robbery death penalty case to come before it.

The provision for appellate review in the Georgia capital sentencing system serves as a check against the random or arbitrary imposition of the death penalty....

### V. ...

... For the reasons expressed in this opinion, we hold that the statutory system under which Gregg was sentenced to death does not violate the

Constitution. Accordingly, the judgment of the Georgia Supreme Court is affirmed.

. . . .

Mr. Justice **Brennan**, dissenting:

The Cruel and Unusual Punishments Clause "must draw its meaning from the evolving standards of decency that mark the progress of maturing society." The [majority] opinions . . . hold that "evolving standards of decency" require focus not on the essence of the death penalty itself but primarily upon the procedures employed by the State to single out persons to suffer the penalty of death. Those opinions hold further that, so viewed, the Clause invalidates the mandatory infliction of the death penalty but not its infliction under sentencing procedures that . . . adequately safeguard against the risk that the death penalty was imposed in an arbitrary and capricious manner.

In *Furman v. Georgia* (1972), I read "evolving standards of decency" as requiring focus upon the essence of the death penalty itself and not primarily or solely upon the procedures under which the determination to inflict the penalty upon a particular person was made. . . .

This Court inescapably has the duty, as the ultimate arbiter of the meaning of our Constitution, to say whether, when individuals condemned to death stand before our Bar, "moral concepts" require us to hold that the law has progressed to the point where we should declare that the punishment of death, like punishments on the rack, the screw, and the wheel, is no longer morally tolerable in our civilized society. My opinion in *Furman v. Georgia* concluded that our civilization and the law had progressed to this point and that therefore the punishment of death, for whatever crime and under all circumstances, is "cruel and unusual" in violation of Eighth and Fourteenth Amendments of the Constitution. . . .

The fatal constitutional infirmity in the punishment of death is that it treats "members of the human race as nonhumans . . . I therefore would hold, on that ground alone, that death is today a cruel and unusual punishment prohibited by the Clause. "Justice of this kind is obviously no less shocking than the crime itself, and the new 'official' murder, far from offering redress for the offense committed against society, adds instead a second defilement to the first."

Mr. Justice **Marshall** dissenting:

In *Furman* I concluded that the death penalty is constitutionally invalid for two reasons. First, the death penalty is excessive. And second, the American people, fully informed as to the purposes of the death penalty and its liabilities, would in my view reject it as morally unacceptable.

Since the decision in *Furman*, the legislatures of 35 States have enacted new statutes authorizing the imposition of the death sentence for certain crimes, and Congress has enacted a law providing the death penalty for air piracy resulting in death. I would be less than candid if I did not acknowledge that these developments have a significant bearing on a realistic assessment of the moral acceptability of the death penalty to the American people. But if the constitutionality of the death penalty turns, as I have urged, on the opinion of an *informed* citizenry, then even the enactment of new death statutes cannot be viewed as conclusive. . . . A recent study, conducted after the enactment of the post-*Furman* statutes has confirmed that the American people know little about the death penalty, and that the opinions of an informed public would differ significantly from those of a public unaware of the consequences and effects of the death penalty.

# CHAPTER 4:

## FREEDOM OF EXPRESSION

### I. THE REVOLUTIONARY ERA

*The idea of freedom of expression during the Revolutionary era was tied closely to the prevailing theory of republican government. The founders wanted to assure open and easy communication between the sovereign people and their representatives in power. Therefore, the people had to be guaranteed the freedom of assembly, the right to petition government for the redress of grievances, and freedom of the press. Eight of the eleven states writing new constitutions protected freedom of the press; nine if New Hampshire's second constitution (1784) is counted. The privilege was not absolute, however, and the limitations may be seen in the following readings. Almost nothing was said about the content of such expressions in the new state constitutions.*

\* \* \* \* \* \* \* \* \* \* \* \* \* \* \* \* \* \* \* \* \* \* \* \* \* \* \* \* \* \*

#### 38. The Right of Assembly and Petition:
#### Excerpts from State Constitutions

*New Hampshire Bill of Rights, XXXII (1784) (Thorpe, IV: 2457)*

The people have a right in an orderly and peaceable manner, to assemble and consult upon the common good, give instructions to their representatives; and to request the legislative body, by way of petition or remonstrance, redress of the wrongs done them, and of the grievances they suffer.

*Pennsylvania Declaration of Rights, XVI (1776) (Thorpe, V: 3084)*

That the people have a right to assemble together, to consult for their common good, to instruct their representatives, and to apply to the legislature for redress of grievances, by address, petition, or remonstrance.

*Pennsylvania Constitution, Art.IX, Sec. 20 (1790) (Thorpe, V: 3101)*

That the citizens have a right, in a peaceable manner, to assemble together for their common good, and to apply to those invested with the powers of government for redress of grievances, or other proper purposes, by petition, address, or remonstrance.

*Virginia Bill of Rights, Sec. 2 (1776) (Thorpe, VII: 3813)*

That all power is vested in, and consequently derived from the people; that magistrates are their trustees and servants, and at all times amenable to them.

*Source: Thorpe, ed.* The Federal and State Constitutions.

## 39. Freedom of Speech and of the Press: Excerpts from State Constitutions

*Georgia Constitution, Art. LXI (1777) (Thorpe, II: 785)*

Freedom of the press and trial by jury to remain inviolate forever.

*Massachusetts Declaration of Rights, XVI (1780) (Thorpe, III: 1892)*

The liberty of the press is essential to the security of freedom in a state it ought not, therefore, to be restricted in this commonwealth.

*Pennsylvania Declaration of Rights, XII (1776) (Thorpe, V: 3083)*

That the people have a right to freedom of speech, and of writing, and publishing their sentiments; therefore the freedom of the press ought not to be restrained.

*Pennsylvania Constitution, Article IX, Sec. 7 (1790) (Thorpe, V: 3100)*

That the printing-presses shall be free to every person who undertakes to examine the proceedings of the legislature, or any branch of government, and no law shall ever be made to restrain the right thereof. The free communication of thoughts and opinions is one of the invaluable rights of man; and every citizen may freely speak, write, and print on any subject, being responsible for the abuse of that liberty. In prosecutions for the publication of papers investigating the official conduct of officers or men in a public capacity, or where the matter published is proper for public information, the truth thereof may be given in evidence; and in all indictments for libels the jury shall have a right to determine the law and the facts, under the direction of the court, as in all other cases.

*Virginia Bill of Rights, Sec. 12 (1776) (Thorpe, VII: 3814)*

That the freedom of the press is one of the great bulwarks of liberty, and can never be restrained but by despotic governments.

*Source: Thorpe, ed.* The Federal and State Constitutions.

## 40. Limits on the Freedom of Speech: Excerpt from a State Constitution

*South Carolina Constitution, Art. XXXVIII (1778) (Thorpe, VI:3257)*

... No person shall disturb or molest any religious assembly; nor shall use any reproachful, reviling, or abusive language against any church, that being the certain way of disturbing the peace, and of hindering the conversion of any to the truth, by engaging them in quarrels and animosities, to the hatred of the professors, and that profession which otherwise they might be brought to assent to. No person whatsoever shall speak anything in their religious assembly irreverently or seditiously of the government of this State ...

*Source: Thorpe, ed.* The Federal and State Constitutions.

## II. RESTRICTIONS ON FREEDOM OF SPEECH

## 41. John Stuart Mill, *On Liberty* (1859)

*Democrats advocate individual freedom. But is there such a thing as too much freedom? The First Amendment protects freedom of expression against congressional abridgment. This is a fundamental democratic right. The Supreme Court has ruled, however, that the First Amendment's protections are not absolute; some forms of expression can be restricted.*

*John Stuart Mill grappled with issues of this kind in his book,* On Liberty. *He observed that, in light of the importance of individual freedom in a democracy, limitations must be placed on government. Otherwise, leaders might abuse their powers. Further, the popular majority might pressure elected officials to adopt laws that oppress non-conformists. Additionally, public opinion itself might operate to enforce conformity to orthodox views and practices. Like Tocqueville, he feared such social tyranny which cannot be legislated out of existence. In short, the problem of liberty is that some behavior obviously cannot be tolerated by society but not all non-conforming behavior should be suppressed. What is the legitimate extent of the majority's power over the minority and the individual? Mill's answer:*

> *. . . . [T]he sole end for which mankind are warranted, individually or collectively, in interfering with the liberty of action of any of their number, is self-protection . . . [T]he only purpose for which power can be rightly exercised over any member of a civilized community, against his will, is to prevent harm to others. His own good, either physical or moral, is not a sufficient warrant. He cannot rightfully be compelled to do or forbear because it will be better for him to do so. . . . The only part of the conduct of any one, for which he is amenable to society, is that which concerns others. In the part which merely concerns himself, his independence is, of right, absolute. Over himself, over his own body and mind, the individual is sovereign.*

*Mill used the example of suppressing opinion, discussion, and expression to demonstrate how this "harm principle" would operate in practice. He contended that freedom of expression has pragmatic as well as normative value.*

\* \* \* \* \* \* \* \* \* \* \* \* \* \* \* \* \* \* \* \* \* \* \* \* \* \* \* \* \* \* \*

. . . . If all mankind minus one, were of one opinion, and only one person were of the contrary opinion, mankind would be no more justified in silencing that one person, than he, if he had the power, would be justified in silencing mankind. . . . [T]he peculiar evil of silencing the expression of an opinion is, that it is robbing the human race; posterity as well as the existing generation; those who dissent from the opinion, still more than those who hold it. If the opinion is right, they are deprived of the opportunity of exchanging error for truth: if wrong, they lose, what is almost as great a benefit, the clearer perception and livelier impression of truth, produced by its collision with error.

. . . . We can never be sure that the opinion we are endeavoring to stifle is a false opinion; and if we were sure, stifling it would be an evil still.

First: the opinion which it is attempted to suppress by authority may possibly be true. Those who desire to suppress it, of course deny its truth; but they are not infallible. They have no authority to decide the question for all mankind, and exclude every other person from the means of judging. To refuse a hearing to an opinion, because they are sure that it is false, is to assume that *their* certainty is the same thing as *absolute* certainty. All silencing of discussion is an assumption of infallibility. Its condemnation may be allowed to rest on this common argument, not the worse for being common.

. . . . There is the greatest difference between presuming an opinion to be true, because, with every opportunity for contesting it, it had not been refuted, and assuming its truth for the purpose of not permitting its refutation. Complete liberty of contradicting and disproving our opinion, is the very condition which justifies us in assuming its truth for purposes of action; and on no other terms can a being with human faculties have any rational assurance of being right.

. . . . [Man's] errors are corrigible. He is capable of rectifying his mistakes, by discussion and experience. Not by experience alone. There must be discussion, to show how experience is to be interpreted. Wrong opinions and practices gradually yield to fact and argument: but facts and arguments, to produce any effect on the mind, must be brought before it. Very few facts are able to tell their own story, without comments to bring out their meaning. The whole strength and value, then, of human judgment, depending on the one property, that it can be set right when it is wrong, reliance can be placed on it only when the means of setting it right are kept constantly at hand. In the case of any person whose judgment is really deserving of confidence, how has it become so? Because he has kept his mind open to criticism of his opinions and conduct. Because it has been his practice to listen to all that could be said against him; to profit by as much of it as was just, and expound to himself, and upon occasion to others, the fallacy of what was fallacious. Because he has felt, that the only way in which a human being can make some approach to knowing the whole of a subject, is by hearing what can be said about it by persons of every variety of opinion, and studying all modes in which it can be looked at by every character of mind. No wise man ever acquired his wisdom in any mode but this; nor is it in the nature of human intellect to become wise in any other manner. . . .

. . . . The beliefs which we have most warrant for, have no safeguard to rest on, but a standing invitation to the whole world to prove them unfounded. . . .

. . . [W]e will now briefly recapitulate.

First, if any opinion is compelled to silence, that opinion may, for aught we can certainly know, be true. To deny this is to assume our own infallibility.

Secondly, though the silenced opinion be an error, it may, and very commonly does, contain a portion of truth; and since the general or prevailing opinion on any subject is rarely or never the whole truth, it is only by the collision of adverse opinions that the remainder of the truth has any chance of being supplied.

Thirdly, even if the received opinion be not only true, but the whole truth; unless it is suffered to be, and actually is, vigorously and earnestly contested, it will, by most of those who receive it, be held in the manner of a prejudice, with little comprehension of feeling of its rational grounds. And not only this, but fourthly, the meaning of the doctrine itself will be in danger of being lost, or enfeebled, and deprived of its vital effect on the character and conduct: the dogma becoming a mere formal profession, inefficacious for good, but cumbering the ground, and preventing the growth of any real and heartfelt conviction from reason or personal experience. . . .

## 42. *Schenck v. United States*
### 249 U.S. 47; 39 S.Ct. 247; 63 L.Ed. 470 (1919)

*During World War I, Congress passed the Espionage Act of 1917 and the Sedition Act of 1918. The Espionage Act made it a crime to circulate false statements to interfere with military success, to attempt to cause disloyalty in the armed forces, or to attempt to obstruct recruiting. The Sedition Act, among other things, made it a crime to incite resistance to the government. Clearly, these laws restricted freedom of speech, but did they violate the First Amendment? The Supreme Court, holding that such First-Amendment freedoms are not absolute, ruled that they did not in the case below.*

*Charles T. Schenck, general secretary of the Socialist Party, was accused of sending some 15,000 pamphlets to men who had been called to military service, urging them to resist the draft. The pamphlet argued that the Conscription Act instituted an unconstitutional form of involuntary servitude in violation of the Thirteenth Amendment. Schenck was convicted in federal court of violating the Espionage Act by attempting to cause insubordination in the armed forces and by obstructing recruitment. Schenck maintained that his conduct was protected by the First Amendment's guarantees of freedom of speech and the press.*

*Writing for the unanimous Supreme Court, Justice Holmes upheld Schenck's conviction on the grounds that the government can restrict freedom of speech if it presents a "clear and present danger" to the nation. Freedom of speech, he suggested, is limited by the wartime demands of national security. In this way, Holmes asserted that speech must be evaluated in context. In the present case, the nature of the times conditioned the act and made it a crime. Recall that in* Gitlow v. New York *(1925), Holmes viewed the times differently. In his* Gitlow *dissent, he claimed that there was no clear and present danger of an actual attempt to overthrow the government by force.*

\* \* \* \* \* \* \* \* \* \* \* \* \* \* \* \* \* \* \* \* \* \* \* \* \* \* \* \* \* \*

Mr. Justice **Holmes** delivered the opinion of the Court:

The document in question upon its first printed side recited the First section of the Thirteenth Amendment, said that the idea embodied in it was violated by the Conscription Act, and that a conscript is little better than a convict. In impassioned language it intimated that conscription was despotism in its worst form and a monstrous wrong against humanity, in the interest of Wall Street's chosen few. . . . Of course the document would not have been sent unless it had been intended to have some effect, and we do not see what effect it could be expected to have upon persons subject to the draft except to influence them to obstruct the carrying of it out. The defendants do not deny that the jury might find against them on this point.

But it is said, suppose that that was the tendency of this circular, it is protected by the First Amendment to the Constitution. Two of the strongest expressions are said to be quoted respectively from well-known public men. It well may be that the prohibition of laws abridging the freedom of speech is not confined to previous restraints, although to prevent them may have been the main purpose. . . . We admit that in many places and in ordinary times the defendants, in saying all that was said in the circular, would have been within their constitutional rights. But the character of every act depends upon the circumstances in which it is done. . . . The most stringent protection of free speech would not protect a man in falsely shouting fire in a theater, and causing a panic. . . . The question in every case is whether the words used are used in such circumstances and are of such a nature as to create a clear and present danger that they will bring about the substantive evils that Congress has a right to prevent. It is a question of proximity and degree. When a nation is at war many things that might be said in time of peace are such a hindrance to its effort that their utterance will not be endured so long as men fight, and that no court could regard them as protected by any constitutional right. It seems to be admitted that if an actual obstruction of the recruiting service were proved, liability for words that produced the effect might be enforced. The Statue of 1917, in Section 4, punishes conspiracies to obstruct as well as actually obstruction. If the act (speaking, or circulating a paper), its tendency and the intent with which it is done, are the same, we perceive no ground for saving that success alone warrants making the act a crime. . . .

### 43. *Near v. Minnesota*
### 283 U.S. 697; 51 S.Ct. 625; 75 L.Ed.1357 (1931)

*As previously noted, in* Barron v. Baltimore *(1833), the Supreme Court held that the provisions of the Bill of Rights do not apply directly against the states. In subsequent years, however, some such protections have been applied against states by way of the Fourteenth Amendment.* Near v. Minnesota *marked the first time that the Court found a state law unconstitutional for violating the freedom of the press that is protected by the Fourteenth Amendment's Due Process Clause.*

*The so-called "Minnesota press gag law" provided for shutting down any newspaper that printed "malicious, scandalous, or defamatory" materials. Such an injunction could only be lifted by the judge who isssued it and he or she would have to be persuaded that the publication would be unobjectionable in the future. Critics pointed out that an injured party could sue the publication for libel after the fact, but this law imposed censorship* **before** *the fact; it restrained publication itself.* The Saturday Press, *published in Minneapolis, charged various public officials with misconduct in office. The law was enforced and publication was enjoined.*

*By a five-to-four vote, the Supreme Court ruled that the law was an unconstitutional abridgment of press freedom as guaranteed by the Fourteenth Amendment.*

\* \* \* \* \* \* \* \* \* \* \* \* \* \* \* \* \* \* \* \* \* \* \* \* \* \* \* \* \*

Mr. Chief Justice **Hughes** delivered the opinion of the Court:

. . . The statute not only operates to suppress the offending newspaper or periodical but to put the publisher under an effective censorship. When a newspaper or periodical is found to be "malicious, scandalous, and defamatory," and is suppressed as such, resumption of publication is punishable as a contempt of court by fine or imprisonment. . . .

If we cut through the mere details of procedure the operation and effect of the statute in substance is that public authorities may bring the owner or publisher of a newspaper or periodical before a judge upon a charge of . . . publishing scandalous and defamatory matter—in particular that the matter consists of charges against public officers of official dereliction—and unless the owner or publisher is able and disposed to bring competent evidence to satisfy the judge that the charges are true and are published with good motives and for justifiable ends, his newspaper or periodical is suppressed and further publication is made punishable as a contempt. This is the essence of censorship.

. . . But it is recognized that punishment for the abuse of the liberty accorded to the press is essential to the protection of the public, and that the common law rules that subject the libeler to responsibility for the public offense, as well as for the private injury, are not abolished by the protection extended in our constitutions. . . . In the present case, . . . [f]or whatever wrong the appellant has committed or may commit, by his publications, the state appropriately affords both public and private redress by its libel laws . . . [T]he statute in question does not deal with punishments; it provides for no punishment, except in case of contempt for violation of the court's order, but for suppression and injunction, that is, for restraint upon publication. . . .

The fact that the liberty of the press may be abused by miscreant purveyors of scandal does not make any the less necessary the immunity of the press form previous restraint in dealing with official misconduct. Subsequent punishment for such abuses as may exist is the appropriate remedy, consistent with constitutional privilege. . . .

For these reasons we hold the statute . . . to be an infringement of the liberty of the press guaranteed by the 14th Amendment. . . .

## 44. *Dennis v. United States*
### 341 U.S. 494; 71 S.Ct. 857; 95 L.Ed. 1137 (1951)

*Eleven leaders of the American Communist Party were convicted under the Smith Act for conspiring to teach and advocate the overthrow of the government by force and violence. In his opinion upholding their convictions, Federal Appeals Court Judge Learned Hand interpreted Justice Holmes' clear-and-present danger test in a way that made it relatively easier to restrict dissent. Hand's test has been called one of "clear and* **probable** *danger." By a six-to-two vote, the Supreme Court also upheld the convictions. Chief Justice Vinson's lead opinion reflected some of Hand's views. Vinson maintained that the danger need not be present; it is enough that there is a group preparing for a probable attempt to overthrow the government "as speedily as circumstances would permit."*

*In* Yates v. United States *(354 U.S. 298, 1957), the Court ruled that mere advocacy of revolution was not enough to convict Communists under the Smith Act; the prosecution would be required to show that others were incited to specific action toward this end. In a related vein, in* Brandenburg v. Ohio *(395 U.S. 44, 1969), the Court held that a state cannot prohibit advocacy of violent change unless the advocacy is likely*

*to incite and produce imminent violence. In sum, under the First
Amendment, one can teach about Communism, s/he can even endorse
the need for revolutionary change. If an individual incites rioting, however, s/he poses a clear and present danger and can be silenced.*

\* \* \* \* \* \* \* \* \* \* \* \* \* \* \* \* \* \* \* \* \* \* \* \* \* \* \* \* \* \* \*

Mr. Chief Justice **Vinson** announced the judgment of the Court.

.... Congress was concerned with those who advocate and organize for
the overthrow of the Government. Certainly those who recruit and com-
bine for the purpose of advocating overthrow intend to bring about that
overthrow. . . .

The obvious purpose of the statute is to protect existing Government
not from change by peaceable, lawful and constitutional means, but from
change by violence, revolution and terrorism. That it is within the *power*
of the Congress to protect the Government of the United States from
armed rebellion is a proposition which requires little discussion. Whatever theoretical merit there may be to the argument that there is a "right"
to rebellion against dictatorial governments is without force where the
existing structure of the government provides for peaceful and orderly
change. We reject any principle of government helplessness in the face of
preparation for revolution. . . .

The very language of the Smith Act . . . is directed at advocacy, not discussion. Thus the trial judge properly charged the jury that they could not
convict if they found that petitioners did "no more than pursue peaceful
studies and discussions or teaching and advocacy in the realm of ideas."
He further charged that it was not unlawful "to conduct in an American
college and university a course explaining the philosophical theories set
forth in the books which have been placed in evidence." . . . Congress did
not intend to eradicate the free discussion of political theories, to destroy
the traditional rights of Americans to discuss and evaluate ideas without
fear of governmental sanction. Rather Congress was concerned with the
very kind of activity in which the evidence showed these petitioners engaged.

. . . [T]he basis of the First Amendment is the hypothesis that speech can
rebut speech, propaganda will answer propaganda, free debate of ideas
will result in the wisest governmental policies. It is for this reason that this
Court has recognized the inherent value of free discourse. An analysis of
the leading cases in this Court . . . however, will demonstrate that . . . the
Court . . . recognized that this is not an unlimited, unqualified right, but
that the societal value of speech must, on occasion, be subordinated to
other values and considerations.

... [In] *Schenck v. United States* (1919)... [w]riting for a unanimous Court, Justice Holmes states that the "question in every case is whether the words used are used in such circumstances and are of such a nature as to create a clear and present danger that they will bring about the substantive evils that Congress has a right to prevent." ...

The rule ... is that where an offense is specified by a statute in nonspeech or nonpress terms, a conviction relying upon speech or press as evidence of violation may be sustained only when the speech or publication created a "clear and present danger" of attempting or accomplishing the prohibited crime. ...

.... In discussing the proper measure of evaluation of this kind of legislation, we suggested that the Holmes-Brandeis philosophy insisted that where was a direct restriction upon speech, a "clear and present danger" that the substantive evil would be caused was necessary before the statute in question could be constitutionally applied. And we stated, "[The First] Amendment requires that one be permitted to believe what he will. It requires that one be permitted to advocate what he will unless there is a clear and present danger that a substantial public evil will result therefrom." But we further suggested that neither Justice Holmes nor Justice Brandeis ever envisioned that a shorthand phrase should be crystallized into a rigid rule to be applied inflexibly without regard to the circumstances of each case. Speech is not an absolute, above and beyond control by the legislature when its judgment, subject to review here, is that certain kinds of speech are so undesirable as to warrant criminal sanction. ... [T]here are no absolutes. ...

.... Overthrow of the Government by force and violence is certainly a substantial enough interest for the Government to limit speech. Indeed, this is the ultimate value of any society, for if a society cannot protect its very structure from armed internal attack, it must follow that no subordinate value can be protected. If, then, this interest may be protected, the literal problem which is presented is what has been meant by the use of the phrase "clear and present danger" of the utterances bringing about the evil within the power of the Congress to punish.

Obviously, the words cannot mean that before the Government may act, it must wait until the *putsh* is about to be executed, the plans have been laid and the signal is awaited. If Government is aware that a group aiming at its overthrow is attempting to indoctrinate its members and to commit them to a course whereby they will strike when the leaders feel the circumstances permit, action by the Government is required. ...

.... The mere fact that from the period 1945 to 1948 petitioners' activities did not result in an attempt to overthrow the Government by force and violence is of course no answer to the fact that there was a group that was ready to make the attempt. The formation by petitioners of such a highly organized conspiracy, with rigidly disciplined members subject to call when the leaders, these petitioners, felt that the time had come for action, coupled with the inflammable nature of world conditions, similar uprisings in other countries, and the touch-and-go nature of our relations with countries with whom petitioners were in the very least ideologically attuned, convince us that their convictions were justified on this score. . . .

. . . . Their conspiracy to organize the Communist Party and to teach and advocate the overthrow of the Government of the United States by force and violence created a "clear and present danger" of an attempt to overthrow the Government by force and violence. They were properly and constitutionally convicted for violation of the Smith Act.

## 45. *New York Times Co. v. United States*
### 403 U.S. 713; 91 S.Ct. 2140; 29 L.Ed. 2d 820 (1971)

*In the course of the escalation of the American military effort in Vietnam, Secretary of Defense Robert McNamara ordered an internal study of how the United States became involved in the conflict. This top secret study was intitled, "History of the U.S. Decision-Making Process on Viet Nam Policy." Daniel Ellsberg, a Pentagon employee, gave copies of the study to the* New York Times *and the* Washington Post. *The* New York Times *began to publish excerpts from these so-called "Pentagon Papers." The Justice Department obtained injunctions enjoining the* Times, *the* Washington Post, *and the* Boston Globe *from publishing additional installments on grounds that such publication would harm national security. The Supreme Court lifted the injunctions by a 6-to-3 vote.*

*The decision was handed down in* Per Curiam *fashion. All nine justices wrote opinions, totaling over eleven-thousand words (the Pentagon Papers themselves ran seven-thousand pages). The justices constructed their arguments carefully for fear that they might otherwise damage the president's authority to safeguard classified information. Ultimately, however, they could not endorse the Justice Department's attempt at prior restraint in light of First-Amendment considerations.*

\* \* \* \* \* \* \* \* \* \* \* \* \* \* \* \* \* \* \* \* \* \* \* \* \* \* \*

*Per Curiam.*

"Any system of prior restraints of expression comes to this Court bearing a heavy presumption against its constitutional validity." *Bantam Books, Inc. v. Sullivan* (1963); see also *Near v. Minnesota* (1931). The government "thus carries a heavy burden of showing justification for the imposition of such a restraint." *Organization for a Better Austin v. Keefe* (1971)....

Mr. Justice **Black**, whom Mr. Justice **Douglas** joins, concurring:

.... [I]t is unfortunate that some of my Brethren are apparently willing to hold that the publication of news may sometimes be enjoined. Such a holding would make a shambles of the First Amendment....

.... Madison and the other Framers of the First Amendment, able men that they were, wrote in language they earnestly believed could never be misunderstood: "Congress shall make no law ... abridging the freedom of the press...." Both the history and language of the First Amendment support the view that the press must be left free to publish news, whatever the source, without censorship, injunctions, or prior restraints.

In the First Amendment the Founding Fathers gave the free press the protection it must have to fulfill its essential role in our democracy. The press was to serve the governed, not the governors. The Government's power to censor the press was abolished so that the press would remain forever free to censure the Government.... In revealing the working of government that led to the Viet Nam war, the newspapers nobly did precisely that which the Founders hoped and trusted they would do.

.... To find that the President has "inherent power" to halt the publication of news by resort to the courts would wipe out the First Amendment and destroy the fundamental liberty and security of the very people the Government hopes to make "secure." ...

The word "security" is a broad, vague generality whose contours should not be invoked to abrogate the fundamental law embodied in the First Amendment....

Mr. Justice **Douglas**, whom Mr. Justice **Black** joins, concurring:

.... [T]he First Amendment provides that "Congress shall make no law ... abridging the freedom of speech or of the press." That leaves, in my view, no room for governmental restraint on the press.

.... The Government says that it has inherent powers to ... obtain an injunction to protect [the] national interest, which in this case is alleged to be national security.

*Near v. Minnesota* repudiated that expansive doctrine in no uncertain terms.

.... Secrecy in government is fundamentally anti-democratic ... Open debate and discussion of public issues are vital to our national health....

Mr. Justice **Brennan**, concurring:

.... [T]he First Amendment tolerates absolutely no prior judicial restraints of the press predicated upon surmise or conjecture that untoward consequence may result.... [T]here is a single, extremely narrow class of cases in which the First Amendniciit's ban on prior judicial restraint may be overridden . . . [S]uch cases may arise only when the Nation "is at war," *Schenck v. United States* (1919), during which times "no one would question but that a government might prevent actual obstruction to its recruiting service or the publication of the sailing dates of transports or the number and location of troops." *Near v. Minnesota* (1931). Even if the present world situation were assumed to be tantamount to a time of war, or if the power of presently available armaments would justify even in peacetime the suppression of information that would set in motion a nuclear holocaust, in neither of these actions has the Government presented or even alleged that publication of . . . the material at issue would cause the happening of an event of that nature. . . . Unless and until the Government has clearly made out its case, the First Amendment commands that no injunction may issue.

Mr. Justice **Stewart**, "whom Mr. Justice **White** joins, concurring:

In the absence of the governmental checks and balances present in other areas of our national life, the only effective restraint upon executive policy and power in the areas of national defense and international affairs may lie in an enlightened citizenry—in an informed and critical public opinion which alone can here protect the values of democratic government. For this reason, it is perhaps here that a press that is alert, aware, and free most vitally serves the basic purpose of the First Amendment. For without an informed and free press there cannot be an enlightened people.

Yet it is elementary that the successful conduct of international diplomacy and the maintenance of an effective national defense require both confidentiality and secrecy. . . .

. . . . We are asked . . . to prevent the publication by two newspapers of material that the Executive Branch insists should not, in the national interest, be published. I am convinced that the Executive is correct with respect to some of the documents involved. But I cannot say that disclosure of any of them will surely result in direct, immediate, and irreparable damage to our Nation or its people. That being so, there can under the First Amendment be but one judicial resolution of the issues before us. I join the judgments of the Court.

Mr. Justice **White**, whom Mr. Justice **Stewart** joins, concurring:

. . . I do not say that in no circumstances would the First Amendment permit an injunction against publishing information about government plans or operations. Nor . . . can I deny that revelation of these documents will do substantial damage to public interests. . . . But I nevertheless agree that the United States has not satisfied the very heavy burden which it must meet to warrant an injunction against publication in these cases . . .

The Government's position is simply stated: The responsibility of the Executive for the conduct of foreign affairs and for the security of the Nation is so basic that the President is entitled to an injunction against publication of a newspaper whenever he can convince a court that the information to be revealed threatens "grave and irreparable" injury to the public interest...

At least in the absence of legislation by Congress, based on its own investigation and findings, I am quite unable to agree that the inherent powers of the Executive and the courts... authorize remedies having such sweeping potential for inhibiting publications by the press....

....That the Government mistakenly chose to proceed by injunction does not mean that it could not successfully proceed in another way.

.... It is... clear that Congress [in considering the Espionage Act in 1917] has addressed itself to the problem of protecting the security of the country and the national defense from unauthorized disclosure of potentially damaging information.... It has not, however, authorized the injunctive remedy against threatened publication. It has apparently been satisfied to rely on criminal sanctions and their deterrent effect on the responsible as well as the irresponsible press....

Mr. Justice **Marshall**, concurring:

.... [I]t is clear that Congress has specifically rejected passing legislation that would have clearly given the President the power he seeks here and made the current activity of the newspapers unlawful. When Congress specifically declines to make conduct unlawful it is not for this Court to redecide those issues—to overrule Congress.

Mr. Chief Justice **Burger**, dissenting:

... [T]his case is not simple... We do not know the facts of the case.... I suggest we are in this posture because these cases have been conducted in unseemly haste....

The newspapers make a derivative claim under the First Amendment; they denominate this right as the public right-to-know; by implication, the *Times* asserts a sole trusteeship of that right by virtue of its journalistic "scoop." ... A great issue of this kind should be tried in a judicial atmosphere conducive to thoughtful reflective deliberation, especially when haste... is unwarranted in light of the long period the *Times*, by its own choice, deferred publication.

It is not disputed that the *Times* has had unauthorized possession of the documents for three to four months, during which it has had its expert analysts studying them, presumably digesting them and preparing the material for publication... No doubt this was for a good reason; the analysis of 7,000 pages of complex material drawn from a vastly greater volume of material would inevitably take time and the writing of good news stories takes time. But why should ... judges [now] be placed under needless pressure? ...

.... [W]e literally do not know what we are acting on. As I see it we have been forced to deal with litigation concerning rights of great magnitude without an adequate record, and surely without time for adequate treatment either in the prior proceedings or in this Court....

... I am in general agreement with much of what Mr. Justice White has expressed with respect to penal sanctions concerning communication or retention of documents or information relating to the national defense.

We all crave speedier judicial processes but when judges are pressured as in these cases the result is a parody of the judicial process.

Mr. Justice **Harlan**, whom the **Chief Justice** and Mr. Justice **Blackmun** join, dissenting:

These cases forcefully call to mind the wise admonition of Mr. Justice Holmes, dissenting in *Northern Securities Company v. United States* (1904): "Great cases like hard cases make bad law." ...

With all respect, I consider that the Court has been almost irresponsibly feverish in dealing with these cases....

The power to evaluate the "pernicious influence" of premature disclosure is not ... lodged in the Executive alone. I agree that, in performance of its duty to protect the values of the First Amendment against political pressures, the judiciary must review the initial Executive determination to the point of satisfying itself that the subject matter of the dispute does lie within the proper compass of the President's foreign relations power.... Moreover, the judiciary may properly insist that the determination that the disclosure of the subject matter would irreparably impair the national security be made by the head of the Executive Department concerned— here the Secretary of State or the Secretary of Defense—after actual personal consideration by that officer.... But in my judgment the judiciary may not properly go beyond these two inquiries and redetermine for itself the probable impact of the disclosure on the national security.... Pending further hearings ... I would continue the restraints on publication. I cannot believe that the doctrine prohibiting prior restraints reaches to the point of preventing courts from maintaining the status quo long enough to act responsibly in matters of such national importance as those involved here.

Mr. Justice **Blackmun**, dissenting:

.... [The] ... courts have been pressed into hurried decision of profound constitutional issues on inadequately developed and largely assumed facts without the careful deliberation that, hopefully, should characterize the American judicial process....

## III. SYMBOLIC SPEECH

### 46. *United States v. O'Brien*
### 391 U.S. 367; 88 S.Ct. 1673; 20 L.Ed. 2d 672 (1968)

*People sometimes try to express their political views through symbolic actions. Does the First Amendment protect symbolic forms of expression? The Court has dealt with this question in a number of cases. In* Stromberg v. California *(283 U.S. 359, 1931), for example, the Court invalidated the State's anti-red-flag law. The Court ruled that the peaceful display of a red flag as a symbol of opposition to the government is a constitutionally protected form of speech. In* Street v. New York *(394 U.S. 577, 1969), the Court overturned the conviction of a man who burned an American flag—in violation of a New York law—to protest the shooting of civil rights activist, James Meredith. In* Tinker v. Des Moines Independent Community School District *(393 U.S. 503, 1969), the Court ruled that school officials acted improperly by suspending students who wore black armbands to express their opposition to American involvement in Vietnam. Such peaceful expressions of political views are protected under the First Amendment. In* Spence v. Washington *(418 U.S. 405, 1974), a student was arrested for violating the State's flag-defacement law after he superimposed a peace symbol on an American flag and flew it upside down from his window to protest the United States' invasion of Cambodia and the shooting of four students by national guardsmen at Kent State University. The Court found his symbolic action to be a protected form of expression.*

*But the Court has not upheld all forms of symbolic expression. In* United States v. O'Brien, *a man burned his draft card to influence others to support his anti-war sentiments. The Supreme Court upheld his conviction for violating a federal law that made it a crime to mutilate draft cards. Chief Justice Warren, writing for a seven-to-one majority, balanced the individual's interest against the government's interest in conducting an efficient and systematic selective service system. Concluding that the regulation was justified, Warren upheld the conviction.*

\* \* \* \* \* \* \* \* \* \* \* \* \* \* \* \* \* \* \* \* \* \* \* \* \* \* \* \* \* \*

Mr. Chief Justice **Warren** delivered the opinion of the Court:

On the morning of March 31, 1966, David Paul O'Brien and three companions burned their Selective Service registration certificates on the steps of the South Boston Courthouse. A sizable crowd, including several agents of the Federal Bureau of Investigation, witnessed the event....

O'Brien stated to FBI agents that he had burned his registration certificate because of his beliefs, knowing that he was violating federal law....

For this act, O'Brien was [convicted] in the United States District Court for the district of Massachusetts.... He stated in argument to the jury that he burned the certificate publicly to influence others to adopt his antiwar beliefs...

...[A]t the time O'Brien burned his certificate an offense was committed by any person, who forges, alters, *knowingly destroys, knowingly mutilates*, or in any manner (changes any such certificate...." (Italics supplied.)

....[A] regulation of the Selective Service System required registrants to keep their registration certificates in their "personal possession at all times." Willful violations... were made criminal by statute....

When a male reaches the age of 18, he is required by the Universal Military Training and Service Act to register with a local draft board. He is assigned a Selective Service number, and within five days he is issued a registration certificate. Subsequently, and based on a questionnaire completed by the registrant, he is assigned a classification denoting his eligibility for induction, and "[a]s soon as practicable" thereafter he is issued a Notice of Classification....

[Both the registration and classification certificates are small white cards approximately 2 by 3 inches....]

....A law prohibiting destruction of Selective Service certificates no more abridges free speech on its face than a motor vehicle law prohibiting the destruction of drivers' licenses, or a tax law prohibiting the destruction of books and records.

O'Brien nonetheless argues [first] that the 1965 Amendment is unconstitutional... as applied to him because his act of burning his registration certificate was protected "symbolic speech" with the First Amendment....

We cannot accept the view that an apparently limitless variety of conduct can be labelled "speech" whenever the person engaging in the conduct intends thereby to express an idea.... This Court has held that when "speech" and "nonspeech" elements are combined in the same course of conduct, a sufficiently important governmental interest in regulating the nonspeech enactment can justify incidental limitations on First Amendment freedoms.... [W]e think it clear that a government regulation is sufficiently justified if it is within the constitutional power of the government; if it furthers an important or substantial governmental interest; if the governmental interest is unrelated to the suppression of free expression; and if the incidental restriction on alleged First Amendment freedom is no greater than is essential to the furtherance of that interest. We find that the 1965 Amendment meets all of these requirements, and consequently that O'Brien can be constitutionally convicted for violating it. . . . Pursuant to [its power to classify and conscript manpower for military service], Congress may establish a system of registration for individuals liable for training and service, and may require such individuals within reason to cooperate in the registration system. The issuance of certificates indicating the registration and eligibility classification of individuals is a legitimate and substantial administrative aid in the functioning of this system. And legislation to insure the continuing availability of issued certificates serves a legitimate and substantial purpose in the system's administration.

. . . .

The many functions performed by Selective Service certificates establish beyond doubt that Congress has a legitimate and substantial interest in preventing their wanton and unrestrained destruction and assuring their continuing availability by punishing people who knowingly and willfully destroy or mutilate them. . . .

We think its apparent that the continuing availability to each registrant of his Selective Service certificates substantially furthers the smooth and proper functioning of the system that Congress has established to raise armies. . . .

. . . . We perceive no alternative means that would more precisely and narrowly assure the continuing availability of issued Selective Service certificates than a law which prohibits their willful mutilation or destruction. . . .

### 47. *Texas v. Johnson*
### 491 U.S. 397; 109 S.Ct. 2533; 105 L.Ed. 2d 342 (1989)

*Burning an American flag arouses strong emotional responses. This, of course, is what makes the action so appealing to some political protestors; it is an ordinary person's way of attracting attention—including media attention—for his or her views. It is doubtful that many people would pay attention if such a person made a speech or issued a position paper articulating only ideas. Should the First Amendment protect flag burning as a symbolic form of expression? By a five-to-four vote, the Supreme Court found that it does in* Texas v. Johnson. *Writing for the majority, Justice Brennan said that "our toleration of [such] criticism . . . is a source of strength." He further stated that "[t]he way to preserve the flag's special role is not to punish those who feel differently about these matters. It is to persuade them that they are wrong."*

*The decision stimulated considerable debate. Critics cited the unique place of honor that the flag holds and regarded flag burning as an intolerable affront to patriotic values. Politicians, recalling how effectively George Bush had used patriotic themes in his successful 1988 presidential campaign against Michael Dukakis, rallied to support the flag. Congress promply enacted the Flag Protection Act of 1989 to make flag desecration a federal crime. Protesters defied the law the day it went into effect and two cases went directly to the Supreme Court for expedited review. Just one year later, the Court invalidated this law in* United States v. Eichman *(496 U.S. 310, 1990). The Court rejected the government's position that flag burning was like "fighting words," and should not enjoy the full protection of the First Amendment, and it held that the federal statute was indistinct from the Texas law. Quoting the* Johnson *decision, Justice Brennan wrote: "If there is a bedrock principle underlying the First Amendment, it is that Government may not prohibit expression of an idea simply because society finds the idea itself offensive or disagreeable."*

*A constitutional amendment was then introduced in Congress that would permit the federal government and the states to prohibit flag mutilation. Opponents warned that to tinker with the First Amendment in this fashion would mutilate the Bill of Rights. Such observers contended that it is more important to protect the freedom the flag represented than it is to protect the flag's cloth. They urged lawmakers to take the politically difficult stand of opposing the proposed amendment. The amendment fell short of the two-thirds majority required in both houses to approve a constitutional revision.*

\* \* \* \* \* \* \* \* \* \* \* \* \* \* \* \* \* \* \* \* \* \* \* \* \* \* \* \*

Justice **Brennan**. . . . wrote the majority opinion:

After publicly burning an American flag as a means of political protest, Gregory Lee Johnson was convicted of desecrating a flag in violation of Texas law. This case presents the question whether his conviction is consistent with the First Amendment. We hold that it is not.

While the Republican National Convention was taking place in Dallas in 1984, respondent Johnson participated in a political demonstration dubbed the "Republican War Chest Tour" . . . to protest the policies of the Reagan administration. . . .

The demonstration ended in front of Dallas City Hall, where Johnson unfurled the American flag, doused it with kerosene and set it on fire. While the flag burned, the protesters chanted, "America, the red, white and blue, we spit on you." After the demonstrators dispersed, a witness to the flag burning collected the flag's remains and buried them in his backyard. No one was physically injured or threatened with injury, though several witnesses testified that they had been seriously offended by the flag burning.

...Johnson ... was charged with ... the desecration of a venerated object in violation of Texas Penal Code ... After a trial, he was convicted, sentenced to one year in prison, and fined $2,000. ...

.... We must first determine whether Johnson's burning of the flag constituted expressive conduct, permitting him to invoke the First Amendment in challenging his conviction ...

The First Amendment literally forbids the abridgement only of "speech," but we have long recognized that its protection does not end at the spoken or written word. ...

In deciding whether particular conduct possesses sufficient communicative elements to bring the First Amendment into play, we have asked whether "[a]n intent to convey a particularized message was present, and [whether] the likelihood was great that the message would be understood by those who viewed it." ... Hence, we have recognized the expressive nature of students' wearing of black armbands to protest American military involvement in Vietnam; ... of a sit-in by blacks in a "whites only" area to protest segregation, ... of the wearing of American military uniforms in a dramatic presentation criticizing American involvement in Vietnam, ... and of picketing about a wide variety of causes. ...

Especially pertinent to the case are our decisions recognizing the communicative nature of conduct relating to flags. Attaching a peace sign to the flag, ... saluting the flag, and displaying a red flag, we have held, all may find shelter under the First Amendment. ... That we have had little difficulty identifying an expressive element in conduct relating to flags should not be surprising. The very purpose of a national flag is to serve as a symbol of our country; ... Pregnant with expressive content, the flag as readily signifies this Nation as does the combination of letters found in "America." ... Texas claims that its interest in preventing breaches of the peace justifies Johnson's conviction for flag desecration. However, no disturbance of the peace actually occurred or threatened to occur because of Johnson's burning of the flag. ...

The State's position, therefore, amounts to a claim that an audience that takes serious offense at particular expression is necessarily likely to disturb the peace and that the expression may be prohibited on this basis. Our precedents do not countenance such a presumption. On the contrary, they recognize that a principal "function of free speech under our system of government is to invite dispute. It may indeed best serve its high purpose when it induces a condition of unrest, creates dissatisfaction with conditions as they are, or even stirs people to anger." ...

Nor does Johnson's expressive conduct fall within that small class of "fighting words" that are "likely to provoke the average person to retaliation, and thereby cause a breach of the peace.".... No reasonable onlooker would have regarded Johnson's generalized expression of dissatisfaction with policies of the Federal Government as a direct personal insult or an invitation to exchange fisticuffs....

We thus conclude that the State's interest in maintaining order is not implicated on these facts. The State need not worry that our holding will disable it from preserving the peace. We do not suggest that the First Amendment forbids a State to prevent "imminent lawless action.".... And, in fact, Texas already has a statute specifically prohibiting breaches of the peace, ... which tends to confirm that Texas need not punish this flag desecration in order to keep the peace....

Johnson's political expression was restricted because of the content of the message he conveyed. We must therefore subject the State's asserted interest in preserving the special symbolic character of the flag to "the most exacting scrutiny."...

[T]he State emphasizes the " 'special place' " reserved for the flag in our Nation....

If there is a bedrock principle underlying the First Amendment, it is that the Government may not prohibit the expression of an idea simply because society finds the idea itself offensive or disagreeable....

We have not recognized an exception to this principle even where our flag has been involved....

We never before have held that the Government may ensure that a symbol be used to express only one view of that symbol....

... To conclude that the Government may permit designated symbols to be used to communicate only a limited set of messages would be to enter territory having no discernible or defensible boundaries....

We are fortified in today's conclusion by our conviction that forbidding criminal punishment for conduct such as Johnson's will not endanger the special role played by our flag or the feelings it inspires....

.... Our decision is a reaffirmation of the principles of freedom and inclusiveness that the flag best reflects, and of the conviction that our toleration of criticism such as Johnson's is a sign and source of our strength....

The way to preserve the flag's special role is not to punish those who feel differently about these matters. It is to persuade them that they are wrong. "To courageous, self-reliant men, with confidence in the power of free and fearless reasoning applied through the process of popular government, no danger flowing from speech can be deemed clear and present, unless the incidence of the evil apprehended is so imminent that it may befall before there is opportunity for full discussion. If there be time to expose through discussion the falsehood and fallacies, to avert the evil by the processes of education, the remedy to be applied is more speech, not enforced silence."... We can imagine no more appropriate response to burning a flag than waving one's own, no better way to counter a flag-burner's message than by saluting the flag that burns, no surer means of perserving the dignity even of the flag that burned than by—as one witness here did—according its remains a respectful burial. We do not consecrate the flag by punishing its desecration, for in doing so we dilute the freedom that this cherished emblem represents. . . .

Justice **Kennedy**, concurring:

I write not to qualify the words Justice Brennan chooses so well, for he says with power all that is necessary to explain our ruling. I join his opinion without reservation, but with a keen sense that this case . . . exacts its personal toll. . . .

The hard fact is that sometimes we must make decisions we do not like. We make them because they are right, right in the sense that the law and the Constitution, as we see them, compel the result. . . .

Chief Justice **Rehnquist** joined by Justices **White** and **O'Connor**, dissenting:

In holding this Texas statute unconstitutional, the Court ignores Justice Holmes' familiar aphorism that a "a page of history is worth a volume of logic" . . . For more than 200 years, the American flag has occupied a unique position as the symbol of our Nation, a uniqueness that justifies a governmental prohibition against flag burning in the way respondent Johnson did here. . . .

No other American symbol has been as universally honored as the flag. . . .

. . . . I cannot agree that the First Amendment invalidates the Act of Congress, and the laws of 48 of the 50 States, which make criminal the public burning of the flag.

. . . . As with "fighting words," so with flag burning, for purposes of the First Amendment: It is "no essential part of any exposition of ideas, and [is] of such slight social value as a step to truth that any benefit that may be derived from [it] is clearly outweighed" by the public interest in avoiding a probable breach of the peace. . . .

. . . The Texas statute deprived Johnson of only one rather inarticulate symbolic form of protest—a form of protest that was profoundly offensive to many—and left him with a full panoply of other symbols and every conceivable form of verbal expression to express his deep disapproval of national policy. . . .

. . . . Surely one of the high purposes of a democratic society is to legislate against conduct that is regarded as evil and profoundly offensive to the majority of people—whether it be murder, embezzlement, pollution, or flag burning. . . .

Justice **Stevens**, dissenting:

. . . . [T]he American flag. It is more than a proud symbol of the courage, the determination, and the gifts of nature that transformed 13 fledgling Colonies into a world power. It is a symbol of freedom, of equal opportunity, of religious tolerance, and of goodwill for other peoples who share our aspirations. . . .

The value of the flag as a symbol cannot be measured. . . .

The ideas of liberty and equality have been an irresistible force . . . If those ideas are worth fighting for—and our history demonstrates that they are—it cannot be true that the flag that uniquely symbolizes their power is not itself worthy of protection from unnecessary desecration. . . .

## IV. OBSCENITY AND FREEDOM OF EXPRESSION

### 48. *Roth v. United States*
### 354 U.S. 476; 77 S.Ct. 1304; 1 L.Ed. 1498 (1957)

*Justice Holmes believed that statements that pose a "clear and present danger" of "substantive evils that Congress has a right to prevent" can be inhibited without violating the First Amendment. Certain political statements may be offensive to majority opinion, but courts generally find that they are constitutionally protected because they have social importance and value. Not so with "fighting words." Public insults calculated to provoke a violent reaction from the listener are unprotected by the First Amendment (Chaplinsky v. New Hampshire, 315 U.S. 568, 1942). What about obscenity?*

*In* Roth v. United States, *the Court upheld the conviction of a New York publisher who was convicted for mailing obscene advertisements and an obscene book in violation of a federal statute. The Court decided by a six-to-three vote that obscenity is not a constitutionally-protected form of speech or press. In his opinion for the Court, Justice Brennan said that the test for obscenity is "whether to the average person, applying contemporary community standards, the dominant theme of the material taken as a whole appeals to prurient interest." Such material is unprotected because it is "utterly without redeeming social importance." Materials possessing even the "slightest redeeming social importance" enjoy constitutional protection. This test, however, proved difficult to operationalize. Who is the "average person"? How are "contemporary community standards" ascertained? What "community" serves as the reference point?*

*Does this material have* any *"redeeming social importance"? In short, it is clear that obscenity can be restricted; its definition is less clear.*

\* \* \* \* \* \* \* \* \* \* \* \* \* \* \* \* \* \* \* \* \* \* \* \* \* \* \* \*

Mr. Justice **Brennan** delivered the opinion of the Court:
. . . The dispositive question is whether obscenity is utterance within the area of protected speech and press. . . . [N]umerous opinions indicate that this Court has always assumed that obscenity is not protected by freedoms of speech and press.

. . . . [T]he unconditional phrasing of the First Amendment was not intended to protect every utterance. This phrasing did not prevent this Court from concluding that libelous utterances are not within the area of constitutionally protected speech, *Beaubarnais v. Illinois*. . . . [T]here is sufficiently contemporaneous evidence to show that obscenity, too, was outside the protection intended for speech and press.

. . . .

All ideas having even the slightest redeeming social importance—unorthodox ideas, controversial ideas, even ideas hateful to the prevailing climate of opinion—have the full protection of the guaranties, unless excludable because they encroach upon the limited area of more important interests. But implicit in the history of the First Amendment is the rejection of obscenity as utterly without redeeming social importance. . . .

We hold that obscenity is not within the area of constitutionally protected speech or press.

. . . . Obscene material is material which deals with sex in a manner appealing to prurient interest. The portrayal of sex, e.g., in art, literature and scientific works, is not itself sufficient reason to deny material the constitutional protection of freedom of speech and press. . . .

. . . . It is . . . vital that the standards for judging obscenity safeguard the protection of freedom of speech and press for material which does not treat sex in a manner appealing to prurient interest.

. . . . [The test of obscenity is]: whether to the average person, applying contemporary community standards, the dominant theme of the material taken as a whole appeals to prurient interest. The [*Regina v. Hicklin*, (1868)] test, judging obscenity by the effect of isolated passages upon the most susceptible persons, might well encompass material legitimately treating with sex, and so it must be rejected as unconstitutionally restrictive of the freedoms of speech and press. On the other hand, the substituted standard provides safeguards adequate to withstand the charge of constitutional infirmity.

. . . . The test in each case is the effect of the book, picture or publication considered as a whole, not upon any particular class, but upon all ... whom it is likely to reach. In other words, you determine its impact upon the average person in the community. The books, pictures and circulars must be judged as a whole, in their entire context. . . .

Many decisions have recognized that . . . [the] terms of obscenity statutes are not precise. This Court, however, has consistently held that lack of precision is not itself offensive to the requirements of due process. "[T]he Constitution does not require impossible standards"; all that is required is that the language "conveys sufficiently definite warning as to the proscribed conduct when measured by common understanding and practices. . . . "

In summary, then, we hold that these statutes, applied according to the proper standard for judging obscenity, do not offend constitutional safeguards against convictions based upon protected material, or fail to give men in acting adequate notice of what is prohibited.

## 49. *Miller v. California*
### 413 U.S. 15; 93 S.Ct. 2067; 37 L.Ed. 419 (1973)

*In* Memoirs v. Massachusetts *(383 U.S. 413, 1966), a state court had banned the controversial novel,* Fanny Hill, *as obscene although the court acknowledged that it might have some "minimal literary value." The Supreme Court held that the book could be banned only if "(a) the dominant theme of the material taken as a whole appeals to a prurient interest in sex; (b) the material is patently offensive because it affronts contemporary community standards relating to the description or representation of sexual matters; and (c) the material is utterly without redeeming social value." Even though the book was deemed to be offensive, it was not "utterly without redeeming social value." For this reason, the Supreme Court reversed the state court.*

*In* Miller v. California, *the Court relaxed these standards and made it relatively easier for a local community to restrict such materials. In* Miller, *sexually-explicit materials were mailed to persons who had not requested nor indicated any interest in receiving such mailings. They complained to the police and California attempted to apply its criminal obscenity law to the situation. By a five-to-four vote, the Court upheld the conviction. In his opinion for the Court, Chief Justice Burger contended that the* Memoirs *decision broke with established precedent and he claimed to be reaffirming the* Roth *holding. In fact,* Roth *protected materials that possessed even the "slightest redeeming social importance" while Burger would extend this protection only to works that have "serious literary, artistic, political or scientific value." (Emphasis added.) He also held that regardless of the nationwide scope of the First Amendment, local communities should be free to develop their own standards of obscenity.*

\* \* \* \* \* \* \* \* \* \* \* \* \* \* \* \* \* \* \* \* \* \* \* \* \* \* \*

Mr. Chief Justice **Burger** delivered the opinion of the Court:

. . . . In *Roth v. United States* (1957), the Court sustained a conviction under a federal statute punishing the mailing of "obscene, lewd, lascivious or filthy . . . " materials. The key to that holding was the Court's rejection of the claim that obscene materials were protected by the First Amendment. Five Justices joined in the opinion stating: " . . . [I]mplicit in the history of the First Amendment is the rejection of obscenity as utterly without redeeming social importance." . . .

. . . [I]n *Memoirs v. Massachusetts* (1966), the Court veered sharply away from *Roth* concept and . . . articulated a new test of obscenity. The plurality held that. . . . "[a] book cannot be proscribed unless it is found to be *utterly* without redeeming social value."

While *Roth* presumed "obscenity" to be "utterly without redeeming social value," *Memoirs* required that to prove obscenity it must be affirmatively established that the materials is "*utterly* without redeeming social value." Thus, . . . the *Memoirs* plurality produced a drastically altered test that called on the prosecution to prove a negative, i.e., that the material was "*utterly* without redeeming social value"—a burden virtually impossible to discharge under our criminal standards of proof. . . .

. . . . [T]he *Memoirs* test has been abandoned as unworkable . . . and no member of the Court today supports the *Memoirs* foundation.

This much has been categorically settled by the Court, that obscene material is unprotected by the First Amendment. . . . We acknowledge, however, the inherent dangers of undertaking to regulate any form of expression. State statutes designed to regulate obscene materials must be carefully limited. . . .

The basic guidelines for the trier of fact must be: (a) whether "the average person, applying contemporary community standards" would find that the work, taken as a whole, appeals to the prurient interest. . . . (b) whether the work depicts or describes, in a patently offensive way, sexual conduct specifically defined by the applicable state law, and (c) whether the work, taken as a whole, lacks serious literary, artistic, political, or scientific value. We do not adopt as a constitutional standard the "*utterly* without redeeming social value" test of *Memoirs v. Massachusetts*. . . .

. . . . At a minimum, prurient, patently offensive depiction or description of sexual conduct must have serious literary, artistic, political, or scientific value to merit First Amendment protection.... For example, medical books for the education of physicians and related personnel necessarily use graphic illustrations and descriptions of human anatomy. In resolving the inevitably sensitive questions of fact and law, we must continue to rely on the jury system....

Under a national Constitution, fundamental First Amendment limitations on the powers of the States do not vary from community to community, but this does not mean that there are, or should or can be, fixed, uniform national standards of precisely what appeals to the "prurient interest" or is "patently offensive." These are essentially questions of fact, and our nation is simply too big and too diverse for this Court to reasonably expect that such standards could be articulated for all 50 States in a single formulation, even assuming the prerequisite consensus exists....

It is neither realistic nor constitutionally sound to read the First Amendment as requiring that the people of Maine or Mississippi accept public depiction of conduct found tolerable in Las Vegas or New York City.... People in different States vary in their tastes and attitudes and this diversity is not to be strangled by the absolutism of imposed uniformity.... We hold the requirement that the jury evaluate the materials with reference to "contemporary standards of the State of California" serves this protective purpose and is constitutionally adequate....

In sum we (a) reaffirm the *Roth* holding that obscene material is not protected by the First Amendment, (b) hold that such material can be regulated by the States ... without a showing that the material is "*utterly* without redeeming social value," and (c) hold that obscenity is to be determined by applying "contemporary community standards," ... not "national standards." ...

## 50. *Federal Communications Commission v. Pacifica Foundation* 438 U.S. 726; 98 S.Ct. 3026; 57 L.Ed. 2d 1073 (1978)

*Can language that is "patently offensive" though not necessarily "obscene" be regulated or barred? The Court's answer depends largely on context. In* Cohen v. California *(403 U.S. 15, 1971), the Court considered Paul Cohen's decision to protest the war in Vietnam by wearing into a Los Angeles courthouse a jacket on which was inscribed the message, "Fuck the Draft." He was convicted for breach of peace. The Supreme Court overturned his conviction saying that unless he intended to provoke a disturbance, he was expressing a political view that was entitled to constitutional protection.*

*In* F.C.C. v. Pacifica, *however, the Court ruled that the Federal Commu-*

*nications Commission can regulate the times when television and radio stations can broadcast offensive material. Comedian George Carlin recorded a monologue entitled "Filthy Words." He satirized social attitudes towards certain words by explaining that there were seven words that one cannot say on the airwaves. He then used these words in a variety of ways throughout the monologue. A New York radio station broadcast this monologue at two in the afternoon and it was heard by a father and his son. The father complained to the F. C. C. and the agency found the monologue patently offensive and ruled that it could not be broadcast when children were likely to be in the audience. The Pacifica Foundation argued that the F. C. C. was violating the First Amendment by regulating the content of a program. Writing for a five-to-four majority, Justice Stevens rejected this argument and said that "both the content and the context of speech are critical elements of First Amendment analysis."*

\* \* \* \* \* \* \* \* \* \* \* \* \* \* \* \* \* \* \* \* \* \* \* \* \* \* \* \* \* \*

Mr. Justice **Stevens** delivered the opinion of the Court:

... [T]he question is whether the First Amendment denies government any power to restrict the public broadcast of indecent language in any circumstances. For if the government has any power, this was an appropriate occasion for its exercise.

The words of the Carlin monologue are unquestionably "speech" within the meaning of the First Amendment. It is equally clear that the Commission's objections to the broadcast were based in part on its content. The order must therefore fall if, as Pacifica argues, the First Amendment prohibits all governmental regulation that depends on the content of speech. Our past cases demonstrate, however, that no such absolute rule is mandated by the Constitution.

The classic exposition of the proposition that both the content and the context of speech are critical elements of First Amendment analysis is Mr. Justice Holmes' statement for the Court in *Schenck v. United States*:

... [T]he character of every act depends upon the circumstances in which it is done. ... The most stringent protection of free speech would not protect a man in falsely shouting fire in a theatre and causing a panic. ... The question in every case is whether the words used are used in such circumstances and are of such a nature as to create a clear and present danger that they will bring about the substantive evils that Congress has a right to prevent. ...

The question in this case is whether a broadcast of patently offensive words dealing with sex and excretion may be regulated because of its content. Obscene materials have been denied the protection of the First Amendment because their content is so offensive to contemporary moral standards. *Roth v. United States....* But the fact that society may find speech offensive is not a sufficient reason for suppressing it. Indeed, if it is the speaker's opinion that gives offense, that consequence is a reason for according it constitutional protection. For it is a central tenet of the First Amendment that the government, must remain neutral in the marketplace of ideas. If there were any reason to believe that the Commission's characterization of the Carlin monologue as offensive could be traced to its political content—or even to the fact that it satirized contemporary attitudes about four-letter words—First Amendment protection might be required. But that is simply not this case.

Although these words ordinarily lack literary, political, or scientific value, they are not entirely outside the protection of the First Amendment. ... Nonetheless, the constitutional protection accorded to a communication containing such patently offensive sexual and excretory language need not be the same in every context. It is a characteristic of speech such as this that both is capacity to offend and its "social value," ... vary with the circumstances. Words that are commonplace in one setting are shocking in another. To paraphrase Mr. Justice Harlan, one occasion's lyric is another's vulgarity.

In this case it is undisputed that the content of Pacifica's broadcast was "vulgar," "offensive," and "shocking." Because content of that character is not entitled to absolute constitutional protection under all circumstances, we must consider its context in order to determine whether the Commission's action was constitutionally permissible.

We have long recognized that each medium of expression presents special First Amendment problems. ... [Broadcasting... has received the most limited First Amendment protection. ... [A] broadcaster may be deprived of his license and his forum if the Commission decides that such an action would serve "the public interest, convenience, and necessity." ...

.... First, the broadcast media have established a uniquely pervasive presence in the lives of all Americans. Patently offensive, indecent material presented over the airwaves confronts the citizen, not only in public, but also in the privacy of the home, where the individual's right to be left alone, plainly outweighs the First Amendment rights on an intruder. Because the broadcast audience is constantly tuning in and out, prior warning cannot completely protect the listener or viewer from unexpected program content. To say that one may avoid further offense by turning off the radio when he hears indecent language is like saying that the remedy for an assault is to run away after the first blow. . . .

Second, broadcasting is uniquely accessible to children, even those too young to read. Although Cohen's written message might have been incomprehensible to a first grader, Pacifica's broadcast could have enlarged a child's vocabulary in an instant. . . . We held in *Ginsberg v. New York*, that the government's interest in the "well-being of it youth" and in supporting "parents' claim to authority in their own household" justified the regulation of otherwise protected expression. The ease with which children may obtain access to broadcast material, . . . amply justifies special treatment of indecent broadcasting.

. . . . The Commission's decision rested entirely on a nuisance rationale under which context is all-important. The concept requires consideration of a host of variables. The time of day was emphasized by the Commission. The content of the program in which the language is used will also affect the composition of the audience, and differences between radio, television, and perhaps closed-circuit transmissions, may also be relevant. As Mr. Justice Sutherland wrote, a "nuisance may be merely a right thing in the wrong place—like a pig in the parlor instead of the barnyard." *Euclid v. Ambler Reality Company*. We simply hold that when the Commission finds that a pig has entered the parlor, the exercise of its regulatory power does not depend on proof that the pig is obscene.

# CHAPTER 5

# FREEDOM OF RELIGION

## I. RELIGION AND THE STATES DURING THE REVOLUTIONARY ERA

*The history of religious freedom in American society is more complex than it might first appear. Many colonists came to America to escape religious persecution and to create a safe haven to practice their religious beliefs. Once established, however, not all were tolerant of religious dissent. State constitutions adopted during the Revolutionary Era reflect the differing opinion on the role of religion in American society; some states favored religious toleration, others authorized public support for a particular religion. This situation was complicated during the Constitutional Era because of concern that the federal government might establish a national church. Much of the debate since then has focused on the meaning of the Establishment and the Free Exercise Clauses of the First Amendment. After the ratification of the Fourteenth Amendment in 1868, the First Amendment's prohibitions could also be applied against the states.*

*Religion was a very important concern for the Revolutionary generation. Many were convinced that it was fundamental to every civil society and that public leadership should only be entrusted to men with firm religious convictions. There was a real difference between those who could participate in the electoral process and those who should hold office. Each of the eleven newly written state constitutions extended the franchise to adult men, with varying property qualifications, without any religious test. Many of these same states limited office-holding itself to Christians or Protestants, thereby excluding non-Christians or non-Protestants by implication. This was accomplished by specifying that only Christians or Protestants could hold an office, or by stipulating the administration of a religious oath. Only three constitutions were free of any religious qualifications for public service.*

\* \* \* \* \* \* \* \* \* \* \* \* \* \* \* \* \* \* \* \* \* \* \* \* \* \* \* \* \* \* \* \*

## 51. Establishment of Religion: State Constitutions

*The Founders also hoped to avoid the abuses of an established church, such as they experienced during the colonial era, but they were divided as to what role the state should play in supporting religion. Four states disqualified active clergy from holding public office. Four states explicitly prohibited any established church. Both Georgia and Maryland held out the possibility of public support. Three states—Massachusetts (1780), New Hampshire (1784), and South Carolina—allowed public support for religion.*

\* \* \* \* \* \* \* \* \* \* \* \* \* \* \* \* \* \* \* \* \* \* \* \* \* \* \* \* \* \* \* \*

*Pennsylvania Declaration of Rights [1776], Article II (Thorpe, V: 3082)*

That all men have a natural and unalienable right to worship Almighty God according to the dictates of their own consciences and understanding: And that no man ought or of right can be compelled to attend any religious worship, or erect or support any place of worship, or maintain any ministry, contrary to, or against, his own free will and consent: Nor can any man, who acknowledges the being of a God, be justly deprived or abridged or any civil right as a citizen on account of his religious sentiments or peculiar mode of religious worship . . .

*South Carolina Constitution [1778], Article XXXVIII (Thorpe, VI: 3255–7)*

That all persons and religious societies who acknowledge that there is one god, and a future state of rewards and punishments, and that God is publicly to be worshipped, shall be freely tolerated. The Christian Protestant religion shall be deemed, and is hereby constituted and declared to be, the established religion of the State. That all denominations of Christian Protestants in this State, demeaning themselves peacefully and faithfully, shall enjoy equal religious and civil privileges . . . No person shall by law, be obligated to pay towards the maintenance and support of a religious worship that he does not freely join in, or has not voluntarily engaged to support.

*Source: Thorpe, ed. The Federal and State Constitutions*

## 52. Free Exercise of Religion: State Constitutions

*The Founders were especially sensitive to the rights of conscience and the free exercise of religion because of the proliferation of different religious groups during the colonial period. Seven new state constitutions recognized the free exercise of religion as a right, two saw it as a duty, and Massachusetts considered it both a right and a duty. Interestingly enough, five of these states conditioned the free exercise of religion, in the words of the New Hampshire Constitution (1784): "provided he doth not disturb the public peace, or disturb others, in their religious worship."*

\* \* \* \* \* \* \* \* \* \* \* \* \* \* \* \* \* \* \* \* \* \* \* \* \* \* \* \* \* \* \* \*

*Massachusetts Declaration of Rights [1780], Article II*
*(Thorpe, III. 1889)*

It is the right as well as the duty of all men in society, publicly, and at stated seasons, to worship the Supreme Being, the great Creator and Preserver of the universe. And no subject shall be hurt, molested, or restrained, in his person, liberty, or estate, for worshipping God in the manner and season most agreeable to the dictates of his own conscience, or for his religious profession of sentiments; provided he doth not disturb the public peace, or obstruct others in their religious worship.

*Source: Thorpe, ed.* The Federal and State Constitutions.

## 53. Virginia's "Act for Establishing Religious Freedom" (1785)

*This act was proposed by Thomas Jefferson in 1777 and adopted by the Virginia legislature, in a slightly amended form, in 1785. At a time when the Anglican Church was not entirely disestablished, Virginians were divided as to whether the state should support religion. Some favored enacting new laws to extend assistance to all religious groups; others, such as Jefferson, opposed any established religion. The following text is taken from the public law:*

\* \* \* \* \* \* \* \* \* \* \* \* \* \* \* \* \* \* \* \* \* \* \* \* \* \* \* \* \* \*

*An Act for Establishing Religious Freedom* (1785)

1. Whereas Almighty God hath created the mind free; that all attempts to influence it by temporal punishments of burthens, or by civil incapacitations, tend only to beget habits of hypocrisy and meanness, and are a departure from the plan of the Holy author of our religion, who being

Lord both of body and mind, yet chose not to propagate it by coercions on either, as was in his Almighty power to do; that the impious presumption of litigators and rulers, civil as well as ecclesiastical, who being themselves but fallible and uninspired men, have assumed dominion over the faith of others, setting up their own opinions and modes of thinking as the only true and infallible, and as such endeavoring to impose them on others, hath established and maintained false religions over the greatest part of the world, and through all time; that to compel a man to furnish contributions of money for the propagation of opinions which he disbelieves, is sinful and tyrannical; that even forcing him to support this or that teacher of his own religious persuasion, is depriving him of the comfortable liberty of giving his contributions to the particular pastor, whose morals he would make his pattern . . . ; that our civil rights have no dependence on our religious opinions, any more than our opinions in physics or geometry; that therefore the proscribing any citizen as unworthy the public confidence by laying upon him an incapacity of being called to offices of trust and emolument, unless he profess of renounce this or that religious opinion, is depriving him injuriously of those privileges and advantages to which in common with his fellow-citizens he has a natural right . . . ; that though indeed these are criminal who do not withstand such temptation, yet neither are those innocent who lay the bait in their way; that to suffer the civil magistrate to intrude his powers into the field of opinion, and to restrain the profession or propagation of principles on supposition of their ill tendency, is a dangerous fallacy, which at once destroys all religious liberty, because he being of course judge of that tendency will make his opinions the rule of judgment, and approve or condemn the sentiments of others only as they shall square with or differ from his own; that it is time enough for the rightful purposes of civil government, for its officers to interfere when principles break out into overt acts against peace and good order; and finally, that truth is great and will prevail if left to herself, that she is the proper and sufficient antagonist to error, and has nothing to fear from the conflict, unless by human interposition disarmed of her natural weapons, free argument and debate, errors ceasing to be dangerous when it is permitted freely to contradict them:

II. **Be it enacted by the General Assembly**, that no man shall be compelled to frequent or support any religious worship, place, or ministry whatsoever, nor shall be enforced, restrained, molested, or burthened in his body or goods, nor shall otherwise suffer on account of his religious opinions or belief; but that all men shall be free to profess, and by argument to maintain, their opinion in matters of religion, and that the same shall in no wise diminish, enlarge, or affect their civil capacities.

III. And though we well know that this assembly, elected by the people for the ordinary purpose of legislation only, have no power to restrain the acts of succeeding assemblies, constituted with powers equal to our own, and that therefore to declare that his act to be irrevocable would be of no effect in law; yet as we are free to declare, and do declare, that the rights hereby asserted are of the natural rights of mankind, and that if any act shall hereafter be passed to repeal the present, or to narrow its operation such act will be an infringement of natural right.

*Source: Rutland, ed.* Papers of James Madison, *VIII: 399–402. For Jefferson's original draft, see: Boyd, ed.* The Papers of Thomas Jefferson, *II: 545–53.*

## II. SEPARATION OF CHURCH AND STATE IN THE EARLY NATIONAL PERIOD

*One of the earliest controversies concerning the separation of church and state on the national level had to do with presidential proclamations calling for a day of public thanksgiving. President Washington initiated the practice, which was followed by President Adams, but President Jefferson discontinued it, because he felt that it violated the principle of the separation of church and state under the Constitution.*

\* \* \* \* \* \* \* \* \* \* \* \* \* \* \* \* \* \* \* \* \* \* \* \* \* \* \* \* \*

### 54. President Washington's Thanksgiving Proclamation, 3 October 1789.

Whereas it is the duty of all Nations to acknowledge the providence of Almighty God, to obey his will, to be grateful for his benefits, and humbly to implore his protection and favor, and Whereas both Houses of Congress have . . . requested me "to recommend to the People of the United States a day of public thanks-giving and prayer to be observed by acknowledging with grateful hearts the many signal favors of Almighty God, especially by affording them an opportunity peaceably to establish a form of government for their safety and happiness."

Now therefore I do recommend and assign Thursday the 26th day of November next to be devoted by the People of these States to the service of that great and glorious Being, who is the beneficent Author of all the good that was, that is, or that will be. That we may then all unite in rendering unto him our sincere and humble thanks, for his kind care and protection of the People of this country previous to their becoming a Nation, for the signal and manifold mercies, and the favorable interpositions of his providence, which we experienced in the course and conclusion of the late war, for the great degree of tranquility, union, and plenty, which we have since enjoyed, for the peaceable and rational manner in which we have been enabled to establish constitutions of government for our safety and happiness, and particularly the national One now lately instituted, for the civil and religious liberty with which we are blessed, and the means we have of acquiring and diffusing useful knowledge and in general for all the great and various favors which he hath been pleased to confer upon us.

And also that we may then unite in most humbly offering our prayers and supplications to the great Lord and Ruler of Nations and beseech him to pardon our national and other transgressions, to enable us all, whether in public or private stations, to perform our several and relative duties properly and punctually, to render our national government a blessing to all the People, by constantly being a government of wise, just and constitutional laws, discreetly and faithfully executed and obeyed, to protect and guide all Sovereigns and Nations (especially such as have shown kindness to us) and to bless them with good government, peace, and concord. To promote the knowledge and practice of true religion and virtue, and the increase of science among them and Us, and generally to grant unto all Mankind such a degree of temporal prosperity as he alone knows to be best.

*Source: John C. Fitzpatrick, ed.* The Writings of George Washington, from the Original Sources, 1745–1799, *39 vols. (Washington, D.C., GPO, 1931–44), XXX: 427–28.*

### 55. President Thomas Jefferson to . . . A Committee of the Danbury Baptist Association (Connecticut) . . . , 1 January 1802

Gentlemen:

. . . Believing with you that religion is a matter which lies solely between man and his God, that he owes account to none other for his faith or his worship, that the legislative powers of government reach actions only, and not opinions, I contemplate with sovereign reverence that act of the whole American people which declared that their legislature should "make no law respecting an establishment of religion, or prohibiting the free exercise thereof," thus building a wall of separation between Church and State. Adhering to this expression of the supreme will of the nation in behalf of the rights of conscience, I shall see with sincere satisfaction the progress of those sentiments which tend to restore to man all his natural rights, convinced he has no natural right in opposition to his social duties.

*Source: A. A. Lipscomb and A. E. Bergh, ed.* The Writings of Thomas Jefferson, *20 vols. (Washington, D.C., GPO, 1903), XVI: 281–82.*

### 56. President Thomas Jefferson to Attorney General Levi Lincoln, 1 January 1802

Adverse to receive addresses, yet unable to prevent them, I have generally endeavored to turn them to some account . . . The Baptist address, now enclosed, admits the condemnation of the alliance between Church and State, under the authority of the Constitution. It furnishes an occasion, too, which I have long wished to find, of saying why I do not want to proclaim fastings and thanksgivings, as my predecessors did. The address, to be sure, does not point at this, and its introduction is awkward. But I foresee no opportunity of doing it more pertinently. I know it will give great offense to the New England clergy; but the advocate of religious freedom is to expect neither peace nor forgiveness from them . . .

*Source: Lipscomb and Bergh, ed.* Writings of Jefferson *X: 305.*

## III. JUDICIAL INTERPRETATIONS OF RELIGIOUS FREEDOM

### 57. *West Virginia State Board of Education v. Barnette* 319 U.S. 624; 63 S.Ct. 1178; 87 L.Ed. 1628 (1943)

*Many of the colonists had fled religious persecution in England. Religious intolerance, however, was not uncommon. Some colonies had religious tests for holding certain jobs and offices. The Framers prohibited such religious tests for national offices in Article VI, but they found it difficult to define further the proper place of religion in the American political system. Some, like George Washington, Patrick, Henry, and others though that religion fosters public morality and favored public support for religious activities. Others, like Thomas Jefferson and James Madison, opposed governmental advancement of religion.*

*The First Amendment provides that, "Congress shall make no law respecting an establishment of religion or prohibiting the free exercise thereof." The Amendment guarantees* **two** *things: freedom to believe what one chooses* **and** *protection against governmental attempts to establish an official religion. In practice, these twin guarantees can seem to work at cross purposes. For example, does the Free Exercise Clause entitle the religious majority in a community to prescribe and conduct prayer ser-*

*vices and other religious exercises in the public schools? Are they not freely exercising their religious beliefs if they do so? On the other hand, does the Establishment Clause prohibit such public-school prayer as state advancement of religious beliefs through public institutions? Jefferson called for a "wall of separation" between church and state to avoid these kinds of problems. On the opposing side are those who think that the Constitution permits the government to support religion as long as no particular sect is favored over others. In other words, the government should be neutral.*

*Chief Justice Burger advanced the argument that the government's role should be that of "benevolent neutrality" in his majority opinion in* Walz v. Tax Commission *(397 U.S. 664, 1970). There the Court upheld the practice of exempting church property from public taxation. Burger said:*

> *. . . . The general principles deducible from the First Amendment and all that has been said by the Court is this: that we will not tolerate either governmentally established religion or governmental interference with religion. Short of these expressly proscribed governmental acts there is room for play in the joints productive of a benevolent neutrality which will permit religious exercise to exist without sponsorship and without interference.*

> *. . . . Adherence to the policy of neutrality that derives from an accommodation of the Establishment and Free Exercise Clauses has prevented the kind of involvement that would tip the balance toward government control of churches or governmental restraint on religious practice.*

*Freedom of religion, like freedom of speech and the press, is not absolute. Courts have upheld laws prohibiting polygamy, the use of hallucinogenics in religious services, and the like. Human sacrifice can be barred. If parents of a critically ill child deny the child conventional medical care, pray instead for the child's recovery, and the child dies, charges can be brought against them. It is one thing to believe what one will; it is another to practice your beliefs in a way that harms others. Recall John Stuart Mill on related matters. In such cases, the Court frequently assesses the relative weights of competing societal and individual interests. The issue of compulsory flag salutes illustrates this point.*

*A number of states passed laws requiring school children to salute the flag. Children who refused to comply could be expelled. In* Minersville School District v. Gobitis *(310 U.S. 586, 1940), the Court, in an opinion by Justice Frankfurther, upheld such a law. There the child of Jehovah's*

*Witnesses refused to salute the flag on grounds that to do so would violate their religious belief that the laws of God are superior to those of government. Frankfurther balanced individual interests in religious freedom against societal interests in promoting national unity and security. The Court allowed the Board's judgment that the compulsory flag salute would advance national unity to prevail. Justice Stone wrote a sharply-critical dissenting opinion.*

*Shortly thereafter, the West Virginia legislature passed a law requiring all schools to offer courses on history, civics, and the Constitution. The Board of Education also required that students salute the flag and recite the Pledge of Allegiance. The irony of forcing someone to recite a pledge in praise of "liberty" was not lost on critics. Nevertheless, failure to conform with this requirement constituted insubordination, punishable by expulsion. Readmittance was barred until the child complied with the requirement. Further, the expelled child was treated as legally absent and parents were subject to fines and imprisonment. In the case below, children of Jehovah's Witnesses again refused to comply with the flag-salute requirement on religious grounds and they were penalized in accordance with the statute. They contended that the requirement abridged their religious freedom as applied to the State by way of the Fourteenth Amendment. (See* Cantwell v. Connecticut, *310 U.S. 296, 1940, where the Court ruled that the Fourteenth Amendment's due process clause protects religious freedom.) Writing for a six-to-three majority, Justice Jackson overruled* Gobitis.

*Compulsory flag salutes continue to generate controversy. During the 1988 presidential campaign, the Democratic candidate, Michael Dukakis, was called upon to defend his opposition to a similar proposal in Massachusetts. The conflict, arising as it did in the midst of a political campaign, probably served to generate more heat than light. More insight into the issue can be gained from a careful reading of Justice Jackson's opinion.*

\* \* \* \* \* \* \* \* \* \* \* \* \* \* \* \* \* \* \* \* \* \* \* \* \* \* \* \*

Mr. Justice **Jackson** delivered the opinion of the Court:

.... As the present Chief Justice [Stone] said in dissent in the *Gobitis* case, the State may "require teaching by instruction and study of all in our history and in the structure and organization of our government, including the guarantees of civil liberty, which tend to inspire patriotism and love of country." Here, however, we are dealing with a compulsion of students to declare a belief. They are not merely made acquainted with the flag salute so that they may be informed as to what it is or even what it means. The issue here is whether this slow and easily neglected route to aroused loyalties constitutionally may be short-cut by substituting compulsory salute and slogan. . . .

Government of limited power need not be anemic government . . . Without promise of a limiting Bill of Rights it is doubtful if our Constitution could have mustered enough strength to enable its ratification. To enforce those rights today is not to choose weak government over strong government. It is only to adhere as a means of strength to individual freedom of mind in preference to officially disciplined uniformity for which history indicates a disappointing and disastrous end. . . . .

The Fourteenth Amendment, as now applied to the States, protects the citizen against the State itself and all of its creatures—Boards of Education not excepted. These have, of course, important, delicate, and highly discretionary functions, but none that they may not perform within the limits of the Bill of Rights. . . .

The very purpose of the Bill of Rights was to withdraw certain subjects from the vicissitudes of political controversy, to place them beyond the reach of majorities and officials and to establish them as legal principles to be applied by the courts. One's right to life, liberty, and property, to free speech, a free press, freedom of worship and assembly, and other fundamental rights may not be submitted to vote; they depend on the outcome of no elections.

. . . . [T]he *Gobitis* opinion . . . reasons that "national unity is the basis of national security," that the authorities have "the right to select appropriate means for its attainment," and hence reaches the conclusion that such compulsory measures toward "national unity" are constitutional. . . .

National unity as an end which officials may foster by persuasion and example is not in question. The problem is whether under our Constitution compulsion as here employed is a permissible means for its achievement.

. . . . Compulsory unification of opinion achieves only the unanimity of the graveyard.

It seems trite but necessary to say that the First Amendment . . . was designed to avoid these ends by avoiding these beginnings. There is no mysticism in the American concept of the State or of the nature or origin of its authority. We set up government by the consent of the governed, and the Bill of Rights denies those in power any legal opportunity to coerce that consent. Authority here is to be controlled by public opinion, not public opinion by authority.

. . . . To believe that patriotism will not flourish if patriotic ceremonies are voluntary and spontaneous instead of a compulsory routine is to make an unflattering estimate of the appeal of our institutions to free minds. . . .

If there is any fixed star in our constitutional constellation, it is that no official, high or petty, can prescribe what shall be orthodox in politics, nationalism, religion, or other matters of opinion or force citizens to confess by word or act their faith therein. If there are any circumstances which permit an exception, they do not now occur to us.

We think the action of the local authorities in compelling the flag salute and pledge transcends constitutional limitations on their power and invades the sphere of intellect and spirit which it is the purpose of the First Amendment to our Constitution to reserve from all official control....

## 58. *Zorach v. Clausen*
### 343 U.S. 306, 72 S. Ct. 679; 96 L.Ed. 954 (1952)

*Congress opens sessions with a prayer. The Supreme Court begins its sessions with the words, "God save the United States and this honorable court." The Ten Commandments are on display in the Supreme Court. "In God We Trust" appears on our money. Such official statements acknowledge religious belief, but the courts have dismissed most challenges to their constitutionality. On the other hand, attempts to require impressionable school children to express such religious sentiments have usually been disallowed. Interest balancing is an inexact process.*

*This point is illustrated by the Court's handling of some "released time" programs. The Court considered such a program in* Illinois ex rel. McCollum v. Board of Education *(333 U.S. 203, 1948). The school board established a program under which public school students could attend religious-instruction classes during regular school hours if their parents requested their participation. Participation was voluntary. The school district did not pay for this instruction. Classes were held in public school buildings and attendance was enforced for those students entered in the program. The Supreme Court invalidated the program on grounds that it involved the use of tax-supported public schools to spread religious beliefs.*

*In* Zorach v. Clausen, *however, the Court upheld the constitutionality of another released time program. A distinctive feature of this program was that religious instruction classes were not held on public school grounds. Writing for a six-to-three majority, Justice Douglas said: "We are a religious people whose institutions presuppose a Supreme Being. ... [This program] respects the religious nature of our people and accommodates the public service to their spiritual needs." Justice Jackson, who wrote the Court's opinion in* Barnette, *wrote a pointed dissent.*

\* \* \* \* \* \* \* \* \* \* \* \* \* \* \* \* \* \* \* \* \* \* \* \* \* \* \* \* \* \*

Mr. Justice **Douglas** delivered the opinion of the Court:

New York City has a program which permits its public schools to release students during the school day so that they may leave the school buildings and school grounds and go to religious centers for religious instruction or devotional exercises. A student is released on written request of his parents. Those not released stay in the classrooms. The churches make weekly reports to the schools, sending a list of children who have been released from public school but who have not reported for religious instruction.

This "released time" program involves neither religious instruction in public school classrooms nor the expenditure of public funds.... The case is therefore unlike *McCollum v. Board of Education* [1948] which involved a "released time" program from Illinois. In that case the classrooms were turned over to religious instructors. We accordingly held that the program violated the First Amendment which (by reason of the Fourteenth Amendment) prohibits the states from establishing religion or prohibiting its free exercise.

Appellants, who are taxpayers and residents of New York City and whose children attend its public schools, challenge the present law, contending it is in essence not different from the one involved in the *McCollum* case. Their argument ... reduces itself to this: the weight and influence of the school is put behind a program for religious instruction....

.... No one is forced to go to the religious classroom and no religious exercise or instruction is brought to the classrooms of the public schools. A student need not take religious instruction. He is left to his own desires ...

There is a suggestion that the system involves the use of coercion to get public school students into religious classrooms. There is no evidence in the record before us that supports that conclusion. The present record indeed tells us that the school authorities are neutral in this regard and do no more than release students whose parents so request....

Moreover, apart from that claim of coercion, we do not see how New York by this type of "released time" program has made a law respecting an establishment of religion within the meaning of the First Amendment. ... There cannot be the slightest doubt that the First Amendment reflects the philosophy that Church and State should be separated.... The First Amendment, however, does not say that in every and all respects there shall be a separation of Church and State. Rather, it studiously defines the manner, the specific ways, in which there shall be no concert or union or dependency one on the other.... Otherwise, ... [c]hurches could not be required to pay even property taxes. Municipalities would not be permitted to render police or fire protection to religious groups. Policemen who helped parishioners into their places of worship would violate the Constitution. Prayers in our legislative halls; the appeals to the Almighty in the messages of the Chief Executive; the proclamations making Thanksgiving Day a holiday; "so help me God" in our courtroom oaths—these and all other references to the Almighty that run through our laws, our public rituals, our ceremonies would be flouting the First Amendment. A fastidious atheist or agnostic could even object to the supplication with which the Court opens each session: "God save the United States and this Honorable Court."

We would have to press the concept of separation of Church and State to these extremes to condemn the present law on constitutional grounds. . . .

We are a religious people whose institutions presuppose a Supreme Being. We guarantee the freedom to worship as one chooses. We make room for as wide a variety of beliefs and creeds as the spiritual needs of man deem necessary. We sponsor an attitude on the part of government that shows no partiality to any one group and that lets each flourish according to the zeal of its adherents and the appeal of its dogma. When the state encourages religious instruction or cooperates with religious authorities by adjusting the schedule of public events to sectarian needs, it follows the best of our traditions. For it then respects the religious nature of our people and accommodates the public service to their spiritual needs. . . . [W]e find no constitutional requirement which makes it necessary for government to be hostile to religion and to throw its weight against efforts to widen the effective scope of religious influence. The government must be neutral when it comes to competition between sects. It may not thrust any sect on any person. It may not make a religious observance compulsory. It may not coerce anyone to attend church, to observe a religious holiday, or to take religious instruction. But it can close its doors or suspend its operations as to those who want to repair to their religious sanctuary for worship or instruction. No more than that is undertaken here. . . .

In the *McCollum* case the classrooms were used for religious instruction and the force of the public school was used to promote that instruction. Here, as we have said, the public schools do no more than accommodate their schedules to a program of outside religious instruction. We follow the *McCollum* case. But we cannot expand it to cover the present released time program unless separation of Church and State means that public institutions can make no adjustments of their schedules to accommodate the religious needs of the people. We cannot read into the Bill of Rights such a philosophy of hostility to religion.

. . . .

Mr. Justice **Jackson**, dissenting:

This released time program is founded upon a use of the State's power of coercion, which, for me, determines its unconstitutionality. Stripped of its essentials, the plan has two stages, first, that the State compel each student to yield a large part of his time for public secular education and, second, that some of it be "released" to him on condition that he devote it to sectarian religious purposes.

. . . .

As one whose children, as a matter of free choice, have been sent to privately supported Church schools, I may challenge the Court's suggestion that opposition to this plan can only be antireligious, atheistic, or agnostic. My evangelistic brethren confuse an objection to compulsion with an objection to religion. It is possible to hold a faith with enough confidence to believe that what should be rendered to God does not need to be decided and collected by Caesar.

. . . . We start down a rough road when we begin to mix compulsory public education with compulsory godliness. . . .

## 59. *Engel v. Vitale*
### 370 U.S. 421; 82 S. Ct. 1261; 8 L.Ed. 2d 601 (1962)

*The Supreme Court's decision in* Engle v. Vitale *stirred a great deal of controversy. The New York State Board of Regents recommended that school districts adopt a denominationally-neutral prayer to be said aloud by students in the presence of a teacher at the start of each school day. The prayer was brief: "Almighty god, we acknowledge our dependence on Thee, and we beg Thy blessings upon us, our parents, our teachers, and our country." The parents of ten students claimed that the program violated their religious beliefs. The Supreme Court, in a six-to-one vote, agreed and found the Regents' Prayer unconstitutional. Writing for the majority, Justice Black said,*

> . . . *[T]he constitutional prohibition against laws respecting an establishment of religion must at least mean that in this country it is no part of the business of government to compose official prayers for any group of the American people to recite as part of a religious service carried on by the government.*

*He went on to say that the government "should stay out of the business of writing or sanctioning official prayers and leave that purely religious function to the people themselves and to those the people choose to look to for religious guidance." Citing "the history of the religious traditions of our people," Justice Stewart dissented.*

*The issue remains controversial. For example, the Alabama state legislature tried to get around the* Engel *decision by passing a law that authorized public school teachers to hold a minute of silence "for meditation or voluntary prayer" at the start of the school day. In* Wallace v. Jaffree *(472 U.S. 38, 1985), the Court invalidated this practice as officially encouraging prayer.*

\* \* \* \* \* \* \* \* \* \* \* \* \* \* \* \* \* \* \* \* \* \* \* \* \* \* \* \*

Mr. Justice **Black** delivered the opinion of the Court:
The respondent Board of Education of Union Free School District No. 9, New Hyde Park, New York, acting in its official capacity under state law, directed the School District's principal to cause the following prayer to be said aloud by each class in the presence of a teacher at the beginning of each school day:

Almighty God, we acknowledge our dependence upon Thee, and we beg Thy blessings upon us, our parents, our teachers and our country.

\* \* \* \* \* \* \* \* \* \* \* \* \* \* \* \* \* \* \* \* \* \* \* \* \* \* \* \*

This daily procedure was adopted on the recommendation of the State Board of Regents, a governmental agency . . . These state officials composed the prayer which they recommended and published. . . .

Shortly after the practice of reciting the Regents' prayer was adopted by the School District, the parents of ten pupils brought this action in a New York State Court insisting that use of this official prayer in the public schools was contrary to the beliefs, religions or religious practices of both themselves and their children . . . [These parents challenged the constitutionality of . . . the use of prayer in public schools . . . on the ground that these actions . . . violate . . . the First Amendment . . . —a command which was "made applicable to the state of New York by the Fourteenth Amendment. . . .

We think that by using its public school system to encourage recitation of the Regents' prayer, the state of New York has adopted a practice wholly inconsistent with the Establishment Clause. There can . . . be no doubt that New York's program of daily classroom . . . prayer is a religious activity. . . .

The petitioners contend among other things that the state laws requiring or permitting use of the Regents' prayer must be struck down as a violation of the Establishment Clause because that prayer was composed by governmental officials as a part of a governmental program to further religious beliefs. . . . [W]e think that the constitutional prohibition against laws respecting an establishment of religion must at least mean that in this country it is no part of the business of government to compose official prayers for . . . the American people to recite as a part of a religious program carried on by government.

It is a matter of history that this very practice of establishing governmentally composed prayers for religious services was one of the reasons which caused many of our early colonists to leave England and seek religious freedom in American. . . .

It is an unfortunate fact of history that when some of the very groups which had most strenuously opposed the established Church of England found themselves sufficiently in control of colonial governments in this country to write their own prayers into law, they passed laws making their own religion the official religion of their respective colonies. Indeed, as late as the time of the Revolutionary War, there were established churches in at least eight of the thirteen former colonies and established religions in at least four of the other five. But the successful Revolution against English political domination was shortly followed by intense opposition to the practice of establishing religion by law. . . .

By the time of the adoption of the Constitution, our history shows that there was a widespread awareness among many Americans of the dangers of a union of church and state. . . . The First Amendment was added to the Constitution to stand as a guarantee that neither the power nor the prestige of the federal government would be used to control, support or influence the kinds of prayer the American people can say—that the people's religions must not be subjected to the pressures of government. . . .

. . . New York's state prayer program officially establishes the religious beliefs embodied in the Regents' prayer. . . . Neither the fact that the prayer may be denominationally neutral, nor the fact that its observance on the part of the students is voluntary can serve to free it from the limitations of the Establishment Clause . . . operative against the states by virtue of the Fourteenth Amendment. . . . The Establishment Clause, unlike the Free Exercise Clause, does not depend upon any showing of direct governmental compulsion and is violated by the enactment of laws which establish an official religion whether those laws operate directly to coerce nonobserving individuals or not. . . . When the power, prestige and financial support of government is placed behind a particular religious belief, the indirect coercive pressure upon religious minorities to conform to the prevailing officially approved religion is plain. But the purposes underlying the Establishment Clause. . . . rested on the belief that a union of government and religion tends to destroy government and to degrade religion. . . . The Establishment Clause thus stands as an expression of principle on the part of the Founders of our Constitution that religion is too personal, too sacred, too holy, to permit its "unhallowed perversion" by a civil magistrate. Another purpose of the Establishment Clause rested upon an awareness of the historical fact that governmentally established religions and religious persecutions go hand in hand. . . . It was in large part to get completely away from this sort of systematic religious persecution that the Founders brought into being our Nation, our Constitution, and our Bill of Rights with its prohibition against any governmental establishment of religion. . . .

. . . It is neither sacrilegious nor antireligious to say that each separate government in this country should stay out of the business of writing or sanctioning official prayers and leave that purely religious function to the people themselves and to those the people choose to look to for religious guidance.

. . . . To those who may subscribe to the view that because the Regents' official prayer is so brief and general there can be no danger to religious freedom in its governmental establishment, however, it may be appropriate to say in the words of James Madison, the author of the First Amendment:

> [I]t is proper to take alarm at the first experiment on our liberties. . . . Who does not see that the same authority which can establish Christianity, in exclusion of all other Religions, may establish with the same ease any particular sect of Christians, in exclusion of all other Sects? . . .

Mr. Justice **Stewart** dissenting:

. . . I think the Court has misapplied a great constitutional principle. I cannot see how an "official religion" is established by letting those who want to say a prayer say it. On the contrary, I think that to deny the wish of these school children to join in reciting this prayer is to deny them the opportunity of sharing in the spiritual heritage of our nation.

. . . . We deal here not with the establishment of a state church, which would, of course, be constitutionally impermissible, but with whether school children who want to begin their day by joining in prayer must be prohibited from doing so. Moreover, I think that the Court's task, in this as in all areas of constitutional adjudication, is not responsibly aided by the uncritical invocation of metaphors like the "wall of separation," a phrase nowhere to be found in the Constitution. What is relevant to the issue here is . . . the history of the religious traditions of our people reflected in countless practices of the institutions and officials of our government.

. . . . It was all summed up by this Court just ten years ago in a single sentence: "We are a religious people whose institutions presuppose a Supreme Being." *Zorach v. Clausen....*

### 60. *Abington School District v. Schempp*
### 374 U.S. 203; 83 S.Ct. 1560; 10 L.Ed. 2d 844 (1963)

*What if the state did not actually compose a prayer for use in public schools? Were other types of religious observances constitutionally acceptable? These kinds of questions were addressed by the Court just one year after* Engel *in* Abington School District v. Schempp.

*A Pennsylvania law provided for reading from the Bible, without comment, followed by the recitation of the Lord's Prayer and the Pledge of Allegiance at the start of the school day. The Schempps, a Unitarian family, claimed that some of the Bible readings violated their religious beliefs. The Supreme Court combined the* Schempp *case with* Murray v. Curlett. *Mrs. Murray and her son, both atheists, thought that a similar Maryland law violated their religious rights on grounds that the daily state-sponsored religious exercises put "a premium on belief as against non-belief." In both cases, then, the families claimed that the laws amounted to government endorsement of particular religious practices. In an eight-to-one decision, the Supreme Court agreed. As he did in* Engel, *Justice Stewart again dissented.*

\* \* \* \* \* \* \* \* \* \* \* \* \* \* \* \* \* \* \* \* \* \* \* \* \* \* \* \* \* \*

Mr. Justice **Clark** delivered the opinion of the Court:

Applying the Establishment Clause principles to the cases at bar we find that the States are requiring the selection and reading at the opening of the school day of verses from the Holy Bible and the recitation of the Lord's Prayer by the students in unison. These exercises are prescribed as part of the curricular activities of students who are required by law to attend school. They are held in the school buildings under the supervision and with the participation of teachers employed in those schools. The trial court ... has found that such an opening exercise is a religious ceremony and was intended by the State to be so. We agree with the trial court's finding as to the religious character of the exercises. Given that finding, the exercises and the law requiring them are in violation of the Establishment Clause.

There is no such specific finding as to the religious character of the exercises ... and the State contends ... that the program is an effort to extend its benefits to all public school children without regard to their religious belief. Included within its secular purposes, it says, are the promotion of moral values, the contradiction to the materialistic trends of our times, the perpetration of our institutions and the teaching of literature. The case came up on demurrer, of course, to a petition which alleged that the uniform practice under the rule had been to read from the King James version of the Bible and that the exercise was sectarian. The short answer . . . is that the religious character of the exercise was admitted by the State. But even if its purpose is not strictly religious, it is sought to be accomplished through readings, without comment, from the Bible. Surely the place of the Bible as an instrument of religion cannot be gainsaid, and the State's recognition of the pervading religious character of the ceremony is evident from the rule's specific permission of the alternative use of the Catholic Douay version as well as the recent amendment permitting nonattendance at the exercises. None of these factors is consistent with the contention that the Bible is here used either as an instrument for nonreligious moral inspiration or as a reference for the teaching of secular subjects.

The conclusion follows that in both cases the laws require religious exercises and such exercises are being conducted in direct violation of the rights of the appellees and petitioners. Nor are these required exercises mitigated by the fact that individual students may absent themselves upon parental request, for the fact furnishes no defense to a claim of unconstitutionality under the Establishment Clause. Further, it is no defense to urge that the religious practices here may be relatively minor encroachments on the First Amendment. The breach of neutrality that is today a trickling stream may all too soon become a raging torrent and, in the words of Madison, "it is proper to take alarm at the first experiment on our liberties."

It is insisted that unless these religious exercises are permitted a "religion of secularism" is established in the schools. We agree of course that the State may not establish a "religion of secularism" in the sense of affirmatively opposing or showing hostility to religion, thus "preferring those who believe in no religion over those who do believe." We do not agree, however, that this decision in any sense has that effect. In addition, it might well be said that one's education is not complete without a study of comparative religion or the history of religion and its relationship to the advancement of civilization. It certainly may be said that the Bible is worthy of study for its literary and historic qualities. Nothing we have said here indicates that such study of the Bible or of religion, when presented objectively as part of a secular program of education, may not be effected consistently with the First Amendment. But the exercises here do not fall into those categories. They are religious exercises, required by the States in violation of the command of the First Amendment that the Government maintain strict neutrality, neither aiding nor opposing religion.

Finally, we cannot accept that the concept of neutrality, which does not permit a State to require a religious exercise even with the consent of the majority of those affected, collides with the majority's right to free exercise of religion. While the Free Exercise Clause clearly prohibits the use of state action to deny the rights of free exercise to *anyone*, it has never meant that a majority could use the machinery of the State to practice its beliefs. . . .

The place of religion in our society is an exalted one, achieved through a long tradition of reliance on the home, the church and the inviolable citadel of the individual heart and mind. We have come to recognize through bitter experience that it is not within the power of government to invade that citadel, whether its purpose or effect be to aid or oppose, to advance or retard. In the relationship between man and religion, the State is firmly committed to a position of neutrality. Though the application of that rule requires interpretation of a delicate sort, the rule itself is clearly and concisely stated in the words of the First Amendment. . . .

Mr. Justice **Stewart**, dissenting:

. . . It is . . . a fallacious oversimplification to regard [the Establishment Clause and the Free Exercise Clause] as establishing a single constitutional standard of "separation of church and state," which can be mechanically applied in every case to delineate the boundaries between government and religion. . . .

. . . . The short of the matter is simply that the two relevant clauses of the First Amendment cannot accurately be reflected in a sterile metaphor which by its very nature may distort rather than illumine the problems involved in a particular case.

. . .

. . . [O]f paramount importance . . . is recognition of the fact that the claim advanced here in favor of Bible reading is sufficiently substantial to make simple reference to the constitutional phrase of "establishment of religion" as adequate an analysis of the cases before us as the ritualistic invocation of the nonconstitutional phrase "separation of church and state." What these cases compel, rather, is an analysis of just what the "neutrality" is which is required by the interplay of the Establishment and Free Exercise Clauses of the First Amendment, as embedded in the Fourteenth.

### 61. *Lemon v. Kurtzman*
### 403 U.S. 602; 91 S.Ct. 2105, 29 L.Ed. 2d 745 (1971)

*Parochial schools help educate children and reduce the financial strain on public schools. State legislatures sometimes try to assist paro-*

*chial schools because they know that public schools would face tremendous financial burdens if parochial schools closed for lack of funds. But how can such "parochaid" be provided without violating the Establishment Clause? Some general rules grew out of a series of cases in which the Court allowed the government to "accommodate" religious activities as long as the government does not sponsor them and does not favor one sect over another.*

*The Constitution has been read to prohibit sectarian religious instruction in the public schools. It has also been read to prohibit organized prayer in the public schools. Further, there is a general constitutionally-derived belief that public funds may not be used to support religious schools. But this latter idea has been rather flexible in application. While public monies cannot be used to aid religion, the Court has sometimes upheld publicly-financed secular programs designed to benefit parochial school children (as opposed to parochial schools).*

*For example, in* Everson v. Board of Education *(330 U.S. 1, 1947), the Supreme Court upheld the use of public funds to pay for transporting children to parochial schools as a way of getting children, "regardless of their religion, safely and expeditiously to and from accredited schools." The primary beneficiaries were the children, not religious institutions, in the Court's view. In* Zorach v. Clausen *(1952), recall that the Court upheld a released-time program in which religious instruction was provided during school hours away from public school grounds. The public schools did no more "than accommodate their schedules to a program of outside religious instruction." Distinguishing accommodation of religion from its establishment, the Court found the program constitutionally acceptable. In another related case,* Board of Education v. Allen *(392 U.S. 236, 1968), the Court upheld a program under which the state was lending textbooks in secular subjects to parochial schools. The Court ruled that, since the books were on secular subjects, they neither inhibited nor advanced religion. And since no funds actually went to the schools, the children were the primary beneficiaries of the program.*

*In* Lemon v. Kurtzman, *the Court attempted to summarize and clarify the judicial criteria employed in evaluating programs that aided parochial schools. A Pennsylvania program reimbursed parochial schools for the salaries of teachers teaching secular subjects and for secular textbooks and instructional materials. The Court rejected the program— and a similar one in Rhode Island in a companion case—by unanimous vote. Chief Justice Burger, writing for the Court, said that such aid must have a secular legislative purpose. It must have a primary effect that neither advances nor inhibits religion. And it must not lead to an "excessive government entanglement" with religion. In this case, the Court concluded that the state could not be sure that the parochial-school teachers were presenting their subjects to students in the required neutral manner unless the state continually monitored teacher performance. Such surveillance would constitute "excessive entanglement" between religious institutions and the state. Burger also found that providing state funds to purchase textbooks and other instructional materials went beyond aiding the children; it was a form of direct aid to the schools.*

*Twelve years later in* Mueller v. Allen *(465 U.S. 388, 1983), the Supreme Court upheld a Minnesota law that gave parents state income tax deductions for tuition, textbook, and transportation costs. Unlike similar programs that had been previously invalidated by the Court (see* Committee for Public Education and Religious Liberty v. Nyquist, *413 U.S. 756, 1973, and* Sloan v. Lemon, *413 U.S. 825, 1973), this tax relief was available to parents regardless of whether their children attended public or nonpublic schools. As a practical matter, however, Minnesota's public schools were tuition free so the main beneficiaries were parents whose children attended private—and usually parochial—schools. Nonetheless, the Court ruled that the Minnesota program met the conditions laid down in the* Lemon *test. Subsequently, President Reagan proposed a* **federal** *tax credit for parents who send their children to nonpublic schools. Opponents pointed to church-and-state issues, budgetary constraints, and the diversion of tax resources away from the public schools that most American children attend. Congress defeated the proposal.*

*To summarize, the Court's "benevolent neutrality" towards parochaid means that the aid will be sustained if it is secular in purpose and in effect and if it does not lead to excessive entanglement between church and state. On the other hand, the Court has disallowed religious exercises in public schools, holding that such religious instruction, prayer services, and so on violate the Establishment Clause.*

*The Court has had relatively less difficulty in upholding aid to church-affiliated colleges and universities. In* Tilton v. Richardson *(403 U.S. 672, 1971), for example, the Court upheld federal construction grants that went to church-related colleges. The grants carried the stipulation that no federally-financed building would be used for religious purposes. Chief Justice Burger's majority opinion explained that there is a difference between aid to colleges, on one hand, and primary and secondary schools, on the other:*

*. . . [C]ollege students are less impressionable and less susceptible to religious indoctrination. . . . The skepticism of the college student is not an inconsiderable barrier to any attempt . . . to subvert the con-*

*gressional objectives and limitations. Furthermore, by their very nature, college and postgraduate courses tend to limit the opportunities for sectarian influence by virtue of their own internal disciplines . . . and seek to evoke free and critical responses from . . . students.*

\* \* \* \* \* \* \* \* \* \* \* \* \* \* \* \* \* \* \* \* \* \* \* \* \* \* \* \*

Mr. Chief Justice **Burger** delivered the opinion of the Court:

[This case] raise[s] questions as to Pennsylvania . . . statutes providing state aid to church-related elementary and secondary schools. . . .

Pennsylvania has adopted a statutory program that provides financial support to nonpublic elementary and secondary schools by way of reimbursement for the cost of teachers' salaries, textbooks, and instructional materials in specified secular subjects. . . . [S]tate aid has been given to church-related educational institutions. We hold that [the] statute [is] unconstitutional.

. . . *In Everson v. Board of Education,* 330 U.S. 1 (1947), this Court upheld a state statute that reimbursed the parents of parochial school children for bus transportation expenses. . . .

. . . . Three . . . tests may be gleaned from our cases. First, the statute must have a secular legislative purpose; second, its principal or primary effect must be one that neither advances nor inhibits religion, *Board of Education v. Allen,* 392 U.S. 236, 243 (1968); finally, the statute must not foster "an excessive government entanglement with religion." [*Walz v. Tax Commission,* 387 U.S. 664, 674 (1970)].

Inquiry into the legislative purposes of the Pennsylvania . . . statute affords no basis for a conclusion that the legislative intent was to advance religion. On the contrary, the statute . . . clearly state[s] that [it is] intended to enhance the quality of the secular education in all schools covered by the compulsory attendance laws. . . . [W]e find nothing here that undermines the stated legislative intent; it must therefore be accorded appropriate deference.

. . . . [T]he cumulative impact of the entire relationship arising under the statute . . . involves excessive entanglement between government and religion.

. . . .

Our prior holdings do not call for total separation between church and state; total separation is not possible in an absolute sense. Some relationship between government and religious organizations is inevitable. . . . Fire inspections, building and zoning regulations, and state requirements under compulsory school-attendance laws are examples of necessary and permissible contacts. . . . Judicial caveats against entanglement must recognize that the line of separation, far from being a "wall," is a blurred, indistinct, and variable barrier depending on all the circumstances of a particular relationship.

This is not to suggest, however, that we are to engage in a legalistic minuet in which precise rules and forms must govern. . . . .

In order to determine whether the government entanglement with religion is excessive, we must examine the character and purposes of the institutions that are benefitted, the nature of the aid that the State provides, and the resulting relationship between the government and the religious authority. . . . Here we find . . . an impermissible degree of entanglement.

. . . .

The Pennsylvania statute . . . provides state aid to church-related schools for teachers' salaries. . . . [T]he church-related elementary and secondary schools are controlled by religious organizations, have the purpose of propagating and promoting a particular religious faith, and conduct their operations to fulfill that purpose. . . .

. . . [T]he very restrictions and surveillance necessary to ensure that teachers play a strictly nonideological role give rise the entanglements between church and state. . . . Reimbursement is not only limited to courses offered in the public schools and materials approved by state officials, but the statute excludes "any subject matter expressing religious teaching, or the morals or forms of worship of any sect." . . .

The Pennsylvania statute . . . has the further defect of providing state financial aid directly to the church-related school. . . . [S]uch programs have almost always been accompanied by varying measures of control and surveillance. . . . [T]he government's post-audit power to inspect and evaluate a church-related school's financial records and to determine which expenditures are religious and which are secular creates an intimate and continuing relationship between church and state.

. . . .

The potential for political divisiveness related to religious belief and practice is aggravated . . . by the need for continuing annual appropriations and the likelihood of larger and larger demands as costs and populations grow. . . .

. . . . We have no long history of state aid to church-related educational institutions comparable to 200 years of tax exemption for churches. Indeed, the state programs before us today represent something of an innovation. . . .

. . . . The sole question is whether state aid to these schools can be squared with the dictates of the Religion Clauses. Under our system the choice has been made that government is to be entirely excluded from the area of religious instruction and churches excluded from the affairs of government. The Constitution decrees that religion must be a private matter for the individual, the family, and the institutions of private choice, and that while some involvement and entanglement are inevitable, lines must be drawn.

## 62. Lynch v. Donnelly
### 465 U.S. 668; 104 S.Ct. 1355; 79 L.Ed. 2d 604 (1984)

*The city of Pawtucket, Rhode Island erected a Christmas display that included, among other elements, a nativity scene. Did the inclusion of this religious symbol constitute government endorsement of religious ideals? By a five-to-four vote, the Supreme Court ruled that it did not.*

*In his lead opinion, Chief Justice Burger concluded that when the entire display was viewed within the context of long-established holiday traditions, the crèche was permissible. He held that the City had a secular purpose, it was not advancing religion, and it had not become excessively entangled with religion. In dissent, Justice Brennan argued that the majority misapplied the* Lemon *test and that the inclusion of a nativity scene in the City's Christmas display puts "the government's imprimatur of approval on the particular religious beliefs exemplified by the crèche." In a separate dissenting opinion, Justice Blackmun observed that the majority did an injustice to the message of the crèche by stripping it of religious significance and equating it with all other commercial symbols and props designed to put shoppers in a money-spending mood.*

\* \* \* \* \* \* \* \* \* \* \* \* \* \* \* \* \* \* \* \* \* \* \* \* \* \* \* \* \* \* \*

Chief Justice **Burger** delivered the opinion of the Court:
.... Each year, in cooperation with the downtown retail merchants' association, the city of Pawtucket, R. I., erects a Christmas display as part of its observance of the Christmas holiday season. The display is situated in a park owned by a nonprofit organization and located in the heart of the shopping district.... The Pawtucket display comprises many of the figures and decorations traditionally associated with Christmas, including, among other things, a Santa Claus house, reindeer pulling Santa's sleigh, candy-striped poles, a Christmas tree, carolers, cutout figures representing such characters as a clown, an elephant, and a teddy bear, hundreds of colored lights, a large banner that reads, "SEASONS GREETINGS," and the crèche at issue here. All components of this display are owned by the city.
The crèche, which has been included in the display for 40 or more

years, consists of the traditional figures, including the Infant Jesus, Mary and Joseph, angels, shepherds, kings, and animals. . . .

This Court has explained that the purpose of the Establishment and Free Exercise Clauses of the First Amendment is "to prevent, as far as possible, the intrusion of either [the church or the state] into the precincts of the other." *Lemon v. Kurtzman* (1971). At the same time, however, the Court has recognized that "total separation is not possible in an absolute sense. Some relationship between government and religious organizations is inevitable." In every Establishment Clause case, we must reconcile the inescapable tension between the objective of preventing unnecessary intrusion of either the church or the state upon the other, and the reality that, as the Court has so often noted, total separation of the two is not possible.

. . . . Nor does the Constitution require complete separation of church and state; it affirmatively mandates accommodation, not merely tolerance, of all religions, and forbids hostility toward any. . . . Anything less would require the "callous indifference" we have said was never intended by the Establishment Clause. *Zorach [v. Clausen* (1952)]. Indeed, we have observed, such hostility would bring us into "war with our national tradition as embodied in the First Amendment's guaranty of the free exercise of religion." . . .

. . . . [In] 1789, [i]n the very week that Congress approved the Establishment Clause as part of the Bill of Rights for submission to the states, it enacted legislation providing for paid chaplains for the House and Senate. . . .

. . . . It would be difficult to identify a more striking example of the accommodation of religious belief intended by the Framers.

. . . .

Other examples of reference to our religious heritage are found in the statutorily prescribed national motto "In God We Trust," which Congress and the President mandated for our currency, and in the language "One nation under God," as part of the Pledge of Allegiance to the American flag. . . .

. . . . The very chamber in which oral arguments on this case were heard is decorated with a notable and permanent—not seasonal—symbol of religion: Moses with the Ten Commandments. Congress has long provided chapels in the Capitol for religious worship and meditation. . . .

This history may help explain why the Court consistently has declined to take a rigid, absolutist view of the Establishment Clause. We have refused "to construe the Religion Clauses with a literalness that would undermine the ultimate constitutional objective *as illuminated by history.*" *Waltz v. Tax Commission* (1970) (Emphasis added). In our modern, complex society, whose traditions and constitutional underpinnings rest on and encourage diversity and pluralism in all areas, an absolutist approach in applying the Establishment Clause is simplistic and has been uniformly rejected by the Court.

Rather than mechanically invalidating all governmental conduct or statutes that confer benefits or give special recognition to religion in general or to one faith—as an absolutist approach would dictate—the Court has scrutinized challenged legislation or official conduct to determine whether, in reality, it establishes a religion or religious faith. . . .

In this case, the focus of our inquiry must be on the crèche in the context of the Christmas season. . . .

The Court has invalidated legislation or governmental action on the ground that a secular purpose was lacking, but only when it has concluded there was no question that the statute or activity was motivated wholly by religious considerations. . . .

. . . . The crèche in the display depicts the historical origins of this traditional event long recognized as a National Holiday. . . .

. . . . The display is sponsored by the city to celebrate the Holiday and to depict the origins of that Holiday. These are legitimate secular purposes. . . .

. . . . We can assume . . . that the display advances religion in a sense; but our precedents plainly contemplate that on occasion some advancement of religion will result from governmental action. The Court has made it abundantly clear, however, that "not every law that confers an 'indirect' 'remote', or 'incidental' benefit upon [religion] is, for that reason alone, constitutionally invalid." [*Committee for Public Education v.*] *Nyquist* [*1973*]. . . .

We are satisfied that the city has a secular purpose for including the crèche, that the city has not impermissibly advanced religion, and that including the crèche does not create excessive entanglement between religion and government. . . .

Justice **Brennan**, with whom Justice **Marshall**, Justice **Blackmun** and Justice **Stevens** join, dissenting:

. . . . [T]he Court properly looks for guidance to the settled test announced in *Lemon v. Kurtzman* (1971). . . .

Applying the three-part test to Pawtucket's crèche, I am persuaded that the city's inclusion of the crèche in its Christmas display simply does not reflect a "clearly . . . secular purpose." . . .

The "primary effect" of including a nativity scene in the city's display is . . . to place the government's imprimatur of approval on the particular religious beliefs exemplified by the crèche. Those who believe in the message of the nativity receive the unique and exclusive benefit of public recognition and approval of their views. . . . The effect on minority religious groups, as well as on those who may reject all religion, is to convey the message that their views are not similarly worthy of public recognition nor entitled to public support. It was precisely this sort of religious chauvinism that the Establishment Clause was intended forever to prohibit. . . .

. . . [I]t is evident that Pawtucket's inclusion of a crèche as part of its annual Christmas display does pose a significant threat of fostering "excessive entanglements." . . . Jews and other non-Christian groups, prompted perhaps by the Mayor's remark that he will include a Menorah in future displays, can be expected to press government for inclusion of their symbols, and faced with such requests, government will have to become involved in accommodating the various demands. . . .

. . .

I refuse to accept the notion implicit in today's decision that non-Christians would find that the religious content of the crèche is eliminated by the fact that it appears as part of the city's otherwise secular celebration of the Christmas holiday. The nativity scene is clearly distinct in its purpose and effect from the rest of the Hodgson Park display for the simple reason that it is the only one rooted in a biblical account of Christ's birth. It is the chief symbol of the characteristically Christian belief that a divine Savior was brought into the world and that the purpose of this miraculous birth was to illuminate a path toward salvation and redemption. . . . When government appears to sponsor such religiously inspired views, we cannot say that the practice is "so separate and so indisputably marked off from the religious function' . . . that [it] may fairly be viewed as reflect[ing] a neutral posture toward religious institutions." . . . To be so excluded on religious grounds by one's elected government is an insult and an injury that, until today, could not be countenanced by the Establishment Clause.

. . . . [T]he Christmas holiday in our national culture contains both secular and sectarian elements. To say that government may recognize the holiday's traditional, secular elements of giftgiving, public festivities, and community spirit, does not mean that government may indiscriminately embrace the distinctively sectarian aspects of the holiday. . . .

. . . . Two features of . . . history are worth noting. First, at the time of the adoption of the Constitution and the Bill of Rights, there was no settled pattern of celebrating Christmas, either as a purely religious holiday or as a public event. Second, the historical evidence, such as it is, offers no uniform pattern of widespread acceptance of the holiday and indeed suggests that the development of Christmas as a public holiday is a comparatively recent phenomenon. . . .

In sum, there is no evidence whatsoever that the Framers would have expressly approved a federal celebration of the Christmas holiday including public displays of a nativity scene; . . . Nor is there any suggestion that publicly financed and supported displays of Christmas crèches are supported by a record of widespread, undeviating acceptance that extends throughout our history. Therefore, our prior decisions which relied upon concrete, specific historical evidence to support a particular practice simply have no bearing on the questions presented in this case. . . .

Justice **Blackmun**, dissenting:

Not only does the Court's resolution of this controversy make light of our precedents, but also, ironically, the majority does an injustice to the crèche and the message it manifests. . . . Before the District Court, an expert witness for the city made a . . . candid point, stating that Pawtucket's display invites people "to participate in the Christmas spirit, brotherhood, peace, and let loose with their money." The crèche has been relegated to the role of a neutral harbinger of the holiday season, useful for commercial purposes, but devoid of any inherent meaning and incapable of enhancing the religious tenor of a display of which it is an integral part. The city has its victory—but it is a Pyrrhic one indeed.

# CHAPTER 6:

# THE RIGHT OF PRIVACY

## I. EARLY ANALYSIS OF THE CONCEPT

### 63. Natural Law and the Revolutionary Generation

*One of the most hotly debated contemporary constitutional issues is the right of privacy. It includes a right to privacy from governmental intrusion, a right to marital privacy, the right to an abortion, the right to die, and other rights which have been claimed but rejected. The word "privacy" is not mentioned in the body of the Constitution, but some argue that it may be inferred from several specific Amendments in the Bill of Rights, and others think that it should be recognized as falling under the Ninth Amendment's provision that "[t]he enumeration in the Constitution of certain rights shall not be construed to deny or disparage others retained by the people." The problem with relying on the Ninth Amendment is distinguishing protected rights from false claims. The Supreme Court prefers to acknowledge rights which may be identified in 1791, when the Bill of Rights was ratified. Those who favor a more expansive definition of rights argue that the Ninth Amendment was meant to shield fundamental "natural rights" which may have been implicit in society in 1791, or that the term "retained by the people" should be used more flexibly to recognize new rights which only become evident as society changes over time.*

*The origin of rights was an especially important question for the Revolutionary generation. As Americans resisted British policies they sought to identify fundamental sources of rights to justify their actions. In addition to claiming protections guaranteed to every Englishman, they also based their claims on the theory of natural rights.*

*In the words of Thomas Jefferson's Declaration of Independence (1776): "We hold these truths to be self-evident, that all men are created equal, that they are endowed by their Creator with certain unalienable Rights, that among these are Life, Liberty, and the pursuit of Happiness." George Mason's Virginia Declaration of Rights (Reading Two, above), as well as the writings of John Locke and Rousseau, also rely on natural rights theory.*

*John Adams (1735–1826) wrote the "Dissertation on the Canon and Feudal Law" in response to the Stamp Act Crisis (1765). The edited selection which follows focuses on Adams's attempt to locate the sources of rights in his society.*

\* \* \* \* \* \* \* \* \* \* \* \* \* \* \* \* \* \* \* \* \* \* \* \* \* \* \* \* \* \* \*

The poor people ... have been much less successful than the great. They have seldom found either leisure or opportunity to form a union or exert their strength; ignorant as they were of arts and letters, they have seldom been able to frame and support a regular opposition. This, however, has been known by the great to be the temper of mankind; and they have accordingly labored, in all ages, to wrest from the populace, as they are contemptuously called, the knowledge of their rights and wrongs, and the power to assert the former or redress the latter. I say RIGHTS, for such they have, undoubtedly, antecedent to all earthly government,—RIGHTS, that cannot be repealed or restrained by human laws—RIGHTS, derived from the great Legislator of the universe.

. . .

We have been afraid to think. We have felt a reluctance to examining into the grounds of our privileges, and the extent in which we have an indisputable right to demand them, against all the power and authority on earth. . . .

. . .

... Let us study the law of nature; search into the spirit of the British constitution; read the histories of ancient ages; contemplate the great examples of Greece and Rome; set before us the conduct of our own British ancestors. ... Let us read and recollect and impress upon our souls the views and ends of our own immediate forefathers. ... Recollect the civil and religious principles and hopes and expectations which supported and carried them through all hardships. ...

. . .

... Let it be known, that British liberties are not the grant of princes or parliaments, but original rights, conditions of original contracts, coequal with prerogative, and coeval with government; that many of our rights are inherent and essential, agreed on as maxims, and established as preliminaries, even before a parliament existed. Let them search for the foundations of British laws and government in the frame of human nature, in the constitution of the intellectual and moral world. There let us see that truth, liberty, justice, and benevolence, are its everlasting basis; and if these could be removed, the superstructure is overthrown. . . .

*Source: Charles F. Adams, ed., The Works of John Adams, 10 vols. (Boston: Little Brown, 1850–56), III: 448–64.*

## 64. The Supreme Court and Natural Law

*The confirmation hearings of Judge Clarence Thomas to replace retiring Justice Thurgood Marshall on the Supreme Court in the fall of 1991 focused attention on the debate over rights under the Constitution. Earlier Judge Thomas had asserted a belief that "natural law" ought to guide judicial decision making, but at the confirmation hearings he declined to elaborate on what he meant. The issue was all but forgotten as more sensational matters dominated the hearings.*

*Citing "natural law" the Supreme Court limited the public role of women in the late nineteenth century. Justice Bradley, writing a concurring opinion holding that the state of Illinois did not violate a woman's constitutional rights by denying her a license to practice law, observed:*

> . . . the civil law, as well as nature herself, has always recognized a wide difference in the respective spheres and destinies of man and woman. . . . The paramount destiny and mission of woman are to fulfil the noble and benign offices of wife and mother. This is the law of the Creator. And the rules of civil society must be adapted to the general constitution of things. . . . (Bradwell v. Illinois, 83 U.S. (16 Wall.) 130, 1873).

*Two years later the Court refused to recognize the right of women to vote as a reasonable reading of the Fourteenth Amendment. (Minor v. Happersett, 88 U.S. (21 Wall.) 162, 1875).*

*When the Court selectively incorporated rights from the Bill of Rights against the states through the Fourteenth Amendment, it did so using the notion of "fundamental principles of liberty." Justice Cardozo argued that such rights should be "implicit in the concept of ordered liberty" and asked if they were not recognized would the " . . . hardship [be] so acute and shocking that our polity will not endure it? Does it violate those "fundamental principles of liberty and justice which lie at the base of our civil and political institutions"? (Palko v. Connecticut, 302 U.S. 319, 1937). The standard, however, was not explicit as to which principles of liberty were "fundamental" or not.*

*The following case,* Lochner v. New York, *198 U.S. 45 (1905), deals with the Court's balancing a person's fundamental "liberty" to contract labor against the state's authority to regulate labor contracts for the individual's or society's safety, health, morals, or the general welfare. The issue is whether a New York law limiting bakers' working hours is an appropriate use of the State's police powers. While* Lochner *is the heart of the Supreme Court's "substantive due process" approach which impeded state regulation of the conditions of labor in the early twentieth century, it is also an excellent example of how a higher-law has been used to influence Supreme Court decision making. The differences between the majority opinion and the dissent underscore this point.*

\* \* \* \* \* \* \* \* \* \* \* \* \* \* \* \* \* \* \* \* \* \* \* \* \* \* \* \* \* \* \*

Mr. Justice **Peckham** delivered the opinion of the Court:

The statute necessarily interferes with the right of contract between the employer and employees, concerning the number of hours in which the latter may labor in the bakery of the employer. The general right to make a contract in relation to his business is part of the liberty of the individual protected by the Fourteenth Amendment.... Under that provision no state can deprive any person of life, liberty, or property without due process of law. The right to purchase or to sell labor is part of the liberty protected by this amendment, unless there are circumstances which exclude the right. There are, however, certain powers, existing in the sovereignty of each state ... somewhat vaguely termed police powers [which] ... relate to the safety, health, morals, and general welfare of the public. Both property and liberty are held on such reasonable conditions as may be imposed by the governing power of the state in the exercise of those powers, and with such conditions the 14th Amendment was not designed to interfere....

The state, therefore, has power to prevent the individual from making certain types of contracts, and in regard to them the Federal Constitution offers no protection.... Therefore, when the state by its legislature, in the assumed exercise of its police powers, has passed an act which seriously limits the right to labor or the right of contract in regard to their means of livelihood between persons who are sui juris (both employer and employee), it becomes of great importance to determine which shall prevail,—the right of the individual to labor for such time as he may choose, or the right of the state to prevent the individual from laboring, or from entering into any contract to labor, beyond a certain time prescribed by the state....

It must, of course, be conceded that there is a limit to the valid exercise of the police power by the state.... In every case that comes before this court, therefore, where legislation of this character is concerned, and where the protection of the Federal Constitution is sought, the question necessarily arises: Is this a fair, reasonable, and appropriate exercise of the police power of the state, or is it an unreasonable, unnecessary, and arbitrary interference with the right of the individual to his personal liberty ... ?

. . .

The question whether this act is valid as a labor law, pure and simple, may be dismissed in a few words. There is no reasonable ground for interfering with the liberty of person or the right of free contract, by determining the hours of labor, in the occupation of a baker. There is no contention that bakers as a class are not equal in intelligence and capacity to men in other trades. . . , or that they are not able to assert their rights and care for themselves without the protecting arm of the state, interfering with their independence of judgment and of action. . . . Viewed in the light of a purely labor law, with no reference whatever to the question of health, we think that a law like the one before us involves neither the safety, the morals, nor the welfare, of the public, and that the interest of the public is not in the slightest degree affected by such an act. The law must be upheld, if at all, as a law pertaining to the health of . . . a baker. . . .

It is a question of which of two powers or rights shall prevail,—the power of the state to legislate or the right of the individual to liberty of person and freedom of contract. The mere assertion that the subject relates . . . to the public health, does not necessarily render the enactment valid. The act must have a more direct relation, as a means to an end, and the end itself must be appropriate and legitimate, before an act can be held to be valid which interferes with the general right of an individual to be free in his person and in his power to contract in relation to his own labor. . . .

We think the limit of police power has been reached and passed in this case. There is . . . no reasonable foundation for holding this to be necessary or appropriate as a health law to safeguard the public health, or the health of individuals who are following the trade of a baker. . . .

. . .

. . . [W]e think that such a law as this, although passed in the assumed exercise of the police power, and as relating to the public health, or the health of the employees named, is not within that power, and is invalid. The act is not, within any fair meaning of the term, a health law, but is an illegal interference with the rights of individual, both employers and employees, to make contracts regarding labor upon such terms as they may think best. . . . Statutes of the nature of that under review, limiting the hours in which grown and intelligent men may labor to earn their living, are mere meddlesome interferences with the rights of the individual, and they are not saved from condemnation by the claim that they are passed in the exercise of the police power and upon the subject of the health of the individual whose rights are interfered with, unless there be some fair ground, reasonable in and of itself, to say there is material danger to the public health, or to the health of the employees, if the hours of labor are not curtailed. . . .

. . .

. . . It seems to us that the real object and purpose were simply to regulate the hours of labor between the master and his employees (all being men, sui juris), in a private business, not dangerous in any degree to morals, or in any real and substantial degree to the health of the employees. Under such circumstances the freedom of the master and employee to contract with each other in relation to their employment, and in defining the same, cannot be prohibited or interfered with, without violating the Federal Constitution. . . .

Mr. Justice **Holmes** dissenting:

. . .

This case is decided upon an economic theory which a large part of the country does not entertain. If it were a question whether I agreed with that theory, I should desire to study it further and long before making up my mind. But I do not conceive that to be my duty, because I strongly believe that my agreement or disagreement has nothing to do with the right of a majority to embody their opinions in law. It is settled by various decisions of this court that state constitutions and state laws may regulate life in many ways which we as legislators might think injudicious, or if you like as tyrannical, as this, and which equally with this, interfere with the liberty to contract. Sunday laws and usury laws are ancient examples. A more modern one is the prohibition of lotteries. The liberty of the citizen to do as he likes so long as he does not interfere with the liberty of others to do the same, which has been a shibboleth for some well-known writers, is interfered with by school laws, by the Post Office, by every state or municipal institution which takes his money for purposes thought desirable, whether he likes it or not. The Fourteenth Amendment does not enact Mr. Herbert Spencer's Social Statics. . . . [A] constitution is not intended to embody a particular economic theory, whether of paternalism and the organic relation of the citizen to the state or of laissez faire. It is made for people of fundamentally differing views, and the accident of our finding certain opinions natural and familiar, or novel, and even shocking, ought not to conclude our judgment upon the question of whether statutes embodying them conflict with the Constitution of the United States.

General propositions do not decide concrete cases. The decision will depend on a judgment or intuition more subtle than any articulate major premise. But I think that the proposition just stated, if it is accepted, will carry us far forward to the end. For every opinion tends to become a law. I think that the word "liberty," in the Fourteenth Amendment, is perverted when it is held to prevent the natural outcome of a dominant opinion, unless it can be said that a rational and fair man necessarily would admit that the statute proposed would infringe fundamental principles as they have been understood by the traditions of our people and our law. It does not need research to show that no such sweeping condemnation can be passed upon the statute before us. A reasonable man might think it a proper measure on the score of health. Men whom I certainly could not pronounce unreasonable would uphold it as a first instalment of a general regulation of the hours of work. . . .

### 65. Justice Brandeis's Dissent in *Olmstead v. United States*
### 277 U.S. 438; 48 S.Ct. 564; 72 L.Ed. 944 (1927)

*A century ago the "right to privacy" was not clearly articulated in the law. In a seminal article, "The Right to Privacy," 4 Harvard Law Review 193 (1890), Samuel Warren and Louis D. Brandeis argued that privacy is the right to be let alone and to control the unauthorized use of one's image or private writings. The right was found in the British common law, emanating from property law and the law of libel, slander, and defamation. They did not examine the constitutional basis for privacy in this article. Justice Brandeis did so, however, in* Olmstead.

*This case involved a large scale boot-legging operation during the Prohibition era, where federal officers obtained incriminating evidence after tapping the suspect's phones. The majority held that such wiretaps did not violate the Fourth Amendment because, in the words of Chief Justice Taft: "There was no searching. There was no seizure. The evidence was secured by the use of the sense of hearing and that only." Furthermore, "[t]he reasonable view is that one who installs in his home a telephone . . . intends to project his voice to those quite outside, and that the wires beyond his house and messages while passing over them are not within the protection of the Fourth Amendment."*

*Justice Brandeis wrote a spirited dissent arguing that the Court should not adhere to a literal interpretation of the Amendment without allow-*

*ing for the impact of changes in technology. A person's expectation of privacy when using the phone must be considered. Federal statutes were later enacted which severely restricted unauthorized wiretaps and modern decisions followed Justice Brandeis's position.*

*The Fourth Amendment has not played a prominent role in the evolution of the right to privacy. In* Katz v. U.S. *(1967), discussed previously, the Court observed: "... the Fourth Amendment cannot be translated into a general constitutional "right to privacy." That Amendment protects individual privacy against certain kinds of governmental intrusion, but its protections go further, and often have nothing to do with privacy at all. But the protection of a person's* **general** *right to privacy—his right to be let alone by other people—is, like the protection of his property and of his life, left largely to the law of the individual states."*

\* \* \* \* \* \* \* \* \* \* \* \* \* \* \* \* \* \* \* \* \* \* \* \* \* \* \* \* \* \* \* \*

Mr. Justice **Brandeis**, dissenting:

... Before any of the persons now charged had been arrested or indicted, the telephones ... had been tapped by federal officers.... The type-written record of the notes of conversations overheard occupies 775 typewritten pages.... [T]he defendants objected to the admission of the evidence obtained by wire-tapping on the ground that the Government's wire-tapping constituted an unreasonable search and seizure, in violation of the Fourth Amendment; and that the use as evidence of the conversations overheard compelled the defendants to be witnesses against themselves, in violation of the Fifth Amendment.

The Government makes no attempt to defend the methods employed by its officers.... [I]t relies on the language of the Amendment; and it claims that the protection given thereby cannot properly be held to include a telephone conversation.

"We must never forget," said Mr. Chief Justice Marshall in *McCulloch v. Maryland,* ... "that it is a constitution we are expounding." Since then, this Court has repeatedly sustained the exercise of power by Congress, under various clauses of that instrument, over objects of which the Fathers could not have dreamed.... Clauses guaranteeing to the individual protection against specific abuses of power, must have a similar capacity of adaptation to a changing world....

When the Fourth and Fifth Amendments were adopted, "the form that evil had theretofore taken," had been necessarily simple. Force and violence were then the only means known to man by which a Government could directly effect self-incrimination. It could compel the individual to testify—a compulsion effected, if need be, by torture. It could secure pos-

session of his papers and other articles incident to his private life—a seizure effected, if need be, by breaking and entry. Protection against such
invasion of "the sanctities of a man's home and the privacies of life" was
provided in the Fourth and Fifth Amendments by specific language. *Boyd
v. United States,* 116 U.S. 616, 630 (1886). But "time works changes, brings
into existence new conditions and purposes." Subtler and more far-reach-
ing means of invading privacy have become available to the Government.
Discovery and invention have made it possible for the Government, by
means far more effective than stretching upon the rack, to obtain disclosure in court of what is whispered in the closet.

Moreover, "in the application of a constitution, our contemplation cannot be only of what has been but of what may be." The progress of science
in furnishing the Government with means of espionage is not likely to
stop with wire-tapping. . . .

. . . In *Ex parte Jackson,* 96 U.S. 727 (1878), it was held that a sealed
letter entrusted to the mail is protected by the Amendments. The mail is
a public service furnished by the Government. The telephone is a public
service furnished by its authority. There is, in essence, no difference between the sealed letter and the private telephone message. . . . The evil
incident to invasion of the privacy of the telephone is far greater than that
involved in tampering with the mails. Whenever a telephone line is
tapped, the privacy of the persons at both ends of the line is invaded and
all conversations between them upon any subject, and although proper,
confidential and privileged, may be overhead. Moreover, the tapping of
one man's telephone line involves the tapping of the telephone of every
other person whom he may call or who may call him. . . .

. . . The protection guaranteed by the [Fourth and Fifth] Amendments is
much broader in scope. The makers of our Constitution undertook to secure conditions favorable to the pursuit of happiness. They recognized the
significance of man's spiritual nature, of his feelings and of his intellect.
They knew that only a part of the pain, pleasure and satisfactions of life
are to be found in material things. They sought to protect Americans in
their beliefs, their thoughts, their emotions and their sensations. They
conferred, as against the Government, the right to be let alone—the most
comprehensive of rights and the right most valued by civilized men. To
protect that right, every unjustifiable intrusion by the Government upon
the privacy of the individual, whatever the means employed, must be
deemed a violation of the Fourth Amendment. And the use, as evidence
in a criminal proceeding, of facts ascertained by such intrusion must be
deemed a violation of the Fifth.

. . . Experience should teach us to be most on our guard to protect liberty when the Government's purposes are beneficent. Men born to free-

dom are naturally alert to repel invasion of their liberty by evil-minded rulers. The greatest dangers to liberty lurk in insidious encroachment by men of zeal, well-meaning but without understanding.

...As Judge Rudkin said below: "Here we are concerned with neither eavesdroppers nor thieves. Nor are we concerned with the acts of private individuals.... We are concerned only with the acts of federal agents whose powers are limited and controlled by the Constitution of the United States." The Eighteenth Amendment has not in terms empowered Congress to authorize anyone to violate the criminal laws of a State. And Congress has never purported to do so.

... The door of a court is not barred because the plaintiff has committed a crime. The confirmed criminal is as much entitled to redress as his most virtuous fellow citizen; no record of crime, however long, makes one an outlaw....

... Decency, security and liberty alike demand that government officials shall be subjected to the same rules of conduct that are commands to the citizen. In a government of laws, existence of the government will be imperilled if it fails to observe the law scrupulously. Our Government is the potent, the omnipresent teacher. For good or for ill, it teaches the whole people by its example. Crime is contagious. If the Government becomes a lawbreaker, it breeds contempt for law; it invites every man to become a law unto himself; it invites anarchy....


## II. MODERN TRENDS


### 66. Justice Harlan's Dissent in *Poe v. Ullman*
### 367 U.S. 497; 81 S.Ct. 1752; 6 L.Ed. 2d 989 (1961)

*The recognition of a constitutionally protected right to privacy took new forms after Justice Brandeis's dissent in* Olmstead. *Relying less on an expectation of privacy in the Fourth Amendment, the Court acknowledged that there were certain human rights which were protected by the Fourteenth Amendment over which a state only had limited powers. The Court decided in 1942 that an Oklahoma law sterilizing habitual criminals violated the Equal Protection Clause of the Fourteenth Amendment. After showing that the law would be used to sterilize persons committing some felonies, but would not be used against persons committing similar crimes which are excluded by the act, thus violating Equal Protection, Justice Douglas observed: "We are dealing with legislation which involves one of the basic civil rights of man. Marriage and procreation are fun-*

*damental to the very existence and survival of the race.... [One who is sterilized by the state] is forever deprived of a basic liberty."*

*The issue before the Court in* Poe v. Ullman *was whether a rarely used state statute deprived married couples of a liberty right under the Fourteenth Amendment to obtain advice from a physician on the use of contraceptives. Two married women, who had suffered physical and emotional distress because of pregnancies, applied to the federal courts for declaratory relief in the late 1950s to prevent Connecticut authorities from enforcing an 1879 law which prohibited the use of contraceptive devices and punished physicians who gave birth-control advice. The majority opinion, written by Justice Frankfurter, dismissed the appeal on the grounds that it was a non-justiciable question. That is, since the plaintiffs were not being prosecuted by the state, and because contraceptives were being sold openly in Connecticut pharmacies which suggested such prosecution unlikely, there was no legal question before the Court. In conclusion, he observed: "This Court cannot be the umpire to debates concerning harmless, empty shadows."*

*Justice Harlan wrote a strong dissent. After arguing that there was a justiciable issue before the Court, he made the following edited observations on the right to privacy.*

\* \* \* \* \* \* \* \* \* \* \* \* \* \* \* \* \* \* \* \* \* \* \* \* \* \* \* \* \*

Mr. Justice **Harlan**, dissenting:

...I consider that this Connecticut legislation,...violates the Fourteenth Amendment. I believe that a statute making it a criminal offense for *married couples* to use contraceptives is an intolerable and unjustifiable invasion of privacy in the conduct of the most intimate concerns of an individual's personal life....

...[T]he guaranties of due process, though having their roots in Magna Carta's *"Per legem terrae"* and considered as procedural safeguards "against executive usurpation and tyranny," have in this country "become bulwarks also against arbitrary legislation."

...[T]he particular enumeration of rights in the first eight Amendments which spells out the reach of Fourteenth Amendment due process, but rather, as was suggested in another context long before the adoption of that Amendment, those concepts which are considered to embrace those rights "which are...*fundamental*; which belong...to the citizens of all free governments"...for "the purposes [of securing] which men enter into society."...Again and again this Court has resisted the notion that the Fourteenth Amendment is no more than a shorthand reference to what is explicitly set out elsewhere in the Bill of Rights....

Due process has not been reduced to any formula. . . . The best that can be said is that through the course of this Court's decisions it has represented the balance which our Nation, built upon postulates of respect for the liberty of the individual, has struck between that liberty and the demands of organized society. . . .

. . . [T]he full scope of the liberty guaranteed by the Due Process Clause cannot be found in or limited by the precise terms of the specific guarantees elsewhere provided in the Constitution. This "liberty" is not a series of isolated points picked out in terms of the taking of property; the freedom of speech, press, and religion; the right to keep and bear arms; the freedom from unreasonable searches and seizures; and so on. It is a rational continuum which, broadly speaking, includes a freedom from all substantial arbitrary impositions and purposeless restraints . . . and which also recognizes, what a reasonable and sensitive judgment must, that certain interests require particularly careful scrutiny of the state needs asserted to justify their abridgment.

. . . Appellants contend that the Connecticut statute deprives them, as it unquestionably does, of a substantial measure of liberty in carrying on the most intimate of all personal relationships, and that it does so arbitrarily and without any rational, justifying purpose. The State, on the other hand, asserts that it is acting to protect the moral welfare of its citizenry, both directly, in that it considers the practice of contraception immoral in itself, and instrumentally, in that the availability of contraceptive materials tends to minimize "the disastrous consequence of dissolute action," that is fornication and adultery.

* * *

Precisely what is involved here is this: the State is asserting the right to enforce its moral judgment by intruding upon the most intimate details of the marital relation with the full power of the criminal law. Potentially, this could allow the deployment of all the incidental machinery of the criminal law, arrests, searches and seizures; inevitably, it must mean at the very least the lodging of criminal charges, a public trial, and testimony as to the *corpus delicti*. Nor could any imaginable elaboration of presumptions, testimonial privileges, or other safeguards, alleviate the necessity for testimony as to the mode and manner of the married couples' sexual relations, or at least the opportunity for the accused to make denial of the charges. In sum, the statute allows the State to enquire into, prove and punish married people for the private use of their marital intimacy. . . .

That aspect of liberty which embraces the concept of the privacy of the home receives explicit Constitutional protection at two places only. These are the Third Amendment, relating to the quartering of soldiers, and the Fourth Amendment, prohibiting unreasonable searches and seizures. . . .

It is clear, of course, that this Connecticut statute does not invade the privacy of the home in the usual sense. . . . What the statute undertakes to do, however, is to create a crime which is grossly offensive to this privacy. . . .

. . . Certainly the safeguarding of the home does not follow merely from the sanctity of property rights. The home derives its pre-eminence as the seat of family life. And the integrity of that life is something so fundamental that it has been found to draw to its protection the principles of more than one explicitly granted Constitutional right. . . .

Of this whole "private realm of family life" it is difficult to imagine what is more private or more intimate than a husband and wife's marital relations. . . .

. . . The right of privacy most manifestly is not an absolute. Thus, I would not suggest that adultery, homosexuality, fornication and incest are immune from criminal enquiry, however privately practiced. So much has been explicitly recognized in acknowledging the State's rightful concern for its people's moral welfare. . . .

## 67. *Griswold v. Connecticut*
### 381 U.S. 479; 85 S.Ct. 1678; 14 L.Ed. 2d 510 (1965)

*In this case, the constitutionality of the same Connecticut birth-control law the Court refused to review in* Poe v. Ullman *was challenged. Connecticut began to enforce the law following the opening of birth-control clinics. Estelle Griswold, the Executive Director of the Planned Parenthood League of Connecticut, was convicted for violating the statute.*

*In a seven-to-two decision, the Supreme Court ruled that the statute violated the right to privacy of husband and wife. Writing for the Court, Justice Douglas maintained that this right of privacy is suggested by the express provisions of the Bill of Rights and that it emanates from the "penumbras" surrounding specific constitutional guarantees. Douglas also made reference to the Ninth Amendment, a critically important point to three concurring justices. Justice Black, joined by Justice Stewart, dissented on the grounds that there is no explicit right to privacy to be found in the literal text of the Constitution.*

*The logic of the* Griswold *decision was applied to a Massachusetts's statute which permitted married persons, but not unmarried individuals, access to contraceptives. The Court struck this law in* Eisenstadt v. Baird *(405 U.S. 438, 1972) because it violated the Equal Protection Clause and because the legislation bore no rational relationship to the stated objectives of the law.*

\* \* \* \* \* \* \* \* \* \* \* \* \* \* \* \* \* \* \* \* \* \* \* \* \* \* \* \*

Mr. Justice **Douglas** delivered the opinion of the Court:

... Coming to the merits, we are met with a wide range of questions that implicate the Due Process Clause of the Fourteenth Amendment....

The foregoing cases suggest that specific guarantees in the Bill of Rights have penumbras, formed by emanations from those guarantees that help give them life and substance.... Various guarantees create zones of privacy. The right of association contained in the penumbra of the First Amendment is one, as we have seen. The Third Amendment in its prohibition against the quartering of soldiers "in any house" in time of peace without the consent of the owner is another facet of that privacy. The Fourth Amendment explicitly affirms the "right of the people to be secure in their persons, houses, papers, and effects, against unreasonable searches and seizures." The Fifth Amendment in its Self-Incrimination Clause enables the citizen to create a zone of privacy which government may not force him to surrender to his detriment. The Ninth Amendment provides: "The enumeration in the Constitution, of certain rights, shall not be construed to deny or disparage others retained by the people." ...

The present case, then, concerns a relationship lying within the zone of privacy created by several fundamental constitutional guarantees. And it concerns a law which, in forbidding the *use* of contraceptives rather than regulating their manufacture or sale, seeks to achieve its goals by means having a maximum destructive impact upon that relationship. Such a law cannot stand in light of the familiar principle, so often applied by this Court, that a "governmental purpose to control or prevent activities constitutionally subject to state regulation may not be achieved by means which sweep unnecessarily broadly and thereby invade the area of protected freedoms." ... Would we allow the police to search the sacred precincts of marital bedrooms for telltale signs of the use of contraceptives? The very idea is repulsive to the notions of privacy surrounding the marriage relationship.

We deal with a right of privacy older than the Bill of Rights—older than our political parties, older than our school system. Marriage is a coming together for better or for worse, hopefully enduring, and intimate to the degree of being sacred....

Mr. Justice **Goldberg**, whom the Chief Justice [**Warren**] and Mr. Justice **Brennan** join, concurring:

... To hold that a right so basic and fundamental and so deep-rooted in our society as the right of privacy in marriage may be infringed because that right is not guaranteed in so many words by the first eight amendments to the Constitution is to ignore the Ninth Amendment and to give it no effect whatsoever. Moreover, a judicial construction that this fundamental right is not protected by the Constitution because it is not mentioned in explicit terms by one of the first eight amendments or elsewhere in the Constitution would violate the Ninth Amendment, which specifically states that "[t]he enumeration in the Constitution, of certain rights, shall not be *construed* to deny or disparage others retained by the people." (Emphasis added.)

... [T]he Ninth Amendment shows a belief of the Constitution's authors that fundamental rights exist that are not expressly enumerated in the first eight amendments and an intent that the list of rights included there not be deemed exhaustive....

Mr. Justice **Black**, with whom Mr. Justice **Stewart** joins, dissented:

The Court talks about a constitutional "right of privacy" as though there is some constitutional provision or provisions forbidding any law ever to be passed which might abridge the "privacy" of individuals. But there is not....

One of the most effective ways of diluting or expanding a constitutionally guaranteed right is to substitute for the crucial word or words of a constitutional guarantee another word or words more or less flexible and more or less restricted in meaning. This fact is well illustrated by the use of the term "right of privacy" as a comprehensive substitute for the Fourth Amendment's guarantee against "unreasonable searches and seizures."...

I realize that many good and able men have eloquently spoken and written ... about the duty of the Court to keep the Constitution in tune with the times. The idea is that the Constitution must be changed from time to time and that this Court is charged with a duty to make those changes. For myself, I must with all deference reject that philosophy. The Constitution makers knew the need for change and provided for it. Amendments ... can be submitted to the people or their selected agents for ratification. The method of change was good for our Fathers, and being somewhat old-fashioned I must add it is good enough for me. And so I cannot rely on the Due Process or the Ninth Amendment or any mysterious and uncertain natural law concept as a reason for striking down this state law....

## 68. *Loving v. Virginia*
### 388 U.S. 1; 87 S.Ct. 1817; 18 L.Ed. 2d 1010 (1967)

*The Court has been especially concerned with protecting fundamental values, such as marriage and nondiscrimination, which is evident in this case dealing with a Fourteenth Amendment challenge to a statute which outlawed interracial marriages. Virginia was one of sixteen states which had miscegenation statutes on the books in the mid-1960s; fifteen states had repealed such acts over the previous fifteen years. The Lovings had been married in the District of Columbia and were convicted of violating the law of the state in which they lived. Virginia argued that the law did not violate the Equal Protection Clause of the Fourteenth Amendment because it was being applied equally to blacks and whites.*

\* \* \* \* \* \* \* \* \* \* \* \* \* \* \* \* \* \* \* \* \* \* \* \* \* \* \* \*

Mr. Chief Justice **Warren** delivered the opinion of the Court:

. . . [T]he Equal Protection Clause requires the consideration of whether the classifications drawn by any statute constitute an arbitrary and invidious discrimination. The clear and central purpose of the Fourteenth Amendment was to eliminate all official state sources of invidious racial discrimination in the States.

There can be no question but that Virginia's miscegenation statutes rest solely upon distinctions drawn according to race. . . .

There is patently no legitimate overriding purpose independent of invidious racial discrimination which justifies this classification. . . . There can be no doubt that restricting the freedom to marry solely because of racial classifications violates the central meaning of the Equal Protection Clause.

These statutes also deprive the Lovings of liberty without due process of law in violation of the Due Process Clause of the Fourteenth Amendment. The freedom to marry has long been recognized as one of the vital personal rights essential to the orderly pursuit of happiness by free men.

## 69. *Roe v. Wade*
### 410 U.S. 113; 93 S.Ct. 705; 35 L.Ed. 2d 147 (1973)

*The Court was asked eight years after deciding* Griswold *to determine if the right to privacy encompassed a woman's choice to obtain an abortion. Texas law prohibited all abortions unless they were needed to preserve the woman's life or health. Jane Doe (the pseudonym used by a Dallas woman) challenged the constitutionality of these anti-abortion statutes. Since her pregnancy was not life threatening, she was unable to obtain a legal abortion in Texas. By a seven-to-two vote, the Court ruled that the law violated her privacy right.*

*Writing for the Court, Justice Blackmun said that the Due Process Clause of the Fourteenth Amendment protects the right of privacy and this right, he added, includes a woman's qualified right to terminate her pregnancy. He observed that the state's interests must be taken into account as well. These interests include protecting the woman's health and protecting potential human life in the form of a viable fetus.*

*Blackmun reasoned that early-term abortions are relatively safe and the fetus is not yet viable. At this point, the state's interest in the matter is slight. Later-term abortions, however, pose greater risks to the women's health. Further, the possibility of fetal viability increases at these later stages. For these reasons, the state's interests become weightier during the later stages of pregnancy. In this light, Blackmun concluded that abortion decisions should be left to the woman and her physician during the first three months of pregnancy. During the second three months, the state can adopt reasonable regulations to protect maternal health and fetuses approaching viability. During the last three months, the state can regulate abortions and even prohibit them unless they are necessary to preserve the woman's life or health.*

\* \* \* \* \* \* \* \* \* \* \* \* \* \* \* \* \* \* \* \* \* \* \* \* \* \* \* \*

Mr. Justice **Blackmun** delivered the opinion of the Court:

... The principal thrust of appellant's attack on the Texas statutes is that they improperly invade a right, said to be possessed by the pregnant woman, to choose to terminate her pregnancy. Appellant would discover this right in the concept of personal "liberty" embodied in the Fourteenth Amendment's Due Process Clause; or in personal, marital, familial, and sexual privacy said to be protected by the Bill of Rights or its penumbras ... or among those rights reserved to the people by the Ninth Amendment. ...

Three reasons have been advanced to explain historically the enactment of criminal abortion laws in the 19th century and to justify their continued existence.

It has been argued occasionally that these laws were the product of a Victorian social concern to discourage illicit sexual conduct. Texas, however, does not advance this justification in the present case. ...

A second reason is concerned with abortion as a medical procedure .... Thus it has been argued that a State's real concern in enacting a criminal abortion law was to protect the pregnant woman, that is, to restrain her from submitting to a procedure that placed her life in serious jeopardy.

Modern medical techniques have altered this situation. ... Consequently, any interest of the State in protecting the woman from an inherently hazardous procedure, except when it would be equally dangerous for her to forego it, has largely disappeared. Of course, impor-

tant state interests in the area of health and medical standards do remain
.... Thus the State retains a definite interest in protecting the woman's
own health and safety when an abortion is proposed at a late stage of
pregnancy.

The third reason is the State's interest—some phrase it in terms of
duty—in protecting prenatal life. Some of the argument for this justification rests on the theory that a new human life is present from the moment
of conception. The State's interest and general obligation to protect life
then extends, it is argued, to prenatal life. Only when the life of the pregnant mother herself is at stake, balanced against the life she carries within
her, should the interest of the embryo or fetus not prevail. . . .

The Constitution does not explicitly mention any right of privacy. In a
line of decisions, however, going back perhaps as far as *Union Pacific R.
Co. v. Botsford* (1891), the Court has recognized that a right of personal
privacy, or a guarantee of certain areas or zones of privacy, does exist
under the Constitution. In varying contexts the Court or individual Justices have indeed found at least the roots of that right in the First Amendment . . . in the Fourth and Fifth Amendments . . . in the penumbras of the
Bill of Rights, . . . in the Ninth Amendment; or in the concept of liberty
guaranteed by the first section of the Fourteenth Amendment. . . . These
decisions make it clear that only personal rights that can be deemed "fundamental" or "implicit in the concept of ordered liberty," *Palko v. Connecticut* (1937), are included in this guarantee of personal privacy. They
also make it clear that the right has some extension to activities relating
to marriage . . . procreation . . . [and] contraception. . . .

This right of privacy, whether it be founded in the Fourteenth
Amendment's concept of personal liberty and restrictions upon state action, as we feel it is, or, as the District Court determined, in the Ninth
Amendment's reservation of rights to the people, is broad enough to encompass a woman's decision whether or not to terminate her pregnancy.
The detriment that the State would impose upon the pregnant woman by
denying this choice altogether is apparent. Specific and direct harm med-
ically diagnosable even in early pregnancy may be involved. Maternity, or
additional offspring, may force upon the woman a distressful life and future. Psychological harm may be imminent. Mental and physical health
may be taxed by child care. There is also the distress, for all concerned,
associated with the unwanted child. . . .

On the basis of elements such as these, appellants and some amici
argue that the woman's right is absolute and that she is entitled to terminate her pregnancy at whatever time, in whatever way, and for whatever
reason she alone chooses. With this we do not agree. . . . The Court's de-

cisions recognizing a right of privacy also acknowledge that some state regulation in areas protected by that right is appropriate. As noted above, a State may properly assert important interests in safeguarding health, in maintaining medical standards, and in protecting potential life. At some point in pregnancy, these respective interests become sufficiently compelling to sustain regulation of the factors that govern the abortion decision. The privacy right involved, therefore, cannot be said to be absolute. . . .

We therefore conclude that the right of personal privacy includes the abortion decision, but that this right is not unqualified and must be considered against state interests in regulation.

. . . Appellee argues that the State's determination to recognize and protect prenatal life from and after conception constitutes a compelling state interest. As noted above, we do not agree fully with either formulation.

### A.

The appellee and certain *amici* argue that the fetus is a "person" within the language and meaning of the Fourteenth Amendment. . . .

The Constitution does not define "person" in so many words. . . . But in nearly all these instances, the use of the word is such that it has application only postnatally. . . . [T]he word "person," as used in the Fourteenth Amendment, does not include the unborn. . . .

Texas urges that, apart from the Fourteenth Amendment, life begins at conception and is present throughout pregnancy, and that, therefore, the State has a compelling interest in protecting that life from and after conception. We need not resolve the difficult question of when life begins. When those trained in the respective disciplines of medicine, philosophy, and theology are unable to arrive at any consensus, the judiciary, at this point in the development of man's knowledge, is not in a position to speculate as to the answer.

### 70. *Maher v. Roe*
### 432 U.S. 464; 97 S.Ct. 2376; 53 L.Ed. 2d 484 (1977)

*The question before the Court in the* Maher *case was whether a state law which denied the indigent public funding for abortions, when such funds were available to pay for childbirth, was a violation of the Equal Protection Clause. The lower court held that it was and observed: "abortion and childbirth, when stripped of the sensitive moral arguments surrounding the abortion controversy, are simply two alternative methods of dealing with pregnancy." Justice Powell, writing for a 6-3 majority, found that the law did not violate equal protection and that it was consistent with the* Roe *decision. Justice Brennan, writing one of the two dissents, warned: "Until today, I had not thought the nature of the fundamental right established in* Roe *was open to question, let alone susceptible of the interpretation advanced by the Court. The fact that the Connecticut scheme may not operate as an absolute bar preventing indigent women from having abortions is not critical. What is critical is that the State had inhibited their fundamental right to make that choice free from state interference."*

\* \* \* \* \* \* \* \* \* \* \* \* \* \* \* \* \* \* \* \* \* \* \* \* \* \* \* \* \* \* \*

Mr. Justice **Powell** delivered the opinion of the Court:

. . . This case involves no discrimination against a suspect class. An indigent woman desiring an abortion does not come within the limited category of disadvantaged classes so recognized by our cases. . . . [T]his Court has never held that financial need alone identifies a suspect class for purposes of equal protection analysis. . . . Accordingly, the central question in this case is whether the regulation "impinges upon a fundamental right explicitly or implicitly protected by the Constitution." . . .

. . . The Texas law in *Roe* was a stark example of impermissible interference with the pregnant woman's decision to terminate her pregnancy. . . .

. . . *Roe* did not declare an unqualified "constitutional right to an abortion". . . . Rather, the right protects the woman from unduly burdensome interference with her freedom to decide whether to terminate her pregnancy. It implies no limitation on the authority of a State to make a value judgment favoring childbirth over abortion, and to implement that judgment by the allocation of public funds.

The Connecticut regulation before us is different in kind from the laws invalidated in our previous abortion decisions. . . . [It] places no obstacles —absolute or otherwise—in the pregnant woman's path to an abortion. An indigent woman who desires an abortion suffers no disadvantage as a consequence of Connecticut's decision to fund childbirth; she continues as before to be dependent on private sources for the service she desires. . . . We conclude that the Connecticut regulation does not impinge upon the fundamental right recognized in *Roe*.

Our conclusion signals no retreat from *Roe* or the cases applying it. . . .

The question remains whether Connecticut's regulation can be sustained under the less demanding test of rationality that applies in the absence of a suspect classification or the impingement of a fundamental right. . . .

*Roe* itself explicitly acknowledged the State's strong interest in protecting the potential life of the fetus.... The State unquestionably has a "strong and legitimate interest in encouraging normal childbirth".... Nor can there be any question that the Connecticut regulation rationally furthers that interest.... The subsidizing of costs incident to childbirth is a rational means of encouraging childbirth.

71. Justice O'Connor's Dissent in
*Akron v. Akron Center for Reproductive Health*
462 U.S. 416; 103 S.Ct. 2481; 76 L.Ed. 2d 687 (1983)

*The dilemma facing the Court after the* Maher *decision was the extent to which a state could regulate abortions within the right guaranteed by* Roe. *In* Akron v. Akron Center for Reproductive Health, *the Court faced abortion regulations that required: 1) all abortions after the first trimester were to be performed only in hospitals; 2) parents of unmarried minors would be notified before such minors could have abortions; 3) the physician was required to make certain statements to the patient, such as that "the unborn child is a human life from the moment of conception"; and 4) except in an emergency, a twenty-four hour delay would be required between signing of the consent form and the actual abortion.*

*Writing for a six-to-three majority, Justice Powell concluded that these regulations failed to advance legitimate state interests. First, noting that a second-trimester abortion "costs more than twice as much in a hospital as in a clinic" without being any safer for the woman's health, Powell concluded that the regulations unreasonably limited a woman's ability to obtain an abortion. Second, he objected that Akron should not make "a blanket determination that all minors under the age of 15 are too immature to make this decision or that an abortion may never be in the minor's best interests without parental approval." Third, he ruled that the "informed consent" requirement that certain statements be made to the pregnant woman intruded on her physician's discretion. Fourth, he found that Akron failed to show a legitimate interest in its "arbitrary and inflexible" twenty-four hour waiting period. Citing the importance of stare decisis in the law, the respect for precedent, Powell reaffirmed* Roe *and invalidated the challenged regulations.*

*Justice O'Connor, joined by Justices White and Rehnquist dissented. She assailed the logic of Justice Blackmun's majority opinion in* Roe *in the process, stating that* Akron *"graphically illustrates why the trimester approach is a completely unworkable method." In addition, she argued that the Court should defer to the legislature on matters of abortion restriction and to apply an "unduly burdensome" standard when balancing the conflicting interests between the state's interest in health and procreation and an individual's interest in obtaining an abortion.*

\* \* \* \* \* \* \* \* \* \* \* \* \* \* \* \* \* \* \* \* \* \* \* \* \* \* \* \* \*

Justice **O'Connor**, dissenting:

In *Roe v. Wade* . . . the Court held that the "right to privacy . . . founded in the Fourteenth Amendment's concept of personal liberty and restrictions upon state action . . . is broad enough to encompass a woman's decision whether or not to terminate her pregnancy." . . . [I]t is apparent from the Court's opinion that neither sound constitutional theory nor our need to decide cases based on the application of neutral principles can accommodate an analytical framework that varies according to the "stages" of pregnancy, where those stages, and their concomitant standards of review, differ according to the level of medical technology available when a particular challenge to state regulation occurs. The Court's analysis of the Akron regulations is inconsistent both with the methods of analysis employed in previous cases dealing with abortion, and with the Court's approach to fundamental rights in other areas.

Our recent cases indicate that a regulation imposed on "a lawful abortion 'is not unconstitutional unless it unduly burdens the right to seek an abortion'." *Maher v. Roe,* 432 U.S. 464, 473 (1977). . . . In my view, this "unduly burdensome" standard should be applied to the challenged regulation throughout the entire pregnancy without reference to the particular "stage" of pregnancy involved. If the particular regulation does not "unduly burde[n]" the fundamental right . . . then our evaluation of that regulation is limited to our determination that the regulation rationally relates to a legitimate state purpose. Irrespective of what we may believe is wise or prudent policy in this difficult area, "the Constitution does not constitute us as 'Platonic Guardians' nor does it vest in this Court the authority to strike down laws because they do not meet our standards of desirable social policy, 'wisdom,' or 'common sense'."

The trimester or "three-stage" approach adopted by the Court in *Roe,* and, in a modified form, employed by the Court to analyze the regulations in these cases, cannot be supported as a legitimate or useful framework for accommodating the woman's right and the State's interests. The decision of the Court today graphically illustrates why the trimester approach is a completely unworkable method of accommodating the conflicting personal rights and compelling state interests that are involved in the abortion context. . . .

It is not difficult to see that despite the Court's purported adherence to the trimester approach adopted in *Roe,* the lines drawn in that decision have now been "blurred" because of what the Court accepts as technological advancement in the safety of abortion procedure. . . .

Just as improvements in medical technology inevitably will move *forward* the point at which the State may regulate for reasons of maternal health, different technological improvements will move *backward* the point of viability at which the State may proscribe abortions except when necessary to preserve the life and health of the mother.

. . . The *Roe* framework, then, is clearly on a collision course with itself. As the medical risks of various abortion procedures decrease, the point at which the State may regulate for reasons of maternal health is moved further forward to actual childbirth. As medical science becomes better able to provide for the separate existence of the fetus, the point of viability is moved further back toward conception. Moreover, it is clear that the trimester approach violates the fundamental aspiration of judicial decision-making through the application of neutral principles "sufficiently absolute to give them roots throughout the community and continuity over significant periods of time. . . . "

. . . Even assuming that there is a fundamental right to terminate pregnancy in some situations, there is no justification in law or logic for the trimester framework adopted in *Roe* and employed by the Court today on the basis of *stare decisis.* For the reasons stated above, the framework is clearly an unworkable means of balancing the fundamental right and the compelling state interests that are indisputably implicated.

. . . The fallacy inherent in the *Roe* framework is apparent: just because the State has a compelling interest in ensuring maternal safety once an abortion may be more dangerous than childbirth, it simply does not follow that the State has *no* interest before that point that justifies state regulation to ensure that first-trimester abortions are performed as safely as possible.

The state interest in potential human life is likewise extant throughout pregnancy. In *Roe,* the Court held that although the State had an important and legitimate interest in protecting potential life, that interest could not become compelling until the point at which the fetus was viable. The difficulty, with this analysis is clear: *potential* life is no less potential in the first weeks of pregnancy than it is at viability or afterward. At any stage in pregnancy, there is the *potential* for human life. Although the Court refused to "resolve the difficult question of when life begins" . . . the Court chose the point of viability-when the fetus is *capable* of life independent of its mother-to permit the complete proscription of abortion. The choice of viability as the point at which the state interest *in potential* life becomes compelling is no less arbitrary then choosing any point before viability or any point afterward. Accordingly, I believe that the State's interest in protecting potential human life exists throughout the pregnancy.

*Roe* did not declare an unqualified 'constitutional right to an abortion'. . . . Rather, the right protects the woman from unduly burdensome interference with her freedom to decide whether to terminate her pregnancy." . . .

The "unduly burdensome" standard is particularly appropriate in the abortion context because of the *nature* and *scope* of the right that is involved. The privacy right involved in the abortion context "cannot be said to be absolute." . . .

The abortion cases demonstrate that an "undue burden" has been found for the most part in situations involving absolute obstacles or severe limitations on the abortion decision. . . .

In determining whether the State imposes an "undue burden," we must keep in mind that when we are concerned with extremely sensitive issues, such as the one involved here, "the appropriate forum for their resolution in a democracy is the legislature. We should not forget that 'legislatures are ultimate guardians of the liberties and welfare of the people in quite as great a degree as the courts'." . . .

We must always be mindful that "[t]he Constitution does not compel a state action to fine-tune its statutes so as to encourage or facilitate abortions. To the contrary, state action 'encouraging childbirth except in the most urgent circumstances' is 'rationally related to the legitimate governmental objective of protecting potential life'." . . .

. . . [T]he Akron ordinance requires that second-trimester abortions be performed in hospitals. . . .

. . . I would apply the "unduly burdensome" test and find that the hospitalization requirement does not impose an undue burden on that decision.

The Court's reliance on increased abortion costs and decreased availability is misplaced. . . .

### 72. *Webster v. Reproductive Health Services*
### 492 U.S. 490; 109 S.Ct. 3040; 106 L.Ed. 2d 410 (1989)

*In* Thornburgh v. American College of Obstetricians and Gynecologists *(476 U.S. 747, 1986), the Court once again invalidated state restrictions on abortions. This time the vote was five-to-four. The majority opinion, written by Justice Blackmun and joined by Justices Brennan, Marshall, Powell, and Stevens, found that: "The States are not free, under the guise of protecting maternal health or potential life, to intimidate women into continuing pregnancies." Justices Rehnquist and White, who dissented in* Roe v. Wade, *again dissented. They were joined by Chief Justice Burger, a member of the original* Roe *majority and Justice O'Connor.*

*As the 1980s drew to a close, speculation focused on how the Court would treat the* Roe *precedent. President Reagan, a "prolife" advocate, made four Supreme Court appointments—Chief Justice Rehnquist and Justices O'Connor, Scalia, and Kennedy. As Reagan neared the end of his presidency, only three Justices—Blackmun, Brennan, and Marshall— remained from the* Roe *majority.*

*In* Webster v. Reproductive Health Services, *the Supreme Court reviewed a Missouri law that said that human life begins at conception, prohibited the use of public facilities and employees to perform abortions not necessary to save the mother's life, proscribed the use of public funds for "encouraging or counseling" a woman to have an abortion not necessary to save her life, and required the physician to perform tests to determine if the unborn child was viable. Without overruling* Roe, *the Court* upheld *the legislation. Chief Justice Rehnquist was joined by Justices White, O'Connor, Scalia, and Kennedy in sustaining these regulations. Justices Blackmun, Brennan, Marshall, and Stevens were in the minority. Blackmun, the author of the* Roe *opinion, said: "Today,* Roe v. Wade *and the fundamental constitutional right of women to decide whether to terminate a pregnancy, survive but are not secure." He claimed that the Court's decision invited states to enact increasingly restrictive abortion laws "in order to provoke more and more test cases" in the hope of providing the Court with an opportunity to overrule* Roe *squarely and return the matter to the states. He characterized the lead opinion as "deceptive" and accused the Court of "foment[ing] disregard for the law and for our standing decisions."*

*One year after* Webster, *Justice Brennan announced his retirement and the Court lost another member of the original* Roe *majority. Judge David Souter, named by President Bush to fill the vacancy, refused to comment on the* Roe *decision at his confirmation hearings.*

*In* Rust v. Sullivan *(1991), the Court ruled that federally funded family planning clinics may be prohibited from providing any information about abortion. This case—which raised free speech as well as abortion issues—was decided by a five-to-four vote. Justice Souter was a member of the majority.*

*Justice Marshall left the Court in 1991, leaving Justice Blackmun as the sole remaining member of the original* Roe *majority. Marshall's successor, Clarence Thomas, claimed at his confirmation hearings that he had no opinion about* Roe. *As such, his treatment of the abortion question in* Planned Parenthood of Southeastern Pennsylvania v. Casey *(1992), another case involving state restrictions on abortions, attracted considerable interest.*

*Regardless of the ultimate judicial fate of* Roe v. Wade, *the legal status of abortion provides a striking illustration of the importance of changes in Court personnel.*

\* \* \* \* \* \* \* \* \* \* \* \* \* \* \* \* \* \* \* \* \* \* \* \* \* \* \* \* \*

Chief Justice **Rehnquist** delivered the opinion of the Court with respect to Parts I, II-A, II-B, and an opinion with respect to Part II-D and III, in which Justices **White** and **Kennedy** joined:

## I

The first provision [of the Statute], or preamble, contains "findings" by the state legislature that "[t]he life of each human being begins at conception," and that "unborn children have protectable interests in life, health, and well-being." ... The Act further requires that all Missouri laws be interpreted to provide unborn children with the same rights enjoyed by other persons, subject to the Federal Constitution and this Court's precedents. ... Among its other provisions, the Act requires that, prior to performing an abortion on any woman whom a physician has reason to believe is 2 or more weeks pregnant, the physician ascertain whether the fetus is viable by performing "such medical examinations and tests as are necessary to make a finding of the gestational age, weight, and lung maturity of the unborn child." ... The Act also prohibits the use of public employees and facilities to perform or assist abortions not necessary to save the mother's life, and it prohibits the use of public funds, employees, or facilities for the purpose of "encouraging or counseling" a woman to have an abortion not necessary to save her life. ...

## IIA

The Act's preamble, as noted, sets forth "findings" by the Missouri legislature that "[t]he life of each human being begins at conception," and that "[u]nborn children have protectable interests in life, health, and well-being." ...

[T]he preamble does not by its terms regulate abortion or any other aspect of appellees' medical practice. The Court has emphasized that *Roe v. Wade* "implies no limitation on the authority of a State to make a value judgment favoring childbirth over abortion." *Maher v. Roe,* 432 U.S., at

474. The preamble can be read simply to express that sort of value judgment. . . .

## IIB

. . . [The Act also] provides that "[i]t shall be unlawful for any public employee within the scope of his employment to perform or assist an abortion, not necessary to save the life of the mother," . . . [and] makes it "unlawful for any public facility to be used for the purpose of performing or assisting an abortion not necessary to save the life of the mother." . . .

As we said earlier this Term in *DeShaney v. Winnebago County Department of Social Services,* 489 U.S. (1989) " . . . our cases have recognized that the Due Process Clauses generally confer no affirmative right to government aid, even when such aid may be necessary to secure life, liberty, or property interests of which the government itself may not deprive the individual." In *Maher v. Roe, supra,* the Court upheld a Connecticut welfare regulation under which medicaid recipients received payments for medical services related to childbirth, but not for nontherapeutic abortions. The Court rejected the claim that this unequal subsidization of childbirth and abortion was impermissible under *Roe v. Wade.* . . .

## IID

. . . [T]he Missouri Act provides:

Before a physician performs an abortion on a woman he has reason to believe is carrying an unborn child of twenty or more weeks gestational age, the physician shall first determine if the unborn child is viable by using and exercising the degree of care, skill, and proficiency commonly exercised by the ordinary skillful, careful, and prudent physician engaged in similar practice under the same or similar conditions. In making this determination of viability, the physician shall perform or cause to be performed such medical examinations and tests as are necessary to make a finding of the gestational age, weight, and lung maturity of the unborn child and shall enter such findings and determination of viability in the medical record of the mother.

. . . We think the viability-testing provision makes sense only if the second sentence is read to require only those tests that are useful to making subsidiary findings as to viability. If we construe this provision to require a physician to perform those tests needed to make the three specified findings *in all circumstances,* including when the physician's reasonable professional judgment indicates that the tests would be irrelevant to determining viability or even dangerous to the mother and the fetus, the second sentence... would conflict with the first sentence's *requirement* that a physician apply his reasonable professional skill and judgment. It would also be incongruous to read this provision, especially the word "necessary," to require the performance of tests irrelevant to the expressed statutory purpose of determining viability....

The viability-testing provision of the Missouri Act is concerned with promoting the State's interest in potential human life rather than in maternal health. [It] creates what is essentially a presumption of viability at 20 weeks, which the physician must rebut with tests indicating that the fetus is not viable prior to performing an abortion. It also directs the physician's determination as to viability by specifying consideration, if feasible, of gestational age, fetal weight, and lung capacity....

We think that the doubt cast upon the Missouri statute... is not so much a flaw in the statute as it is a reflection of the fact that the rigid trimester analysis of the course of a pregnancy enunciated in *Roe* has resulted in subsequent cases... making constitutional law in this area a virtual Procrustean bed....

*Stare decisis* is a cornerstone of our legal system, but it has less power in constitutional cases, where, save for constitutional amendments, this Court is the only body able to make needed changes.... We have not refrained from reconsideration of a prior construction of the Constitution that has proved "unsound in principle and unworkable in practice."... We think the *Roe* trimester framework falls into that category.

In the first place, the rigid *Roe* framework is hardly consistent with the notion of a Constitution cast in general terms, as ours is, and usually speaking in general principles, as ours does. The key elements of the *Roe* framework—trimesters and viability—are not found in the text of the Constitution or in any place else one would expect to find a constitutional principle. Since the bounds of the inquiry are essentially indeterminate, the result has been a web of legal rules that have become increasingly intricate, resembling a code of regulations rather than a body constitutional doctrine....

In the second place, we do not see why the State's interest in protecting potential human life should come into existence only at the point of viability, and that there should therefore be a rigid line allowing state regulation after viability but prohibiting it before viability....

### III

Both appellants and the United State as *Amicus Curiae* have urged that we overrule our decision in *Roe v. Wade*.... The facts of the present case, however, differ from those at issue in *Roe*. Here, Missouri has determined that viability is the point at which its interest in potential human life must be safeguarded. In *Roe,* on the other hand, the Texas statute criminalized the performance of all abortions, except when the mother's life was at stake. This case therefore affords us no occasion to revisit the holding of Roe, which was that the Texas statute unconstitutionally infringed the right to an abortion derived from the Due Process Clause ... and we leave it undisturbed. To the extent indicated in our opinion, we would modify and narrow *Roe* and succeeding cases.

Justice **O'Connor** concurred in the judgment and in Parts I, IIA, IIB ... :

Unlike the plurality [Chief Justice Rehnquist, and Justices White and Kennedy] I do not understand these viability testing requirements to conflict with any of the Court's past decisions concerning state regulation of abortion. Therefore, there is no necessity to accept the State's invitation to reexamine the constitutional validity of *Roe v. Wade.* Where there is no need to decide a constitutional question, it is venerable principle of this Court's adjudicatory processes not to do so for "[t]he Court will not 'anticipate a question of constitutional law in advance of the necessity of deciding it.'" *Ashwander v. TVA,* 297 U.S. 288 (1936) (Brandeis J., concurring). . . . When the constitutional invalidity of a State's abortion statute actually turns on the constitutional validity of *Roe v. Wade,* there will be time enough to reexamine *Roe.* And to do so carefully. . . .

Justice **Scalia** concurred in the judgment and in Parts I, IIA, IIB. . . :

The outcome of today's case will doubtless be heralded as a triumph of judicial statesmanship. It is not that, unless it is statesmanlike needlessly to prolong this Court's self-awarded sovereignty over a field where it has little proper business since the answers to most of the cruel questions posed are political and not judicial—a sovereignty which therefore quite properly, but to the great damage of the Court, makes it the object of the sort of organized public pressure that political institutions in a democracy ought to receive.

Justice O'Connor's assertion ... that a "fundamental rule of judicial restraint" requires us to avoid reconsidering *Roe,* cannot be taken seriously. By finessing *Roe* we do not, as she suggests ... adhere to the strict and venerable rule that we should avoid" 'decid[ing] questions of a constitutional nature'." ... What is involved ... is not the rule of avoiding constitutional issues where possible, but the quite separate principle that we will not "formulate a rule of constitutional law broader than is required by the precise facts to which it is to be applied'." The latter is a sound general principle, but one often departed from when good reason exists. . . .

The real question, then, is whether there are valid reasons to go beyond the most stingy possible holding today. It seems to me there are not only valid but compelling ones. Ordinarily, speaking no more broadly than is absolutely required avoids throwing settled law into confusion; doing so today preserves a chaos that is evident to anyone who can read and count ... [O]ur retaining control, through *Roe,* of what I believe to be, and many of our citizens recognized to be, a political issue, continuously distorts the public perception of the role of this Court. We can now look forward to at least another Term with carts full of mail from the public, and streets full of demonstrators, urging us—their unelected and life-tenured judges who have been awarded those extraordinary, undemocratic characteristics precisely in order that we might follow the law despite the popular will—to follow the popular will. ...

It was an arguable question today whether ... the Missouri law contravened this Court's understanding of *Roe v. Wade,* and I would have examined *Roe* rather than examining the contravention. Given the Court's newly contracted abstemiousness, what will it take, one must wonder, to permit us to reach that fundamental question? ... It ... appears that the mansion of constitutionalized abortion-law, constructed overnight in *Roe v. Wade,* must be disassembled door-jamb by door-jamb, and never entirely brought down, no matter how wrong it may be.

Justice **Blackmun**, joined by Justices **Brennan** and **Marshall**, dissenting:

Today, *Roe v. Wade* ... and the fundamental constitutional right of women to decide whether to terminate a pregnancy, survive but are not secure. Although the Court extricates itself from this case without making a single, even incremental, change in the law of abortion, the plurality and Justice Scalia would overrule *Roe* (the first silently, the other explicitly) and would return to the States virtually unfettered authority to control the quintessentially intimate, personal, and life-directing decision whether to carry a fetus to term. ... [A] plurality of this Court implicitly invites every state legislature to enact more and more restrictive abortion regulations in order to provoke more and more test cases, in the hope that sometime down the line the Court will return the law of procreative freedom to the severe limitations that generally prevailed in this country before January 22, 1973. Never in my memory has a plurality announced a judgment of this Court that so foments disregard for the law and for our standing decisions.

Nor in my memory has a plurality gone about its business in such a deceptive fashion. ... With feigned restraint, the plurality announces that its analysis leaves *Roe* "undisturbed," albeit "modif[ied] and narrow[ed]." ... But this disclaimer it totally meaningless. The plurality opinion is filled with winks, and nods, and knowing glances to those who would do away with *Roe* explicitly, but turns a stone face to anyone in search of what the plurality conceives as the scope of a woman's right under the Due Process

Clause to terminate a pregnancy free from the coercive and brooding influence of the State. The simple truth is that *Roe* would not survive the plurality's analysis, and that the plurality provides no substitute for *Roe's* protective umbrella.

I fear for the future. I fear for the liberty and equality of the millions of women who have lived and come of age in the 16 years since *Roe* was decided. I fear for the integrity of, and public esteem for, this Court.

I dissent.

... Finally, the plurality asserts that the trimester framework cannot stand because the State's interest in potential life is compelling throughout pregnancy, not merely after viability. ... The opinion contains not one word of rationale for its view of the State's interest. This "it-is-so-because-we-say-so" jurisprudence constitutes nothing other than an attempted exercise of brute force; reason, much less persuasion, has no place.

For my own part, I remain convinced, as six other Members of this Court 16 years ago were convinced, that the *Roe* framework, and the viability standard in particular, fairly, sensibly, and effectively functions to safeguard the constitutional liberties of pregnant women while recognizing and accommodating the State's interest in potential human life. The viability line reflects the biological facts and truths of fetal development; it marks that threshold moment prior to which a fetus cannot survive separate from the woman and cannot reasonably and objectively be regarded as a subject of rights or interests distinct from, or paramount to, those of the pregnant woman. At the same time, the viability standard takes account of the undeniable fact that as the fetus evolves into its postnatal form, and as it loses its dependence on the uterine environment, the State's interest in the fetus' potential human life, and in fostering a regard for human life in general, becomes compelling. ...

## III. THE EXPANSION OF THE RIGHT TO PRIVACY

### 73. *Bowers v. Hardwick*
### 478 U.S. 186; 106 S.Ct. 2841; 92 L.Ed. 2d 140 (1986)

*The following case explores the limits of privacy. While most people would accept the notion that a "man's home is his castle," or that the marital relationship merits special respect, there is no consensus as to the outer limits of privacy. Homosexuals asserted that the right to privacy should also incorporate private consensual sexual practices between adults. They pointed out that sodomy laws had been liberalized in recent years and that some states were not enforcing existing laws.*

*A Georgia law banned sodomy. It was being enforced only against homosexuals. In this case a police officer was admitted to Hardwick's house where he saw Hardwick in another room committing sodomy with another consenting, adult male. Hardwick was arrested, but the local district attorney declined to prosecute. In an attempt to bring a test case, he sued in a federal district court seeking an injunction to restrain the State from enforcing the law, arguing that it deprived him of his rights to privacy and intimate association. The district court dismissed the suit, but a federal appeals court reversed. Georgia then requested review from the Supreme Court.*

*By a five-to-four vote, the Court upheld the statute. Justice White's lead opinion concluded that the Constitution does not provide "a fundamental right to engage in homosexual sodomy." Justice Powell provided the fifth vote in a separate concurring opinion, but he suggested that Hardwick should have raised Eighth Amendment claims—the statute authorized a court "to imprison a person for up to 20 years for a single private, consensual act of sodomy." Justice Blackmun dissented, stressing the importance of the expectation of privacy that a person enjoys in his or her home. He maintained that Justice White understated the nature of the right that was really at issue in this case. Blackmun believed that this case was about "the most comprehensive of rights and the right most valued by civilized men, namely, the right to be let alone."*

*Following his retirement from the Court, Powell acknowledged that he originally voted to strike down the statute but, in light of the fact that it had not been enforced for several decades, he switched and voted to uphold it. Reflecting upon this decision in 1990, he told a group of New York University law students, "I probably made a mistake in that one."*

\* \* \* \* \* \* \* \* \* \* \* \* \* \* \* \* \* \* \* \* \* \* \* \* \* \*

Justice **White** delivered the opinion of the Court:

This case does not require a judgment on whether laws against sodomy between consenting adults in general, or between homosexuals in particular, are wise or desirable. It raises no question about the right or propriety of state legislative decisions to repeal their laws that criminalize homosexual sodomy, or of state-court decisions invalidating those laws on state constitutional grounds. The issue presented is whether the Federal Constitution confers a fundamental right upon homosexuals to engage in sodomy and hence invalidates the laws of the many States that still make such conduct illegal and have done so for a very long time. . . .

We first register our disagreement with the Court of Appeals and with respondent that the Court's prior cases have construed the Constitution to confer a right of privacy that extends to homosexual sodomy and for all intents and purposes have decided this case. . . .

. . . We think it evident that none of the rights announced in those cases bears any resemblance to the claimed constitutional right of homosexuals to engage in acts of sodomy that is asserted in this case. No connection between family, marriage, or procreation on the one hand and homosexual activity on the other has been demonstrated. . . .

. . . [R]espondent would have us announce, as the Court of Appeals did, a fundamental right to engage in homosexual sodomy. This we are quite unwilling to do. . . .

. . . [T]he Court has sought to identify the nature of the right qualifying for heightened judicial protection. In *Palko v. Connecticut* . . . it was said that this category includes those fundamental liberties that are "implicit in the concept of ordered liberty," such that "neither liberty nor justice would exist if [they] were sacrificed." A different description of fundamental liberties appeared in *Moore v. East Cleveland* . . . where they are characterized as those liberties that are "deeply rooted in this Nation's history and tradition."

It is obvious to us that neither of these formulations would extend a fundamental right to homosexuals to engage in acts of consensual sodomy. Proscriptions against that conduct have ancient roots. . . . Sodomy was a criminal offense at common law and was forbidden by the laws of the original 13 States when they ratified the Bill of Rights. In 1868, when the Fourteenth Amendment was ratified, all but 5 of the 37 States in the Union had criminal sodomy laws. In fact, until 1961, all 50 States outlawed sodomy, and today, 24 States and the District of Columbia continue to provide criminal penalties for sodomy performed in private and between consenting adults. . . .

Nor are we inclined to take a more expansive view of our authority to discover new fundamental rights imbedded in the Due Process Clause. The Court is most vulnerable and comes nearest to illegitimacy when it deals with judge-made constitutional law having little or no cognizable roots in the language or design of the Constitution. . . .

Respondent, however, asserts that the result should be different where the homosexual conduct occurs in the privacy of the home. He relies on *Stanley v. Georgia,* 394 U.S. 557 (1969), where the Court held that the First Amendment prevents conviction for possessing and reading obscene material in the privacy of one's home. . . .

*Stanley* did protect conduct that would not have been protected outside the home, and it partially prevented the enforcement of state obscenity laws; but the decision was firmly grounded in the First Amendment. The right pressed upon us here has no similar support in the text of the Constitution, and it does not qualify for recognition under the prevailing principles for construing the Fourteenth Amendment.... Victimless crimes, such as the possession and use of illegal drugs, do not escape the law where they are committed at home.... And if respondent's submission is limited to the voluntary sexual conduct between consenting adults, it would be difficult, except by fiat, to limit the claimed right to homosexual conduct while leaving exposed to prosecution adultery, incest, and other sexual crimes even though they are committed in the home. We are unwilling to start down that road....

Justice **Blackmun**, with whom Justices **Brennan**, **Marshall**, and **Stevens** join, dissenting:

This case is no more about "a fundamental right to engage in homosexual sodomy," as the Court purports to declare, than *Stanley v. Georgia* (1969) was about a fundamental right to watch obscene movies, or *Katz v. United States* (1967) was about a fundamental right to place interstate bets from a telephone booth. Rather, this case is about "the most comprehensive of rights and the right most valued by civilized men," namely, "the right to be let alone." *Olmstead v. United States* (1928) (Brandeis, J., dissenting.)

The statute at issue ... denies individuals the right to decide for themselves whether to engage in particular forms of private, consensual sexual activity. The Court concludes that [the statute] is valid essentially because "the laws of ... many States ... still make such conduct illegal and have done so for a very long time." ... I believe we must analyze respondent's claim in the light of the values that underlie the constitutional right to privacy. If that right means anything, it means that, before Georgia can prosecute its citizens for making choices about the most intimate aspects of their lives, it must do more than assert that the choice they have made is an "abominable crime not fit to be named among Christians."

... A fair reading of the statute and of the complaint clearly reveals that the majority has distorted the question this case presents.

... [T]he Court's almost obsessive focus on homosexual activity is particularly hard to justify in light of the broad language Georgia has used.... The sex or status of the persons who engage in [sodomy] is irrelevant as a matter of state law. In fact ... the coverage of the law [was designed] to reach heterosexual as well as homosexual activity. I therefore see no basis for the Court's decision to treat this case as an "as applied" challenge to [the statute] ... solely on the grounds that it prohibits homosexual activity....

... The Court claims that its decision today merely refuses to recognize a fundamental right to engage in homosexual sodomy; what the Court really has refused to recognize is the fundamental interest all individuals have in controlling the nature of their intimate associations with others.

The behavior for which Hardwick faces prosecution occurred in his own home, a place to which the Fourth Amendment attaches special significance. . . .

. . . "The right of the people to be secure in their . . . houses," expressly guaranteed by the Fourth Amendment, is perhaps the most "textual" of the various constitutional provisions that inform our understanding of the right to privacy, and thus I cannot agree with the Court's statement that "[t]he right pressed upon us here has no . . . support in the text of the Constitution." Indeed, the right of an individual to conduct intimate relationships in the intimacy of his or her own home seems to me to be the heart of the Constitution's protection of privacy.

. . . Essentially, petitioner argues, and the Court agrees, that the fact that the acts described in [the statute] "for hundreds of years, if not thousands, have been uniformly condemned as immoral" is a sufficient reason to permit a State to ban them today. . . .

I cannot agree that either the length of time a majority has held its convictions or the passions with which it defends them can withdraw legislation from this Court's scrutiny. . . . It is precisely because the issue raised by this case touches the heart of what makes individuals what they are that we should be especially sensitive to the rights of those whose choices upset the majority.

The assertion that "traditional Judeo-Christian values proscribe" the conduct involved . . . cannot provide an adequate justification for [the statute]. That certain, but by no means all, religious groups condemn the behavior at issue gives the State no license to impose their judgments on the entire citizenry. The legitimacy of secular legislation depends instead on whether the State can advance some justification for its law beyond its conformity to religious doctrine. . . . A State can no more punish private behavior because of religious intolerance than it can punish such behavior because of racial animus. . . .

. . . Statutes banning public sexual activity are entirely consistent with protecting the individual's liberty interest in decisions concerning sexual relations: the same recognition that those decisions are intensely private which justifies protecting them from governmental interference can justify protecting individuals from unwilling exposure to the sexual activities of others. But the mere fact that intimate behavior may be punished when it takes place in public cannot dictate how States can regulate intimate behavior that occurs in intimate places. . . .

This case involves no real interference with the rights of others, for the mere knowledge that other individuals do not adhere to one's value system cannot be a legally cognizable interest . . . let alone an interest that can justify invading the houses, hearts, and minds of citizens who choose to live their lives differently.

. . . I can only hope that . . . the Court soon will reconsider its analysis and conclude that depriving individuals of the right to choose for themselves how to conduct their intimate relationships poses a far greater threat to the values most deeply rooted in our Nation's history than tolerance of nonconformity could ever do. Because I think the Court toady betrays those values, I dissent.

Justice **Stevens**, with whom Justices **Brennan** and **Marshall** join, dissenting:

. . . [A] proper analysis of its constitutionality requires consideration of two questions: First, may a State totally prohibit the described conduct by means of a neutral law applying without exception to all persons subject to its jurisdiction? If not, may the State save the Statute by announcing that it will only enforce the law against homosexuals? . . .

Society has every right to encourage its individual members to follow particular traditions in expressing affection for one another and in gratifying their personal desires. . . . But when individual married couples are isolated from observation by others, the way in which they voluntarily choose to conduct their intimate relations is a matter for them—not the State—to decide. The essential "liberty" that animated the development of the law in cases like *Griswold, Eisenstadt,* and *Carey* surely embraces the right to engage in nonreproductive, sexual conduct that others may consider offensive or immoral.

. . . [O]ur prior cases thus establish that a State may not prohibit sodomy within "the sacred precincts of marital bedrooms," *Griswold* . . . or, indeed, between unmarried heterosexual adults. *Eisenstadt.* . . . In all events, it is perfectly clear that the State of Georgia may not totally prohibit the conduct proscribed by [the statute].

The second possibility is similarly unacceptable. A policy of selective application [against homosexuals] must be supported by a neutral and legitimate interest—something more substantial than a habitual dislike for, or ignorance about, the disfavored group. Neither the State nor the Court identified any such interest in this case. . . .

### 74. *Cruzan v. Director, Missouri Department of Health*
### 497 U.S. 261; 110 S.Ct. 2841; 111 L.Ed. 2d 224 (1990)

*This case explores the question whether "privacy" includes "a right to die." The parents of a young woman, who had been in an irreversible coma since a 1983 automobile accident, argued that her right to die should be recognized and they wanted permission to remove a surgically implanted gastronomy tube, which was keeping her alive by providing her with food and water. This case is complicated by the fact that the parents were asserting a right on behalf of a daughter who had not expressed a written opinion on the issue before the accident. Her roommate testified that she said in a conversation that she would not want to live in a vegetative state. The decision makes it clear that a person's right to die may be respected only if that individual expressly stated her intention in conformity with a state's living will statute.*

*There are an estimated 10,000 patients being maintained in a persistent vegetative state today. Advocates for the severly handicapped expressed concern that if the Court recognized a right to die their right to live would be jeopardized. Others recall the 1976 Quinlan case where the New Jersey Supreme Court allowed her guardian to disconnect a respirator, in recognition of her right to refuse treatment and in anticipation that she would die without it, only to have her survive.*

\* \* \* \* \* \* \* \* \* \* \* \* \* \* \* \* \* \* \* \* \* \* \* \* \* \* \* \*

Chief Justice **Rehnquist** delivered the opinion of the Court:

[T]he [Supreme Court of Missouri] recognized a right to refuse treatment embodied in the common-law doctrine of informed consent, but expressed skepticism about the application of that doctrine in the circumstances of this case.... [It] also declined to read a broad right of privacy into the State Constitution which would "support the right of a person to refuse medical treatment in every circumstance," and expressed doubt as to whether such a right existed under the United States Constitution.... It then decided that the Missouri Living Will statute ... embodied a state policy strongly favoring the preservation of life.... The court found that Cruzan's statements to her roommate regarding her desire to live or die under certain conditions were "unreliable for the purpose of determining her intent ... and thus insufficient to support the co-guardians claim to exercise substituted judgment on Nancy's behalf." ... It rejected the argument that Cruzan's parents were entitled to order the termination of her medical treatment, concluding that "no person can assume that choice for an incompetent in the absence of the formalities required under Missouri's Living Will statutes or the clear and convincing, inherently reliable evidence absent here." ...

We granted certiorari to consider the question of whether Cruzan has a right under the United States Constitution which would require the hospital to withdraw life-sustaining treatment from her under these circumstances.

... [T]he common-law doctrine of informed consent is viewed as generally encompassing the right of a competent individual to refuse medical treatment.... State courts have available to them for decision a number of sources—state constitution, statutes, and common law—which are not available to us. In this Court, the question is simply and starkly whether the United States Constitution prohibits Missouri from choosing the rule of decision which it did. This is the first case in which we have been squarely presented with the issue of whether the United States Constitution grants what is in common parlance referred to as a "right to die." ...

The Fourteenth Amendment provides that no State shall "deprive any person of life, liberty, or property, without due process of law." The principle that a competent person has a constitutionally protected liberty interest in refusing unwanted medical treatment may be inferred from our prior decisions....

Petitioners go on to assert that an incompetent person should possess the same right in this respect as is possessed by a competent person....

The difficulty with petitioners' claim is that in a sense it begs the question: an incompetent person is not able to make an informed and voluntary choice to exercise a hypothetical right to refuse treatment or any other right. Such a "right" must be exercised for her, if at all, by some sort of surrogate.... Missouri requires that evidence of the incompetent's wishes as to the withdrawal of treatment be proved by clear and convincing evidence. The question, then, is whether the United States Constitution forbids the establishment of this procedural requirement by the State. We hold that it does not.

... The Supreme Court of Missouri held that in this case the testimony adduced at trial did not amount to clear and convincing proof of the patient's desire to have hydration and nutrition withdrawn....

... No doubt is engendered by anything in this record but that Nancy Cruzan's mother and father are loving and caring parents. If the State were required by the United States Constitution to repose a right of "substituted judgement" with anyone, the Cruzans would surely qualify. But we do not think the Due Process Clause requires the State to repose judgement on these matters with anyone but the patient herself....

Justice **Brennan**, with whom Justices **Marshall** and **Blackmun** join, dissenting:

... Because I believe that Nancy Cruzan has a fundamental right to be free of unwanted artificial nutrition and hydration, which right is not outweighed by any interests of the State, and because I find that the improperly biased procedural obstacles imposed by the Missouri Supreme Court impermissibly burden that right, I respectfully dissent. Nancy Cruzan is entitled to die with dignity.

... The question before the Court is a relatively narrow one: whether the Due Process Clause allows Missouri to require a now-incompetent patient in an irreversible persistent vegetative state to remain on life-support absent rigorously clear and convincing evidence that avoiding the treatment represents the patient's prior, express choice. . . .

. . . Missouri may constitutionally impose only those procedural requirements that serve to enhance the accuracy of a determination of Nancy Curzan's wishes or are at least consistent with an accurate determination. The Missouri "safeguard" that the Court upholds today does not meet that standard. The determination needed in this context is whether the incompetent person would choose to live in a persistent vegetative state on life-support to avoid this medical treatment. Missouri's rule of decision imposes a markedly asymmetrical evidentiary burden. Only evidence of specific statements of treatment choice made by the patient when competent is admissible to support a finding that the patient, now in a persistent vegetative state, would wish to avoid further medical treatment. . . .

The testimony of close friends and family members . . . may often be the best evidence available of what the patient's choice would be. It is they with whom the patient is most likely will have discussed such questions and they who know the patient best. . . .

. . . Missouri and this Court have displaced Nancy's own assessment of the processes associated with dying. They have discarded evidence of her will, ignored her values, and deprived her of the right to a decision as closely approximating her own choice as humanly possible. . . .

# APPENDIX A:

# THE CONSTITUTION OF
# THE UNITED STATES

## PREAMBLE

We the People of the United States, in Order to form a more perfect Union, establish Justice, insure domestic Tranquility, provide for the common defence, promote the general Welfare, and secure the Blessings of Liberty to ourselves and our Posterity, do ordain and establish this Constitution for the United States of America.

## ARTICLE I

**Section 1.** All legislative Powers herein granted shall be vested in a Congress of the United States, which shall consist of a Senate and House of Representatives.

**Section 2.** The House of Representatives shall be composed of Members chosen every second Year by the People of the several States, and the Electors in each State shall have the Qualifications requisite for Electors of the most numerous Branch of the State Legislature.

No Person shall be a Representative who shall not have attained to the age of twenty five Years, and been seven Years a Citizen of the United States, and who shall not, when elected, be an Inhabitant of that State in which he shall be chosen.

[Representatives and direct Taxes shall be apportioned among the several States which may be included within this Union, according to their respective Numbers, which shall be determined by adding to the whole Number of free Persons, including those bound to Service for a Term of Years, and excluding Indians not taxed, three fifths of all other Persons.][1] The actual Enumeration shall be made within three Years after the first Meeting of the Congress of the United States, and within every subsequent

Term of ten Years, in such Manner as they shall by Law direct. The Number of Representatives shall not exceed one for every thirty Thousand, but each State shall have at Least one Representative; and until such enumeration shall be made, the State of New Hampshire shall be entitled to chuse three, Massachusetts eight, Rhode-Island and Providence Plantations one, Connecticut five, New-York six, New Jersey four, Pennsylvania eight, Delaware one, Maryland six, Virginia ten, North Carolina five, South Carolina five, and Georgia three.

When vacancies happen in the Representation from any State, the Executive Authority thereof shall issue Writs of Election to fill such Vacancies.

The House of Representatives shall chuse their Speaker and other Officers; and shall have the sole Power of Impeachment.

**Section 3.** The Senate of the United States shall be composed of two Senators from each State, [chosen by the Legislature thereof,][2] for six Years; and each Senator shall have one Vote.

Immediately after they shall be assembled in Consequence of the first Election, they shall be divided as equally as may be into three Classes. The Seats of the Senators of the first Class shall be vacated at the Expiration of the second Year, of the second Class at the Expiration of the fourth Year, and of the third Class at the Expiration of the sixth Year, so that one third may be chosen every second Year; [and if Vacancies happen by Resignation, or otherwise, during the Recess of the Legislature of any State, the Executive thereof may make temporary Appointments until the next Meeting of the Legislature, which shall then fill such Vacancies.][3]

No Person shall be a Senator who shall not have attained to the Age of thirty Years, and been nine Years a Citizen of the United States, and who shall not, when elected, be an Inhabitant of the State for which he shall be chosen.

The Vice President of the United States shall be President of the Senate, but shall have no Vote, unless they be equally divided.

The Senate shall chuse their other Officers, and also a President pro tempore, in the Absence of the Vice President, or when he shall exercise the Office of President of the United States.

The Senate shall have the sole Power to try all Impeachments. When sitting for that Purpose, they shall be on Oath or Affirmation. When the President of the United States is tried the Chief Justice shall preside: And no Person shall be convicted without the Concurrence of two thirds of the Members present.

Judgment in Cases of Impeachment shall not extend further than to removal from Office, and disqualification to hold and enjoy any Office of honor, Trust or Profit under the United States: but the Party convicted shall nevertheless be liable and subject to Indictment, Trial, Judgment and Punishment, according to Law.

**Section 4.** The Times, Places and Manner of holding Elections for Senators and Representatives, shall be prescribed in each State by the Legislature thereof; but the Congress may at any time by Law make or alter such Regulations, except as to the Places of chusing Senators.

The Congress shall assemble at least once in every Year, and such Meeting shall [be on the first Monday in December],[4] unless they shall by Law appoint a different Day.

**Section 5.** Each House shall be the Judge of the Elections, Returns and Qualification of its own Members, and a Majority of each shall constitute a Quorum to do Business; but a smaller Number may adjourn from day to day, and may be authorized to compel the Attendance of absent Members, in such Manner, and under such Penalties as each House may provide.

Each House may determine the Rules of its Proceedings, punish its Members for disorderly Behaviour, and, with the Concurrence of two thirds, expel a Member.

Each House shall keep a Journal of its Proceedings, and from time to time publish the same, excepting such Parts as may in their Judgment require Secrecy; and the Yeas and Nays of the Members of either House on any question shall, at the Desire of one fifth of those Present, be entered on the Journal.

Neither House, during the Session of Congress, shall, without the Consent of the other, adjourn for more than three days, nor to any other Place than that in which the two Houses shall be sitting.

**Section 6.** The Senators and Representatives shall receive a Compensation for their Services, to be ascertained by Law, and paid out of the Treasury of the United States. They shall in all Cases, except Treason, Felony and Breach of the Peace, be privileged from Arrest during their Attendance at the Session of their respective Houses, and in going to and returning from the same; and for any Speech or Debate in either House, they shall not be questioned in any other Place.

No Senator or Representative shall, during the Time for which he was elected, be appointed to any civil Office under the Authority of the United States, which shall have been created, or the Emoluments whereof shall have been encreased during such time; and no Person holding any Office under the United States, shall be a Member of either House during his Continuance in Office.

**Section 7.** All Bills for raising Revenue shall originate in the House of

Representatives; but the Senate may propose or concur with amendments as on other Bills.

Every Bill which shall have passed the House of Representatives and the Senate, shall, before it become a Law, be presented to the President of the United States; If he approve he shall sign it, but if not he shall return it, with his Objections to that House in which it shall have originated, who shall enter the Objections at large on their Journal, and proceed to reconsider it. If after such Reconsideration two thirds of that House shall agree to pass the Bill, it shall be sent, together with the Objections, to the other House, by which it shall likewise be reconsidered, and if approved by two thirds of that House, it shall become a Law. But in all such Cases the Votes of both Houses shall be determined by yeas and Nays, and the Names of the Persons voting for and against the Bill shall be entered on the Journal of each House respectively. If any Bill shall not be returned by the President within ten Days (Sunday excepted) after it shall have been presented to him, the Same shall be a Law, in like Manner as if he had signed it, unless the Congress by their Adjournment prevent its Return, in which Case it shall not be a Law.

Every Order, Resolution, or Vote to which the Concurrence of the Senate and House of Representatives may be necessary (except on a question of Adjournment) shall be presented to the President of the United States; and before the Same shall take Effect, shall be approved by him, or being disapproved by him, shall be repassed by two thirds of the Senate and House of Representatives, according to the Rules and Limitations prescribed in the Case of a Bill.

**Section 8.** The Congress shall have Power To lay and collect Taxes, Duties, Imposts and Excises, to pay the Debts and provide for the common Defence and general Welfare of the United States; but all Duties, Imposts and Excises shall be uniform throughout the United States;

To borrow Money on the credit of the United States;

To regulate Commerce with foreign Nations, and among the several States, and with the Indian Tribes;

To establish an uniform Rule of Naturalization, and uniform Laws on the subject of Bankruptcies throughout the United States;

To coin Money, regulate the Value thereof, and of foreign Coin, and fix the Standard of Weights and Measures;

To provide for the Punishment of counterfeiting the Securities and current Coin of the United States;

To establish Post Offices and post Roads;

To promote the Progress of Science and useful Arts, by securing for limited Times to Authors and Inventors the exclusive Right to their respective Writings and Discoveries;

To constitute Tribunals inferior to the supreme Court;

To define and punish Piracies and Felonies commited on the high Seas, and Offences against the Law of Nations;

To declare War, grant Letters of Marque and Reprisal, and make Rules concerning Captures on Land and Water;

To raise and support Armies, but no Appropriation of Money to that Use shall be for a longer Term than two Years;

To provide and maintain a Navy;

To make Rules for the Government and Regulation of the land and naval Forces;

To provide for calling forth the Militia to execute the Laws of the Union, suppress Insurrections and repel Invasions;

To provide for organizing, arming, and disciplining, the Militia, and for governing such Part of them as may be employed in the Service of the United States, reserving to the States respectively, the Appointment of the Officers, and the Authority of training the Militia according to the discipline prescribed by Congress;

To exercise exclusive Legislation in all Cases whatsoever, over such District (not exceeding ten Miles square) as may, by Cession of Particular States, and the Acceptance of Congress, become the Seat of the Government of the United States, and to exercise like Authority over all Places purchased by the Consent of the Legislature of the State in which the Same shall be, for the Erection of Forts, Magazines, Arsenals, dock-Yards, and other needful Buildings;—And

To make all Laws which shall be necessary and proper for carrying into Execution the foregoing Powers, and all other Powers vested by this Constitution in the Government of the United States, or in any Department or Officer thereof.

**Section 9.** The Migration or Importation of such Persons as any of the States now existing shall think proper to admit, shall not be prohibited by the Congress prior to the Year one thousand eight hundred and eight, but a Tax or duty may be imposed on such Importation, not exceeding ten dollars for each Person.

The Privilege of the Writ of Habeas Corpus shall not be suspended, unless when in Cases of Rebellion or Invasion the public Safety may require it.

No Bill of Attainder or ex post facto Law shall be passed.

No capitation, or other direct, Tax shall be laid, unless in Proportion to the Census of Enumeration herein before directed to be taken.[5]

No Tax or Duty shall be laid on Articles exported from any State.

No Preference shall be given by any Regulation of Commerce or Revenue to the Ports of one State over those of another; nor shall Vessels bound to, or from, one State, be obliged to enter, clear or pay Duties in another.

No Money shall be drawn from the Treasury, but in Consequence of Appropriations made by Law; and a regular Statement and Account of the Receipts and Expenditures of all public Money shall be published from time to time.

No Title of Nobility shall be granted by the United States; And no Person holding any Office of Profit or Trust under them, shall, without the Consent of the Congress, accept of any present, Emolument, Office, or Title, of any kind whatever, from any King, Prince or foreign State.

**Section 10.** No State shall enter into any Treaty, Alliance, or Confederation; grant Letters of Marque and Reprisal; coin Money; emit Bills of Credit; make any Thing but gold and silver Coin a Tender in Payment of Debts; pass any Bill of Attainder, ex post facto Law, or Law impairing the Obligation of Contracts or grant any Title of Nobility.

No State shall, without the Consent of the Congress, lay any Imposts or Duties on Imports or Exports, except what may be absolutely necessary for executing it's inspection Laws; and the net Produce of all Duties and Imposts, laid by any State on Imports or Exports, shall be for the Use of the Treasury of the United States; and all such Laws shall be subject to the Revision and Controul of the Congress.

No State shall, without the Consent of Congress, lay any Duty of Tonnage, keep Troops, or Ships of War in time of Peace, enter into any Agreement or Compact with another State, or with a foreign Power, or engage in War, unless actually invaded, or in such imminent Danger as will not admit of delay.

## ARTICLE II

**Section 1.** The executive Power shall be vested in a President of the United States of America. He shall hold his Office during the Term of four Years, and, together with the Vice President, chosen for the same Term, be elected, as follows.

Each State shall appoint, in such Manner as the Legislature thereof may direct, a Number of Electors, equal to the whole Number of Senators and Representatives to which the State may be entitled in the Congress; but no Senator or Representative, or Person holding an Office of Trust or Profit under the United States, shall be appointed an Elector.

[The Electors shall meet in their respective States, and vote by Ballot for two Persons, of whom one at least shall not be an Inhabitant of the same State with themselves. And they shall make a List of all the Persons voted for, and of the Number of Votes for each; which List they shall sign and certify, and transmit sealed to the Seat of the Government of the United States, directed to the President of the Senate. The President of the Senate shall, in the Presence of the Senate and House of Representatives, open all the Certificates, and the Votes shall then be counted. The Person having the greatest Number of Votes shall be the President, if such Number be a Majority of the whole Number of Electors appointed; and if there be more than one who have such Majority, and have an equal Number of Votes, then the House of Representatives shall immediately chuse by Ballot one of them for President; and if no Person have a Majority, then from the five highest on the list the said House shall in like Manner chuse the President. But in chusing the President, the Votes shall be taken by States, the Representation from each State having one Vote; a quorum for this Purpose shall consist of a Member or Members from two thirds of the States, and a Majority of all the States shall be necessary to a Choice. In every Case, after the Choice of the President, the Person having the greatest Number of Votes of the Electors shall be the Vice President. But if there should remain two or more who have equal Votes, the Senate shall chuse from them by Ballot the Vice President.][6]

The Congress may determine the Time of chusing the Electors, and the Day on which they shall give their Votes; which Day shall be the same throughout the United States.

No Person except a nautral born Citizen, or a Citizen of the United States, at the time of the Adoption of this Constitution, shall be eligible to the Office of President; neither shall any Person be eligible to that Office who shall not have attained to the Age of thirty five Years, and been fourteen Years a Resident within the United States.

In Case of the Removal of the President from Office, or of his Death, Resignation, or Inability to discharge the Powers and Duties of the said Office,[7] the Same shall devolve on the Vice President, and the Congress may by Law provide for the Case of Removal, Death, Resignation or Inability, both of the President and Vice President, declaring what Officer shall then act as President, and such Officer shall act accordingly, until the Disability be removed, or a President shall be elected.

The President shall, at stated Times, receive for his Services, a Compensation, which shall neither be encreased nor diminished during the Period for which he shall have been elected, and he shall not receive within that Period any other Emolument from the United States, or any of them.

Before he enter on the Execution of his Office, he shall take the following Oath or Affirmation:—"I do solemnly swear (or affirm) that I will faithfully execute the Office of President of the United States, and will to the best of my Ability, preserve, protect and defend the Constitution of the United States."

**Section 2.** The President shall be Commander in Chief of the Army and

Navy of the United States, and of the Militia of the several States, when called into the actual Service of the United States; he may require the Opinion, in writing, of the principal Officer in each of the executive Departments, upon any Subject relating to the Duties of their respective Offices, and he shall have Power to grant Reprieves and Pardons for Offenses against the United States, except in Cases of Impeachment.

He shall have Power, by and with the Advice and Consent of the Senate, to make Treaties, provided two thirds of the Senators present concur; and he shall nominate, and by and with the Advice and Consent of the Senate, shall appoint Ambassadors, other public Ministers and Consuls, Judges of the supreme Court, and all other Officers of the United States, whose Appointments are not herein otherwise provided for, and which shall be established by Law: but the Congress may by Law vest the Appointment of such inferior Officers, as they think proper, in the President alone, in the Courts of Law, or in the Heads of Departments.

The President shall have Power to fill up all Vacancies that may happen during the Recess of the Senate, by granting Commissions which shall expire at the End of their next Session.

**Section 3.** He shall from time to time give to the Congress Information of the State of the Union, and recommend to their Consideration such Measures as he shall judge necessary and expedient; he may, on extraordinary Occasions, convene both Houses, or either of them, and in Case of Disagreement between them, with Respect to the Time of Adjournment, he may adjourn them to such Time as he shall think proper; he shall receive Ambassadors and other public Ministers; he shall take Care that the Laws be faithfully executed, and shall Commission all the Officers of the United States.

**Section 4.** The President, Vice President and all Civil Officers of the United States, shall be removed from office on Impeachment for, and Conviction of, Treason, Bribery, or other high Crimes and Misdemeanors.

## ARTICLE III

**Section 1.** The judicial Power of the United States, shall be vested in one supreme Court, and in such inferior Courts as the Congress may from time to time ordain and establish. The Judges, both of the supreme and inferior Courts, shall hold their Offices during good Behaviour, and shall, at stated Times, receive for their Services, a Compensation, which shall not be diminished during their Continuance in Office.

**Section 2.** The judicial Power shall extend to all Cases, in Law and Equity, arising under this Constitution, the Laws of the United States, and

Treaties made, or which shall be made, under their Authority;—to all Cases affecting Ambassadors, other public Ministers and Consuls;—to all Cases of admiralty and maritime Jurisdiction;—to Controversies to which the United States shall be a Party;—to Controversies between two or more States;—between a State and Citizens of another State;[8]—between Citizens of different States;—between Citizens of the same State claiming Lands under Grants of different States, and between a State, or the Citizens thereof, and foreign States, Citizens or Subjects.[8]

In all Cases affecting Ambassadors, other public Ministers and Consuls, and those in which a State shall be Party, the supreme Court shall have original Jurisdiction. In all the other Cases before mentioned, the supreme Court shall have appellate Jurisdiction, both as to Law and Fact, with such Exceptions, and under such Regulations as the Congress shall make.

The Trial of all Crimes, except in cases of Impeachment, shall be by Jury; and such Trial shall be held in the State where the said Crimes shall have been committed; but when not committed within any State, the Trial shall be at such Place or Places as the Congress may by Law have directed.

**Section 3.** Treason against the United States, shall consist only in levying War against them, or in adhering to their Enemies, giving them Aid and Comfort. No Person shall be convicted of Treason unless on the Testimony of two Witnesses to the same overt Act, or on Confession in open Court.

The Congress shall have Power to declare the Punishment of Treason, but no Attainder of Treason shall work Corruption of Blood, or Forfeiture except during the Life of the Person attainted.

## ARTICLE IV

**Section 1.** Full Faith and Credit shall be given in each State to the public Acts, Records, and judicial Proceedings of every other State. And the Congress may by general Laws prescribe the Manner in which such Acts, Records and Proceedings shall be proved, and the Effect thereof.

**Section 2.** The Citizens of each State shall be entitled to all Privileges and Immunities of Citizens in the several States.

A Person charged in any State with Treason, Felony, or other Crime, who shall flee from Justice, and be found in another State, shall on Demand of the executive Authority of the State from which he fled, be delivered up, to be removed to the State having Jurisdiction of the Crime.

[No Person held to Service or Labour in one State, under the Laws thereof, escaping into another, shall, in Consequence of any Law or Regulation therein, be discharged from such Service or Labour, but shall be delivered up on Claim of the Party to whom such Service or Labour may be due.]⁹

**Section 3.** New States may be admitted by the Congress into this Union; but no new State shall be formed or erected within the Jurisdiction of any other State; nor any State be formed by the Junction of two or more States, or Parts of States, without the Consent of the Legislatures of the States concerned as well as of the Congress.

The Congress shall have Power to dispose of and make all needful Rules and Regulations respecting the Territory or other Property belonging to the United States; and nothing in this Constitution shall be so construed as to Prejudice any Claims of the United States, or of any particular State.

**Section 4.** The United States shall guarantee to every State in this Union a Republican Form of Government, and shall protect each of them against Invasion; and on Application of the Legislature, or of the Executive (when the Legislature cannot be convened) against domestic Violence.

## ARTICLE V

The Congress, whenever two thirds of both Houses shall deem it necessary, shall propose Amendments to this Constitution, or, on the Application of the Legislatures of two thirds of the several States, shall call a Convention for proposing Amendments, which, in either Case, shall be valid to all Intents and Purposes, as Part of this Constitution, when ratified by the Legislatures of three fourths of the several States, or by Conventions in three fourths thereof, as the one or the other Mode of Ratification may be proposed by the Congress; Provided [that no Amendment which may be made prior to the Year One thousand eight hundred and eight shall in any Manner affect the first and fourth Clauses in the Ninth Section of the first Article; and]¹⁰ that no State, without its Consent, shall be deprived of its equal Suffrage in the Senate.

## ARTICLE VI

All Debts contracted and Engagements entered into, before the Adoption of this Constitution, shall be as valid against the United States under this Constitution, as under the Confederation.

This Constitution, and the Laws of the United States which shall be made in Pursuance thereof; and all Treaties made, or which shall be made, under the Authority of the United States, shall be the supreme Law of the Land; and the Judges in every State shall be bound thereby, any Thing in the Constitution or Laws of any State to the Contrary notwithstanding.

The Senators and Representatives before mentioned, and the Members of the several State Legislatures, and all executive and judicial Officers, both of the United States and of the several States, shall be bound by Oath or Affirmation, to support this Constitution; but no religious Test shall ever be required as a Qualification to any Office or public Trust under the United States.

## ARTICLE VII

The Ratification of the Conventions of nine States, shall be sufficient for the Establishment of this Constitution between the States so ratifying the Same. Done in Convention by the Unanimous Consent of the States present the Seventeenth Day of September in the Year of our Lord one thousand seven hundred and Eighty seven and of the Independence of the United States of America the Twelfth In witness whereof We have hereunto subscribed our Names, George Washington, President and deputy from Virginia.

| | |
|---|---|
| New Hampshire: | John Langdon, Nicholas Gilman. |
| Massachusetts: | Nathaniel Gorham, Rufus King. |
| Connecticut: | William Samuel Johnson, Roger Sherman. |
| New York: | Alexander Hamilton. |
| New Jersey: | William Livingston, David Brearley, William Paterson, Jonathan Dayton. |
| Pennsylvania: | Benjamin Franklin, Thomas Mifflin, Robert Morris, George Clymer, Thomas FitzSimons, Jared Ingersoll, James Wilson, Gouverneur Morris. |

| Delaware: | George Read, |
| | Gunning Bedford Jr., |
| | John Dickinson, |
| | Richard Bassett, |
| | Jacob Broom. |
| Maryland: | James McHenry, |
| | Daniel of St. Thomas Jenifer, |
| | Daniel Carroll. |
| Virginia: | John Blair, |
| | James Madison Jr. |
| North Carolina: | William Blount, |
| | Richard Dobbs Spaight, |
| | Hugh Williamson. |
| South Carolina: | John Rutledge, |
| | Charles Cotesworth Pinckney, |
| | Charles Pinckney, |
| | Pierce Butler. |
| Georgia: | William Few, |
| | Abraham Baldwin. |

[The language of the original Constitution, not including the Amendments, was adopted by a convention of the states on Sept. 17, 1787, and was subsequently ratified by the states on the following dates: Delaware, Dec. 7, 1787; Pennsylvania, Dec. 12, 1787; New Jersey, Dec. 18, 1787; Georgia, Jan. 2, 1788; Connecticut, Jan. 9, 1788; Massachusetts, Feb. 6, 1788; Maryland, April 28, 1788; South Carolina, May 23, 1788; New Hampshire, June 21, 1788.

Ratification was completed on June 21, 1788.

The Constitution subsequently was ratified by Virginia, June 25, 1788; New York, July 26, 1788; North Carolina, Nov. 21, 1789; Rhode Island, May 29, 1790; and Vermont, Jan. 10, 1791.]

# AMENDMENTS

## Amendment I
*(First ten amendments ratified Dec. 15, 1791.)*

Congress shall make no law respecting an establishment of religion, or prohibiting the free exercise thereof; or abridging the freedom of speech, or of the press; or the right of the people peaceably to assemble, and to petition the Government for a redress of grievances.

## Amendment II

A well regulated Militia, being necessary to the security of a free State, the right of the people to keep and bear Arms, shall not be infringed.

## Amendment III

No Soldier shall, in time of peace be quartered in any house, without the consent of the Owner, nor in time of war, but in a manner to be prescribed by law.

## Amendment IV

The right of the people to be secure in their persons, houses, papers, and effects, against unreasonable searches and seizures, shall not be violated, and no Warrants shall issue, but upon probable cause, supported by Oath or affirmation, and particularly describing the place to be searched, and the persons or things to be seized.

## Amendment V

No person shall be held to answer for a capital, or otherwise infamous crime, unless on a presentment or indictment of a Grand Jury, except in cases arising in the land or naval forces, or in the Militia, when in actual service in time of War or public danger; nor shall any person be subject for the same offence to be twice put in jeopardy of life or limb; nor shall be compelled in any criminal case to be a witness against himself, nor be deprived of life, liberty, or property, without due process of law; nor shall private property be taken for public use, without just compensation.

## Amendment VI

In all criminal prosecutions, the accused shall enjoy the right to a speedy and public trial, by an impartial jury of the State and district wherein the crime shall have been committed, which district shall have been previously ascertained by law, and to be informed of the nature and cause of the accusation; to be confronted with the witnesses against him; to have compulsory process for obtaining witnesses in his favor, and to have the Assistance of Counsel for his defence.

## Amendment VII

In Suits at common law, where the value in controversy shall exceed twenty dollars, the right of trial by jury shall be preserved, and no fact tried by a jury, shall be otherwise re-examined in any Court of the United States, than according to the rules of the common law.

### Amendment VIII

Excessive bail shall not be required, nor excessive fines imposed, nor cruel and unusual punishments inflicted.

### Amendment IX

The enumeration in the Constitution, of certain rights, shall not be construed to deny or disparage others retained by the people.

### Amendment X

The powers not delegated to the United States by the Constitution, nor prohibited by it to the States, are reserved to the States respectively, or to the people.

### Amendment XI *(Ratified Feb. 7, 1795)*

The Judicial power of the United States shall not be construed to extend to any suit in law or equity, commenced or prosecuted against one of the United States by Citizens of another State, or by Citizens or Subjects of any Foreign State.

### Amendment XII *(Ratified June 15, 1804)*

The Electors shall meet in their respective states and vote by ballot for President and Vice-President, one of whom, at least, shall not be an inhabitant of the same state with themselves; they shall name in their ballots the person voted for as President, and in distinct ballots the person voted for as Vice-President, and they shall make distinct lists of all persons voted for as President, and of all persons voted for as Vice-President, and of the number of votes for each, which lists they shall sign and certify, and transmit sealed to the seat of the government of the United States, directed to the President of the Senate;—The President of the Senate shall, in the presence of the Senate and House of Representatives, open all the certificates and the votes shall then be counted;—The person having the greatest number of votes for President, shall be the President, if such number be a majority of the whole number of Electors appointed; and if no person have such majority, then from the persons having the highest numbers not exceeding three on the list of those voted for as President, the House of Representatives shall choose immediately, by ballot, the President. But in choosing the President, the votes shall be taken by states, the representation from each state having one vote; a quorum for this purpose shall consist of a member or members from two-thirds of the states, and a majority of all the states shall be necessary to a choice. [And if the House of Representatives shall not choose a President whenever the right of choice shall devolve upon them, before the fourth day of March next following, then the Vice-President shall act as President, as in the case of the death or other constitutional disability of the President—]¹¹ The person having the greatest number of votes as Vice-President, shall be the Vice-President, if such number be a majority of the whole number of Electors appointed, and if no person have a majority, then from the two highest numbers on the list, the Senate shall choose the Vice-President; a quorum for the purpose shall consist of two-thirds of the whole number of Senators, and a majority of the whole number shall be necessary to a choice. But no person constitutionally ineligible to the office of President shall be eligible to that of Vice-President of the United States.

### Amendment XIII *(Ratified Dec. 6, 1865)*
**Section 1.** Neither slavery nor involuntary servitude, except as a punishment for crime whereof the party shall have been duly convicted, shall exist within the United States, or any place subject to their jurisdiction.

**Section 2.** Congress shall have power to enforce this article by appropriate legislation.

### Amendment XIV *(Ratified July 9, 1868)*
**Section 1.** All persons born or naturalized in the United States and subject to the jurisdiction thereof, are citizens of the United States and of the State wherein they reside. No State shall make or enforce any law which shall abridge the privileges or immunities of citizens of the United States; nor shall any State deprive any person of life, liberty, or property, without due process of law; nor deny to any person within its jurisdiction the equal protection of the laws.

**Section 2.** Representatives shall be apportioned among the several States according to their respective numbers, counting the whole number of persons in each State, excluding Indians not taxed. But when the right to vote at any election for the choice of electors for President and Vice President of the United States, Representatives in Congress, the Executive and Judicial officers of a State, or the members of the Legislature thereof, is denied to any of the male inhabitants of such State, being twenty-one years of age,¹² and citizens of the United States, or in any way abridged, except for participation in rebellion, or other crime, the basis of representation therein shall be reduced in the proportion which the number of such male citizens shall bear to the whole number of male citizens twenty-one years of age in such State.

**Section 3.** No person shall be a Senator or Representative in Congress, or elector of President and Vice President, or hold any office, civil or military, under the United States, or under any State, who, having previously taken an oath, as a member of Congress, or as an officer of the United

States, or as a member of any State legislature, or as an executive or judicial officer of any State, to support the Constitution of the United States, shall have engaged in insurrection or rebellion against the same, or given aid or comfort to the enemies thereof. But Congress may by a vote of two-thirds of each House, remove such disability.

**Section 4.** The validity of the public debt of the United States, authorized by law, including debts incurred for payment of pensions and bounties for services in suppressing insurrection or rebellion, shall not be questioned. But neither the United States nor any State shall assume or pay any debt or obligation incurred in aid of insurrection or rebellion against the United States, or any claim for the loss or emancipation of any slave; but all such debts, obligations and claims shall be held illegal and void.

**Section 5.** The Congress shall have power to enforce, by appropriate legislation, the provisions of this article.

## Amendment XV *(Ratified Feb. 3, 1870)*

**Section 1.** The right of citizens of the United States to vote shall not be denied or abridged by the United States or by any State on account of race, color, or previous condition of servitude.

**Section 2.** The Congress shall have power to enforce this article by appropriate legislation.

## Amendment XVI *(Ratified Feb. 3, 1913)*

The Congress shall have power to lay and collect taxes on incomes, from whatever source derived, without apportionment among the several States, and without regard to any census or enumeration.

## Amendment XVII *(Ratified April 8, 1913)*

The Senate of the United States shall be composed of two Senators from each State, elected by the people thereof, for six years; and each Senator shall have one vote. The electors in each State shall have the qualifications requisite for electors of the most numerous branch of the State legislatures.

When vacancies happen in the representation of any State in the Senate, the executive authority of such State shall issue writs of election to fill such vacancies: *Provided,* That the legislature of any State may empower the executive thereof to make temporary appointments until the people fill the vacancies by election as the legislature may direct.

This amendment shall not be so construed as to affect the election or term of any Senator chosen before it becomes valid as part of the Constitution.

**Amendment XVIII** *(Ratified Jan. 16, 1919)*

[**Section 1**. After one year from the ratification of this article the manufacture, sale, or transportation of intoxicating liquors within, the importation thereof into, or the exportation thereof from the United States and all territory subject to the jurisdiction thereof for beverage purposes is hereby prohibited.

**Section 2**. The Congress and the several States shall have concurrent power to enforce this article by appropriate legislation.

**Section 3**. This article shall be inoperative unless it shall have been ratified as an amendment to the Constitution by the legislatures of the several States, as provided in the Constitution, within seven years from the date of the submission hereof to the States by the Congress.][13]

**Amendment XIX** *(Ratified Aug. 18, 1920)*

The right of citizens of the United States to vote shall not be denied or abridged by the United States or by any State on account of sex.

Congress shall have power to enforce this article by appropriate legislation.

**Amendment XX** *(Ratified Jan. 23, 1933)*

**Section 1**. The terms of the President and Vice President shall end at noon on the 20th day of January, and the terms of Senators and Representatives at noon on the 3d day of January, of the years in which such terms would have ended if this article had not been ratified; and the terms of their successors shall then begin.

**Section 2**. The Congress shall assemble at least once in every year, and such meeting shall begin at noon on the 3d day of January, unless they shall by law appoint a different day.

**Section 3**.[14] If, at the time fixed for the beginning of the term of the President, the President elect shall have died, the Vice President elect shall become President. If a President shall not have been chosen before the time fixed for the beginning of his term, or if the President elect shall have failed to qualify, then the Vice President elect shall act as President until a President shall have qualified; and the Congress may by law provide for the case wherein neither a President elect nor a Vice President elect shall have qualified, declaring who shall then act as President, or the manner in which one who is to act shall be selected, and such person shall act accordingly until a President or Vice President shall have qualified.

**Section 4**. The Congress may by law provide for the case of the death of any of the persons from whom the House of Representatives may choose a President whenever the right of choice shall have devolved upon them, and for the case of the death of any of the persons from whom the

Senate may choose a Vice President whenever the right of choice shall have devolved upon them.

**Section 5.** Sections 1 and 2 shall take effect on the 15th day of October following the ratification of this article.

**Section 6.** This article shall be inoperative unless it shall have been ratified as an amendment to the Constitution by the legislatures of three-fourths of the several States within seven years from the date of its submission.

### Amendment XXI *(Ratified Dec. 5, 1933)*

**Section 1.** The eighteenth article of amendment to the Constitution of the United States is hereby repealed.

**Section 2.** The transportation or importation into any State, Territory or possession of the United States for delivery or use therein of intoxicating liquors, in violation of the laws thereof, is hereby prohibited.

**Section 3.** This article shall be inoperative unless it shall have been ratified as an amendment to the Constitution by conventions in the several States, as provided in the Constitution, within seven years from the date of the submission hereof to the States by the Congress.

### Amendment XXII *(Ratified Feb. 27, 1951)*

**Section 1.** No person shall be elected to the office of the President more than twice, and no person who has held the office of President, or acted as President, for more than two years of a term to which some other person was elected President shall be elected to the office of the President more than once. But this Article shall not apply to any person holding the office of President when this Article was proposed by the Congress, and shall not prevent any person who may be holding the office of President, or acting as President, during the term within which this Article become operative from holding the office of President or acting as President during the remainder of such term.

**Section 2.** This Article shall be inoperative unless it shall have been ratified as an amendment to the Constitution by the legislatures of three-fourths of the several States within seven years from the date of its submission to the States by the Congress.

### Amendment XXIII *(Ratified March 29, 1961)*

**Section 1.** The District constituting the seat of Government of the United States shall appoint in such manner as the Congress may direct:

A number of electors of President and Vice President equal to the whole number of Senators and Representatives in Congress to which the District would be entitled if it were a State, but in no event more than the least populous State; they shall be in addition to those appointed by the States, but they shall be considered, for the purposes of the election of President and Vice President, to be electors appointed by a State; and they shall meet in the District and perform such duties as provided by the twelfth article of amendment.

**Section 2.** The Congress shall have power to enforce this article by appropriate legislation.

**Amendment XXIV** *(Ratified Jan. 23, 1964)*

**Section 1.** The right of citizens of the United States to vote in any primary or other election for President or Vice President, for electors for President or Vice President, or for Senator or Representative in Congress, shall not be denied or abridged by the United States or any State by reason of failure to pay any poll tax or other tax.

**Section 2.** The Congress shall have power to enforce this article by appropriate legislation.

**Amendment XXV** *(Ratified Feb. 10, 1967)*

**Section 1.** In case of the removal of the President from office or of his death or resignation, the Vice President shall become President.

**Section 2.** Whenever there is a vacancy in the office of the Vice President, the President shall nominate a Vice President who shall take office upon confirmation by a majority vote of both Houses of Congress.

**Section 3.** Whenever the President transmits to the President pro tempore of the Senate and the Speaker of the House of Representatives has written declaration that he is unable to discharge the powers and duties of his office, and until he transmits to them a written declaration to the contrary, such powers and duties shall be discharged by the Vice President as Acting President.

**Section 4.** Whenever the Vice President and a majority of either the principal officers of the executive departments or of such other body as Congress may by law provide, transmit to the President pro tempore of the Senate and the Speaker of the House of Representatives their written declaration that the President is unable to discharge the powers and duties of his office, the Vice President shall immediately assume the powers and duties of the office as Acting President.

Thereafter, when the President transmits to the President pro tempore of the Senate and the Speaker of the House of Representatives his written declaration that no inability exists, he shall resume the powers and duties of his office unless the Vice President and a majority of either the principal officers of the executive department or of such other body as Congress may by law provide, transmit within four days to the President pro tempore of the Senate and the Speaker of the House of Representatives their written declaration that the President is unable to discharge the powers and duties of his office. Thereupon Congress shall decide the issue, assembling within forty-eight hours for that purpose if not in session. If the Congress, within twenty-one days after receipt of the latter written declaration, or, if Congress is not in session, within twenty-one days after Congress is required to assemble, determines by two-thirds vote of both houses that the President is unable to discharge the powers and duties of his office, the Vice President shall continue to discharge the same as Acting President; otherwise, the President shall resume the powers and duties of his office.

### Amendment XXVI *(Ratified July 1, 1971)*

**Section 1.** The right of citizens of the United States, who are eighteen years of age or older, to vote shall not be denied or abridged by the United States or by any State on account of age.

**Section 2.** The Congress shall have power to enforce this article by appropriate legislation.

### Amendment XXVII *(Ratified May 1992)*

No law varying the compensation for the services of the Senators and Representatives shall take effect, until an election of Representatives shall have intervened.

---

**Footnotes**

1. The part in brackets was changed by section 2 of the Fourteenth Amendment.
2. The part in brackets was changed by section 1 of the Seventeenth Amendment.
3. The part in brackets was changed by the second paragraph of the Seventeenth Amendment.
4. The part in brackets was changed by section 2 of the Twentieth Amendment.
5. The Sixteenth Amendment gave Congress the power to tax incomes.
6. The material in brackets has been superseded by the Twelfth Amendment.
7. This provision has been affected by the Twenty-fifth Amendment.
8. These clauses were affected by the Eleventh Amendment.
9. This paragraph has been superseded by the Thirteenth Amendment.
10. Obsolete.
11. The part in brackets has been superseded by section 3 of the Twentieth Amendment.
12. See the Twenty-sixth Amendment.
13. This Amendment was repealed by section 1 of the Twenty-first Amendment.
14. See the Twenty-fifth Amendment.

Source:  U.S. Congress, House, Committee on the Judiciary, *The Constitution of the United States of America, As Amended Through July 1971*, H. Doc. 93-215, 93rd Cong., 2nd sess., 1974.

# APPENDIX B:

## THE BILL OF RIGHTS:
## A VERY SELECTIVE BIBLIOGRAPHY

### Richard B. Bernstein and Ellis Katz

(from, *To Preserve These Rights:
User's Guide to the Bill of Rights
Poster Exhibit*, produced by the
Pennsylvania Humanities Council.)

*Most of the writers on the first ten amendments are fierce advocates.
They feel so deeply about such issues as the freedom of the press and
speech, the separation of church and state, the right to bear arms, the
right to trial by jury, the death penalty, and the right of privacy that
many of them cannot hide their prejudices. Some are not even inclined
to be objective... their intense feelings and beliefs have clearly conditioned their conclusions.*

Gaspare J. Saladino

Gaspare J. Saladino, "The Bill of Rights: A Bibliographic Essay," in Stephen Schechter and Richard B. Bernstein, eds., *Forgotten Partners: The
States and the Bill of Rights* (Albany, N.Y.: New York State Commission on
the Bicentennial of the U.S. Constitution, 1990).

### More Comprehensive Bibliographies

The reader who wants to pursue a particular subject further should
consult Saladino's bibliography cited above. It is an excellent review of
the historical literature dealing with the drafting and ratification of the Bill
of Rights and the never-ending search to discover the intent of the framers
of the Bill of Rights. One should also be familiar with the extensive bibliography (182 pages) in Henry J. Abraham, *The Judicial Process* (New
York: Oxford University Press, 1980). It is organized by subtopics and
should provide enough sources for even the most ambitious general
reader.

### General Works on the Constitution and the Bill of Rights

One of two indispensable one-volume constitutional histories is Alfred H. Kelly, Winfred Harbison, and Herman Belz, *The American Constitution: Its Origins and Development,* 6th ed. (New York: W. W. Norton, 1983).

The best introduction to the scholarship of one of the notable constitutional historians is Leonard W. Levy, *Original Intent and the Framers' Constitution* (New York: Macmillan Publishing Co., 1988).

A valuable analysis of the principles of constitutionalism in American history, contending that the principal influence on the making of the Constitution and the Bill of Rights was the American colonial experience, is Donald S. Lutz, *The Origins of American Constitutionalism* (Baton Rouge, La.: Louisiana State University Press, 1988).

A useful starting place for the general reader is to consult the individual essays in Leonard Levy, Kenneth L. Karst, and Dennis J. Mahoney, *Encyclopedia of the American Constitution* (4 volumes) (New York: Macmillan Publishing Co., 1986); and the historical documents in Philip B. Kurland and Ralph Lerner, eds., *The Founders' Constitution* (5 volumes) (Chicago: University of Chicago Press, 1987), especially volume 5, which deals with the Bill of Rights. Both of these important works should be available at most college and public libraries. A useful and well-written introduction to how the U.S. Supreme Court has interpreted the Bill of Rights is Henry J. Abraham, *Freedom and the Court* (New York: Oxford University Press, 1988). Two recent and very useful books on the Bill of Rights are Glenn A. Phelps and Robert A. Poirier, *Contemporary Debates on Civil Liberties* (Lexington, Mass.: D. C. Heath and Co., 1985), and Herbert M. Levine and Jean Edward Smith, *Civil Liberties and Civil Rights Debated* (Englewood Cliffs, N J.: Prentice-Hall, 1988). Each book is a collection of short essays debating the meaning of particular provisions of the Bill of Rights.

Two learned essays on the origins of the Constitution and the Bill of Rights are in William E. Nelson and Robert C. Palmer, *Liberty and Community in Early America* (Dobbs Ferry, N.Y.: Oceana Publications, 1987). Palmer argues that bills of rights were originally intended to be "checklists" for citizens to determine if their elected officials deserved to be returned to office; the idea of rights as judicially enforceable evolved only gradually.

Two useful books on the background, drafting, and ratification of the Bill of Rights are Edmund Dumbauld, *The Bill of Rights and What it Means Today* (Norman, Okla.: University of Oklahoma Press, 1957), and Robert A. Rutland, *The Birth of the Bill of Rights 1776–1791* (Chapel Hill, N. C.: University of North Carolina Press, 1955). Both works discuss the English antecedents of the American Bill of Rights, the colonial experience, and the actual drafting and ratification of the Bill of Rights. Another excellent source, designed for the "ordinary citizen," is the collection of essays in Jon Kukla, ed., *The Bill of Rights: A Lively Heritage* (Richmond, Va.: Virginia State Library and Archives, 1987).

A learned, detailed and rigorous study of state constitution-making in the Revolutionary period, including discussion of state bills of rights, is Willi Paul Adams, *The First American Constitutions* (Chapel Hill, N. C.: University of North Carolina Press, 1980).

A massive, lively, richly detailed, and idiosyncratic history is Irving Brant, *The Bill of Rights: Its Origin and Meaning* (Indianapolis, Ind.: Bobbs-Merrill, 1965).

A fine short biography of one of the key figures in the making of the Bill of Rights is Jack N. Rakove, *James Madison and the Creation of the American Republic* (Glenview, Ill.: Scott, Foresman/Little, Brown, 1990) (paperback).

A symposium presenting essays on the intellectual, political, and historiographical contexts of the Bill of Rights is Stephen L. Schechter and Richard B. Bernstein, eds., *Contexts of the Bill of Rights* (Albany, N.Y.: New York State Commission on the Bicentennial of the United States Constitution, 1990).

More legal than the Rutland volume cited above, but valuable for that reason as the clearest exposition of the framing of the Bill of Rights, is Bernard Schwartz, *The Great Rights of Mankind: A History of the American Bill of Rights* (New York: Oxford University Press, 1977).

A leading contemporary treatise on constitutional law and constitutional theory is Laurence H. Tribe, *American Constitutional Law*, 2d edition (Mineola, N.Y.: Foundation Press, 1988).

The other indispensable one-volume constitutional history of the United States (see Kelly, Harbison, and Belz above) is Melvin I. Urofsky, *A March of Liberty: A Constitutional History of the United States* (New York: Alfred A. Knopf, 1988).

The best introduction to the Constitution for the secondary school student and teacher, arranged in question-and-answer format and written clearly with emphasis on explaining and untangling legal reasoning while avoiding jargon, is John Sexton and Nat Brandt, *How Free Are We? What the Constitution Says We Can and Cannot Do* (New York: M. Evans, 1986) (paperback).

### Freedoms of Speech, Press and Assembly

An excellent work on the First Amendment's guarantee of the freedoms of speech, press, and assembly continues to be Zechariah Chafee, Jr., *Free Speech in the United States* (Cambridge, Mass.: Harvard University Press, 1948), although it is over 40 years old. Another useful work, despite its age, is Milton R. Konvitz, *Expanding Liberties: The Emergence of New Civil Liberties and Rights in Postwar America* (New York: Viking Books, 1967). More recent, albeit more limited, books include: Henry M. Clor, *Obscenity and Public Morality* (Chicago: University of Chicago Press, 1969), a useful account of how the Supreme Court has attempted to deal with the problem of obscenity; Fred W. Friendly, *Minnesota Rag* (New York: Random House, 1981), the fascinating story behind the case of *Near v. Minnesota,* a very important case involving the freedom of the press; and Richard Polenberg, *Fighting Faiths: The Abrams Case, The Supreme Court and Free Speech* (New York: Penguin Books, 1987), which recounts the story of Jacob Abrams and other radicals whose convictions under the Espionage Act were upheld by the United States Supreme Court in 1919.

A revised and greatly expanded version of Levy's controversial and pathbreaking 1960 work, *Legacy of Suppression: Freedom of Speech and Press in Early American History,* is Leonard W. Levy, *Emergence of a Free Press* (New York: Oxford University Press, 1985) (paperback, 1986).

### Freedom of Religion and the Establishment Clause
The single most valuable history of church and state in America and the adoption of the First Amendment is Thomas J. Curry, *The First Freedoms* (New York: Oxford University Press, 1986).

A useful introduction to the religion clauses of the First Amendment is Francis Graham Lee, ed., *Wall of Controversy: Church-State Conflict in America* (Malabar, Fla.: Krieger Publishing Co., 1986), which contains excerpts from important Supreme Court decisions and documents relating to the "original intent" of the religion clauses of the First Amendment. Richard Morgan, *The Supreme Court and Religion* (New York: Free Press, 1974) is an extended, readable analysis of the Court's religion decisions.

### The Right to Bear Arms and the Quartering of Soldiers
There are few good book-length treatments of the Second Amendment. An exception is Stephen P. Halbrook, *That Every Man Be Armed: The Evolution of a Constitutional Right* (Albuquerque, N. Mex.: University of New Mexico Press, 1984). For two articles that take somewhat different perspectives, see David T. Hardy, "Armed Citizens, Citizen Armies: Toward a Jurisprudence of the Second Amendment," *Harvard Journal of Law and Public Policy* 9 (1986): 559–638; and Lawrence Delbert Cress, "A Well-Regulated Militia: The Origins and Meaning of the Second Amendment," in Jon Kukla, ed., *The Bill of Rights: A Lively Heritage* (Richmond, Va.: Virginia State Library and Archives, 1987), pp. 55–65. On the historical importance of the Third Amendment's bar on the quartering of soldiers,

see B. Carmon Hardy, "A Free People's Intolerable Grievance: The Quartering of Troops and the Third Amendment," in Kukla, *op. cit.,* pp. 67–82.

### Criminal Procedure

Two fine but very different books on the constitutional rights of criminal defendants are Jonathan Casper, *American Criminal Justice: The Defendant's Perspective* (Englewood Cliffs, N.J.: Prentice-Hall, 1972) and Fred P. Graham, *The Self-Inflicted Wound* (New York: Macmillan Publishing Co., 1970). Casper's book is based on interviews with actual criminal defendants. Rather than finding courtroom drama where constitutional guarantees are carefully protected, Casper finds a bureaucratic process in which everyone has an interest in disposing of cases rather than in arriving at just decisions. Graham, who is both an attorney and a well-known journalist, provides a constitutional-political account of the Warren Court's revolution in criminal procedure.

A Pulitzer Prize-winning study of the privilege against self-incrimination is Leonard W. Levy, *Origins of the Fifth Amendment* (New York: Oxford University Press, 1968) (paperback, New York: Macmillan Publishing Co., 1988).

### Property Rights

For much of American history, the U.S. Supreme Court used its power of judicial review to protect property rights. This historical record is well documented in Wallace Mendelson, *Capitalism, Democracy and the Supreme Court* (New York: Appleton-Century-Crofts, 1960). A good collection of essays that advocates a more active role for the contemporary Supreme Court in protecting property is James A. Dorn and Henry G. Manne, eds., *Economic Liberties and the Constitution* (Fairfax, Va.: George Mason University Press, 1987).

### The Ninth and Tenth Amendments

The standard work on the Ninth Amendment is still Bennett B. Patterson, *The Forgotten Ninth Amendment* (Indianapolis, Ind.: Bobbs-Merrill, 1955). A more recent anthology of both historical documents and contemporary scholarship is Randy Barnett, ed., *Rights Retained by the People: The History and Meaning of the Ninth Amendment* (Washington, D.C.: Cato Institute, 1989). For a strong argument that the Tenth Amendment was designed to limit the authority of the national government, see Raoul Berger, *Federalism: The Founders' Design* (Norman, Okla.: University of Oklahoma Press, 1987). For an articulation of the view that federalism is a political rather than a constitutional question, see Jesse H. Choper, "The

Scope of National Power Vis-a-Vis the States: The Dispensability of Judicial Review," *Yale Law Journal 86* (1977): 1552. One should also see Charles F. Hobson, "The Tenth Amendment and the New Federalism of 1789" in Jon Kukla, *op. cit.,* pp. 152–63.

### Privacy and Abortion

For a stimulating debate on the abortion issue, see Philip B. Heymann and Douglas E. Barzlay, "Roe v. Wade and Its Critics" and Patrick T. Conley and Robert J. McKenna, "The Supreme Court on Abortion: A Dissenting Opinion," both reprinted in Glenn A. Phelps and Robert A. Poirier, eds., *Contemporary Debates on Civil Rights and Liberties* (Lexington, Mass.: D. C. Heath and Company, 1988), pp. 198–210.

### The Fourteenth Amendment and the Nationalization of the Bill of Rights

As originally written and ratified, the Bill of Rights applied only as limitations upon actions by the national government. For the process of how the protections of the Bill of Rights came to limit state action, see Henry J. Abraham, *Freedom and the Court* (especially Chapter 2) cited previously, and Richard C. Cortner, *The Supreme Court and the Second Bill of Rights* (Madison, Wis.: University of Wisconsin Press, 1981).

An award-winning study of the origins of the Fourteenth Amendment that moves beyond the sterile debate about whether the Framers intended to incorporate or not to incorporate the federal Bill of Rights is William E. Nelson, *The Fourteenth Amendment: From Political Principle to Judicial Doctrine* (Cambridge, Mass.: Harvard University Press, 1988).

### Equality Under the Law

As definitive a study of the subject as we can expect, especially valuable for understanding the context out of which the Thirteenth, Fourteenth, and Fifteenth Amendments emerged, is Eric Foner, *Reconstruction: America's Unfinished Revolution* (New York: Harper & Row, 1988) (paperback, 1989). Eric Foner, A *Short History of Reconstruction* (abridged edition of the above) (hardcover and paperback; New York: Harper & Row, 1990).

A fine study on the struggle for racial equality is J. Harvie Wilkinson III, *From Brown to Bakke: The Supreme Court and School Integration 1954–1978* (New York: Oxford University Press, 1979), which traces this difficult issue from the Supreme Court's 1954 decision in *Brown v. Board of Education* through the affirmative action controversy of the *Bakke* case in 1978.

A modern classic on the African American struggle for equality, culminating with *Brown v. Board of Education*, is Richard Kluger, *Simple Justice* (New York: Alfred A. Knopf, 1975) (paperback, New York: Vintage, 1977).

On how the equal protection clause of the Fourteenth Amendment has been applied to other minorities, see Ruth Bader Ginsburg, "The Burger Court's Grapplings with Sex Discrimination," in Vincent Blasi, ed., *The Burger Court: The Counter-Revolution That Wasn't* (New Haven: Yale University Press, 1983), pp. 132–156, and Wendy W. Williams, "Sex Discrimination: Closing the Law's Gender Gap," in Herman Schwartz, ed., *The Burger Years: Rights and Wrongs in the Supreme Court 1969—1986* (New York: Penguin Books, 1987), pp. 109–124.

### The Struggle for Civil Rights and Liberties

A reprint of Levy's 1963 monograph demolishes the conventional picture of Jefferson as a civil libertarian, conceding only his commitment to separation of church and state. Valuable also as a case study in exploding historical myth-making is Leonard W. Levy, *Jefferson and Civil Liberties: The Darker Side* (Chicago: Elephant Books/Ivan R. Dee, 1989).

Merely having a written bill of rights is no assurance that citizens will enjoy individual freedom. The struggle to make the Bill of Rights meaningful is documented in several books. Two fine books on the role of the American Civil Liberties Union are Charles Lam Markmann, *The Noblest Cry: A History of the American Civil Liberties Union* (New York: St. Martin's Press, 1965) and the more recent Samuel Walker, *In Defense of American Liberties: A History of the ACLU* (New York: Oxford University Press, 1990). On the struggle for racial equality, see Taylor Branch, *Parting the Waters: America in the King Years* (New York: Simon and Schuster, 1988), and, of course, Martin Luther King, Jr., *Stride Toward Freedom: The Montgomery Story* (New York: Harper and Row, 1958). On the stories behind the headlines of pathbreaking civil liberties decisions by the U.S. Supreme Court, see Peter Irons, *The Courage of Their Convictions* (New York: Free Press, 1988). Other case studies in the development of civil rights and liberties include: Dan T. Carter, *Scottsboro: A Tragedy of the American South* (Baton Rouge, La.: Louisiana State University Press, 1969); Anthony Lewis, *Gideon's Trumpet* (New York: Random House, 1965) (paperback, New York: Vintage, 1966); and E. Barrett Prettyman, Jr., *Death and the Supreme Court* (New York: Avon Books, 1964).

# APPENDIX C:

## READINGS FOR STUDENTS

### Helen H. Carey and Judith E. Greenberg

(from, *To Preserve These Rights:
User's Guide to
the Bill of Rights Poster Exhibit*,
produced by the Pennsylvania
Humanities Council.)

This list is only a starting point. We hope that it will encourage students
to look for other books, newspaper and magazine articles, and nonprint
sources of information about the Bill of Rights.

*Bar/School Partnership Handbooks*. (Reprinted from *Update on Law-Related Education*). "Liberty," "Equality," "Justice," "Power." Chicago: American Bar Association, n.d.

Bender, David L., and Bruno Leone, eds. *Criminal Justice*. St. Paul, Minn.:
Greenhaven Press, 1981.

Daniels, Roger. *The Decision to Relocate the Japanese Americans*. Mel-
bourne, Fla.: Robert E. Krieger Publishing Co., 1986.

Feinberg, Barbara Silberdick. *The Constitution: Yesterday, Today, and
Tommorrow*. New York: Scholastic Inc., 1987.

*Freedom of the Press: A Simulation of Legal Issues in Journalism*. Legal
Studies Simulations. Culver City, Calif.: Social Studies School Service.

Harrell, M., and B. Anderson. *Equal Justice Under the Law: The Supreme
Court in American Life*. Washington, D.C.: Supreme Court Historical Society, 1982. (Instructor's Guide by Isadore Starr is also available.)

Hentoff, Nat. *The First Freedom: The Tumultuous History of Free Speech in America*. Garden City, N.Y.: Doubleday & Co., 1980.

Hoobler, Dorothy, and Thomas Hoobler. *Your Right to Privacy*. New York: Franklin Watts, Inc., 1986.

Irons, Peter. *Justice At War*. New York: Oxford University Press, 1983.

Kerber, Linda K. " 'Ourselves and Our Daughters Forever': Women and the Constitution," *this Constitution* 6 (Spring 1985): 25–34.

Kluger, Richard. *Simple Justice: The History of Brown v. Board of Education and Black America's Struggle for Equality*. New York: Alfred A. Knopf, 1977.

Lewis, Anthony. *Gideon's Trumpet*. New York: Bantam Books, 1964.

Lindop, Edmund. *The Bill of Rights and Landmark Cases*. New York: Franklin Watts, Inc., 1989.

Lockwood, Alan L., and David E. Harris. *Reasoning with Democratic Values: Ethical Problems in U.S. History*. New York: Teachers College Press, 1985.

Manak, James, P. "Drink, Drank, Drunk: Can We Stop Highway Slaughter Without Infringing Individual Rights?" *Update on Law-Related Education* (Spring 1986). Chicago: American Bar Association.

National Archives Education Branch Staff. *The Bill of Rights: Evolution of Personal Liberties*. Boca Raton, Fla., Social Issues Resources Services, Inc., 1988.

"Religion, Morality, and American Education," *Bill of Rights in Action* 17, No. 1 (February—March 1983).

Rader, Robert J. *Mock Trials*. (Five Simulations: Custody, Delinquency, Murder, Burglary, Vandalism.) New York: Law Instructor Publications, 1982. (Available through Social Studies School Service, Culver City, Calif.)

Taylor, C. L. *Censorship*. New York: Franklin Watts, Inc., 1986.

*The Crime Question: Rights and Responsibilities of Citizens.* (Part of the Law-in-Social-Studies Series). Culver City, Calif.: Constitutional Rights Foundation, 1984.

*Update on Law-Related Education.* "Discipline and Due Process in the Schools" (Fall 1977), "Free Press in America" (Fall 1985), "The First Amendment at Mid-Decade" (Spring 1985), "The Revolution in Search and Seizure" (Winter 1985), "Privacy vs. Power" (Spring 1982). Chicago: American Bar Association.

*We the People ... do ordain and establish this Constitution for the United States of America.* Calabasas, Calif.: Center for Civic Education, 1987.

Woods, Geraldine, and Harold Woods. *The Right to Bear Arms.* New York: Franklin Watts, Inc., 1986.

# APPENDIX D:

## FILMOGRAPHY

Compiled by Linda Blackaby, Director,
Neighborhood Film/Video Project,
International House of Philadelphia
and Rose Tallow, Development/Public Relations
Associate, Pennsylvania Humanities Council

(from, *To Preserve These Rights:*
*User's Guide to the*
*Bill of Rights Poster Exhibit,*
produced by the Pennsylvania
Humanities Council.)

Please note that these and other useful films may be available at your public library.

*Books Our Children Read*
Michelle Marder Kamhi, 1984, 28 min.
   This film offers an impartial treatment of the issues surrounding the banning of books. Parents, teachers, and students express their attitudes in this award-winning program.
Distributor: Films Incorporated, 5547 N. Ravenswood Avenue, Chicago, IL 60640 (800) 323–4222

*The Civil War: Anguish of Emancipation*
Living Corporation of America, 1972, 27 min.
   A dramatic reenactment, centering on the issuance of the Emancipation Proclamation, which reveals the agonizing dilemma that confronted Abraham Lincoln as he struggled to resolve the Civil War. All of the dialogue is taken verbatim from manuscripts, letters, diaries, and journals of the period.
Distributor: Coronet/MTI Film and Video, 108 Wilmont Road, Deerfield, IL 60015 (800) 621–2131

*The Constitution: The Compromise That Made a Nation*
Living Corporation of America, 1975, 27 min.

A dramatic recreation of the tense exchanges between the colonial leaders who met in a secret session in Philadelphia in May of 1789. Viewers are plunged into the passionate argument—finally resolved by the "Great Compromise"—that preceded the framing of the Constitution.
Distributor: Coronet/MTI Film and Video, 108 Wilmont Road, Deerfield, IL 60015 (800) 621–2131

*The Constitution: That Delicate Balance*
Stuart Sucherman, Executive Director, 13 programs, 60 min. each

Providing a springboard for examining public policy and the Constitution, each program presents a hypothetical case study based on contemporary constitutional issues. Several of the programs deal with Bill of Rights issues.
Distributor: Intellimation, P.O. Box 1922, Santa Barbara, CA 93116 (800) 532–7637

*Crime, Punishment, and Kids . . .*
NBC News, 1987, 50 min.

The great majority of serious juvenile crimes in America are committed by a small core of young offenders who seem destined for a life of crime. This film discusses the conflict between the public's right to safety and society's ideal of reforming young delinquents.
Distributor: Films Incorporated, 5547 N. Ravenswood Avenue, Chicago, IL 60640 (800) 323–4222

*Eyes on the Prize, Parts I and II*
Henry Hampton, Executive Producer, Blackside Inc., 1989, 1990

The film history of the Civil Rights movement in the United States, as shown on PBS.
Distributor: PBS Video, 1320 Braddock Place, Alexandria, VA 22314 (703) 739–5380

*Focus on the Constitution*
ABC Video Enterprises, 1987, 3 programs, 19 min. each

This series takes a historical look at the challenges faced by the framers in establishing a new government, and discusses the Constitution's applications in today's society. The three-part series examines "The Amendments," "Federalism," and "The Presidency."
Distributor: Coronet/MTI Film and Video, 108 Wilmont Road, Deerfield, IL 60015 (800) 621–2131

*The Grand Jury: An Institution Under Fire*
Joel Sucher and Steven Fischler, 1977, 60 min.

An investigative documentary tracing the history of the Grand Jury system and exploring allegations of its abuse.
Distributor: Cinema Guild, 1697 Broadway, New York, NY 10019 (212) 246–5522

*Guns, Guns, Guns*
NBC News, 1988, 58 min.

Connie Chung narrates this disturbing examination of the role that guns play in modern society. This film provides a useful starting point for discussion on the right to bear arms.
Distributor: Films Incorporated, 5547 N. Ravenswood Avenue, Chicago, IL 60640 (800) 323–4222

*The Klan: A Legacy of Hate in America*
Guggenheim, 1982, 30 min.

This film graphically reveals the 120-year infamy of the Ku Klux Klan's reign of terror. It also exposes the spread of the Klan's influence, membership, and savagery today.
Distributor: Films Incorporated, 5547 N. Ravenswood Avenue, Chicago, IL 60640 (800) 323–4222

*Legacy of a Dream*
Martin Luther King, Jr. Foundation, 1981, 29 min.

Narrated by James Earl Jones, this well-known documentary chronicles the career of Martin Luther King, Jr., and the civil rights movement. It summarizes King's public life and delineates his central role in the struggle for civil rights, including voting rights and desegregation.
Distributor: Films Incorporated, 5547 N. Ravenswood Avenue, Chicago, IL 60640 (800) 323–4222

*The Lemon Grove Incident*
Frank Christopher, 1985, 58 min.

In 1930 the school board in Lemon Grove, California, announced plans for a separate school for Mexican American students. The Hispanic community protested the decision, and filed and eventually won a lawsuit against the school board, marking the nation's first successful legal challenge to school segregation.
Distributor: The Cinema Guild, 1697 Broadway, Suite 802, New York, NY 10019 (212) 246–5522

*Malcolm X*
Warner Brothers, 1972, 92 min.

This feature-length documentary, narrated by James Earl Jones, details the life and thought of Malcolm X, the Black nationalist leader and visionary of the 1960s.

Distributor: Swank Motion Pictures, 350 Vanderbilt Motor Parkway, Hauppauge, NY 11787 (516) 434–1560, (800) 876–3344

*Moyers: In Search of the Constitution*
WNET/13, 1987, 10 programs, 60 min. each

In this ten-program series, host Bill Moyers explores the Constitution's role in the United States' history and future through interviews with people who interpret and teach about it, and whose lives have been changed by it, including Justice William J. Brennan, Jr., Judge Robert H. Bork, and Justice Sandra Day O'Connor.

Distributor: PBS Video, 1320 Braddock Place, Alexandria, VA 22314 (703) 739–5380

*The Secret File*
WGBH, Frontline, 1987, 58 min.

This film tells the real-life story of Penn Kimball, a university professor, former New York Times editor, Rhodes Scholar, and Eagle Scout, who discovered that for 30 years U.S. government files existed declaring him a disloyal American. This film looks at Kimball's fight to clear his name and considers whether the government has the right to gather and classify information on American citizens.

Distributor: Films Incorporated, 5547 N. Ravenswood Avenue, Chicago, IL 60640 (800) 323–4222

*Skokie: Rights or Wrong*
Sheila Chamovitz, 25 min.

*Skokie* documents the legal and moral crisis posed when the American Nazi Party chose to demonstrate in Skokie, Illinois, home to many concentration-camp survivors. Featured are scenes of the angry demonstration and interviews with American Nazi leaders, their ACLU attorneys, Holocaust survivors, and Jesse Jackson.

Distributor: New Day Films, 121 West 27th Street, Suite 902, New York, NY 10001 (212) 645–8210

*Traveling Hopefully*
John Avildsen, 1982, 30 min.

A documentary, profiling Roger Baldwin, principal founder of the ACLU.

Baldwin's thoughts, essence, and life's work are powerfully presented in this film, which includes testimony and archival footage from the Scopes Trial, Klan marches, and the American Nazis in Skokie.
Distributor: Films Incorporated, 5547 N. Ravenswood Ave., Chicago, IL 60604 (800) 323–4222

*Unfinished Business*
Steven Okazaki, 1984, 60 min.

In 1942 the U.S. government forcibly evicted over 110,000 Americans of Japanese descent from their homes on the West Coast and herded them into internment camps. *Unfinished Business* focuses on three men who defied the government's order to evacuate. They were convicted and imprisoned as a result. Historical scenes show wartime anti-Japanese hysteria, the process of evacuation and incarceration, and life in the camps. Present-day scenes show the three men as they fight to overturn their original convictions in the final round of a 40-year-old battle.
Distributor: Mouchette Films, 548 Fifth Street, San Francisco, CA 97107 (415) 495–3934

Teachers may wish to recommend to their students the following films that feature Bill of Rights issues: *Absence of Malice* (freedom of the press); *Advise and Consent* (balance of powers); *All the President's Men* (freedom of the press); *Beyond a Reasonable Doubt* (capital punishment); *Cheyenne Autumn* (rights of Native Americans); *The Conversation* (right to privacy); *Gideon's Trumpet* (right to counsel); *Harlan County USA* (right to organize collectively); *Inherit the Wind* (separation of church and state); *Intruder in the Dust* (civil rights); *Roe v. Wade* (women's rights); *To Kill a Mockingbird* (civil rights); *Twelve Angry Men* (trial by jury).

# APPENDIX E:

## CHRONOLOGY FOR
## THE BILL OF RIGHTS

*October 1774*
The First Continental Congress (1774–1775) approves a "Declaration of Rights" based on "the immutable laws of nature, the principles of the English constitution, and the several charters or compacts of the colonies." This Declaration states the basic proposition that all men are entitled to life, liberty, and property, and that they cannot be deprived of these rights without their consent. The Declaration also specifies particular rights: of assembly and petition; of freedom of the press and religion; and of the people to participate in legislative councils and to be tried by a jury of their peers. The right to be free from a standing army "in time of peace . . . [without] consent of the legislature of that colony, in which such army is kept" is also included in this Declaration.

*May 1776*
The Second Continental Congress (1775–1781) recommends that each colony form their own state government. A general convention of delegates in Williamsburg, Virginia, summoned to create a state government, calls for declaring "the United Colonies free and independent states" and for appointing a committee to prepare a declaration of rights.

*June 1776*
The Virginia Declaration of Rights is passed at the General Convention of Virginia, authored mainly by George Mason. The rights of the individual include male suffrage for those who could give evidence of an interest in and attachment to the community; protections against self-accusation; the right to know the nature and cause of arrest; and the right to a speedy trial and an impartial jury. Excessive bails, fines, and cruel and unusual punishments are prohibited, as are general warrants of search and seizure. Freedom of the press and religion are ensured. The Virginia Declaration

of Rights expands the concept of the personal rights of citizens as had no other previous document.

*July 4, 1776*
The Second Continental Congress adopts the Declaration of Independence.

*1776–1784*
All thirteen original colonies, declaring themselves to be states, either adopt a new bill of rights, incorporate the previous provisions of such bills in their new state constitutions, or expand the barriers to arbitrary government already written into their colonial charters.

*November 1777*
The Continental Congress agrees on a constitution establishing the Articles of Confederation to be presented to the state legislatures for approval or rejection.

*March 1781*
By March 1, 1781, all states had ratified the Articles of Confederation.

*1787*
Congress passes the Ordinance of 1787, part of the Northwest Ordinance, which includes specific guarantees of personal freedoms: freedom of religion; trial by jury; habeas corpus; reasonable bail; moderate fines; prohibitions against cruel and unusual punishment; inviolability of contract; protection for private property; and prohibition of slavery in the Northwest territory. For the first time, civil rights becomes a factor in national legislation.

*May 25, 1787*
The Constitutional Convention opens in Philadelphia.

*September 1787*
George Mason, a delegate to the Constitutional Convention from Virginia, writes "Objections to this Constitution of Government" during the waning days of the Convention. Mason asserts, "There is no Declaration of Rights, and the laws of the general government being paramount to the laws and constitution of the several States, the Declaration of Rights in the separate States are no security." Mason protests the lack of a declaration for liberty of the press, trial by jury in civil cases, and against standing armies in time of peace.

*September 17, 1787*
The Constitution is signed without a Bill of Rights and Mason, Elbridge Gerry of Massachusetts, and Edmund Randolph of Virginia refuse to sign, emphasizing the omission. The Constitution goes to the states for ratification.

*December 20, 1787*
Thomas Jefferson, United States Minister to France, writes to John Adams: " . . . a bill of rights is what the people are entitled to against every government on earth, general or particular, & what no just government should refuse, or rest on inference."

*1787–1788*
As the states ratify the Constitution, it becomes clear to all but a few die-hard Federalists that a federal bill of rights is necessary. James Madison agrees even though he had originally argued against any additional amendments. Five state ratifying conventions strongly recommend that a bill of rights be added to the Constitution.

*July 2, 1788*
The Constitution is ratified by the requisite nine states. The Congress under the Articles of Confederation prepares for the change in government.

*February 4, 1789*
In the new government's first election, George Washington is chosen as president and John Adams as vice-president by the presidential electors.

*June 8, 1789*
Madison introduces a series of amendments to the Constitution in the House of Representatives, explaining that they would promote "tranquility of the public mind, and the stability of the Government."

*September 25, 1789*
The First Congress submits to the states twelve amendments to the Constitution. Amendments I and II, concerning the apportionment of seats in the House of Representatives and the compensation of congressmen, will be rejected by the states. Amendments III through XII will be ratified and known as the Bill of Rights.

*November 20, 1789*
New Jersey ratifies the Bill of Rights.

*November 21, 1789*
As a result of congressional action to amend the Constitution, North Carolina ratifies the original document by a vote of 194 to 77.

*December 19, 1789*
Maryland ratifies the Bill of Rights.

*December 22, 1789*
North Carolina ratifies the Bill of Rights.

*January 18, 1790*
South Carolina ratifies the Bill of Rights.

*January 25, 1790*
New Hampshire ratifies the Bill of Rights.

*January 28, 1790*
Delaware ratifies the Bill of Rights.

*February 24, 1790*
New York ratifies the Bill of Rights.

*March 10, 1790*
Pennsylvania ratifies the Bill of Rights.

*June 7, 1790*
Rhode Island ratifies the Bill of Rights.

*November 3, 1791*
Vermont ratifies the Bill of Rights.

*December 15, 1791*
Virginia ratifies the Bill of Rights, making it part of the United States Constitution.

Three of the original thirteen states did not ratify the Bill of Rights until the 150th anniversary of its submission to the states. Massachusetts ratified on March 2, 1939; Georgia on March 18, 1939; and Connecticut on April 19, 1939.

This chronology is based on Robert Allen Rutland *The Birth of the Bill of Rights: 1776–1791* (Boston: Northeastern University Press, 1982) and *this Constitution: A Bicentennial Chronicle* (Project '87 of the American Historical Association/the American Political Science Association, Washington, D.C.) *18* (Spring/Summer 1988). (Reprinted from, *To Preserve These Rights: User's Guide to the Bill of Rights Poster Exhibit*, produced by the Pennsylvania Humanities Council.)